D1094352

BALANCHINE

BALANCHINE

by *BERNARD TAPER*   *Harper & Row, Publishers*
New York, Evanston, and London

The author expresses his appreciation to THE NEW YORKER, where portions of this biography appeared in somewhat different form.

The material quoted on page 129 appeared in the article "Diaghilev and His Period" in the August 1949 issue of DANCE NEWS. Copyright 1949 by DANCE NEWS, and reprinted with their permission. The quotation on page 120 from SERGE DIAGHILEV by Serge Lifar is reprinted with permission of G. P. Putnam's Sons.

First Edition

Library of Congress Catalog Card Number: 62–14549

Designed by The Etheredges

CONTENTS

CHOREOGRAPHER IN HIS ELEMENT

The rehearsal studio of a ballet company is something of a cross between a convent and a prizefight gym. Before the dancers go into action, they paw a resin box in a corner, like fighters, and when they make their way about the room between classes or rehearsal sessions, they are apt—even the most petite of ballerinas—to walk with a pugilist's flat-footed but springy gait, shoulders swaying with a bit of swagger, arms hanging loosely. There is the acrid sweat smell of the gym, and the same formidable presence of lithe, steel-muscled, incredibly trim and capable bodies ruthlessly forcing themselves to become even trimmer and more capable. But there is also an aura of asceticism, of spirituality—a spirituality achieved paradoxically, by means of single-minded concentration on the body. The mirror covering one whole wall from ceiling to floor would seem to speak of gross vanity, but the dancers, though they may have embarked on their careers from vain motives, have learned to rid themselves of conceit when they work. They use the mirror dispassionately, measuring their reflected selves with almost inhuman objectivity against the conception of an ideal to which they have dedicated their lives. The ideal, of course, is that of a particular kind of beauty, a centuries-old, thoroughly artificial way of moving, which, when shaped into ballets by a choreographer, becomes art of a special sort—an elusive, evanescent art, as fleeting as fireworks or soap bubbles, that nevertheless has the power not only to entrance beholders but even, in some mysterious manner, to convey an experience of lasting significance.

To see George Balanchine in such an environment, rehearsing his New York City Ballet Company or, better yet, creating one of the new ballets he brings forth bountifully, season after season, is to have a rare pleasure— the pleasure of seeing someone who appears completely attuned to his world. In his person, Balanchine suggests the quintessence of the ballet studio's paradoxical combination of qualities. A noble-looking man, with a proud, elegant bearing—"a *grand seigneur*," Cecil Beaton has called him—Balanchine does not hesitate to throw himself on the studio floor in the course of

3

demonstrating to his dancers some movement in one of his ballets, and he will often work himself into a dray-horse lather of perspiration during a rehearsal or choreographic session. In him, an intense, dedicated vision of a perfection of grace merges with an unquestioning willingness to submit to the arduous discipline, the specific physical efforts, required to attain—or, at any rate, approach—this vision. "First comes the sweat," Balanchine says, speaking in a low, agreeable voice, tinged with the accents of his native Russia. "Then comes the beauty—if you're *vairy* lucky and have said your prayers." Someone once observed of ballet that it is "a science on top of which an art is precariously balanced." Balanchine would agree, although he would prefer to substitute the word "craft" for the more resounding "science."

In the half-century since his introduction to this craft, at the age of ten, in the Imperial School of Ballet, in St. Petersburg, he has knocked about in many parts of the world, but wherever, in the course of his wanderings, he has been able to find a ballet studio, with a complement of dancers in need of something new to dance, there he has been at home and in his element. The ballet studio—whether it be in Russia, France, Denmark, Italy, Monaco, Argentina, England or the United States—is his true native heath. It is much more to him than just the setting in which he works; it provides the vital stimulus to his creativity—the rare and indefinable kind of creativity that has made him the most esteemed and prolific inventor of ballets in our time, whose works are to be found in the repertory of every major ballet company in the West. "I'm not one of those people who can create in the abstract, in some nice quiet room at home," he says. "If I didn't have a studio to go to, with dancers waiting for me to give them something to do, I would forget I was a choreographer. I need to have real, living bodies to look at. I see how this one can stretch and that one can jump and another one can turn, and then I begin to get a few ideas."

As a man, aside from ballet, the impression Balanchine makes is of someone who is pleasant, mercurial, authoritative and fundamentally enigmatic. In tastes and interests, he falls into no category; he is highbrow, lowbrow and middlebrow all mixed up together in a blend of his own. He likes Braque, Pushkin, Eisenhower, Stravinsky, Jack Benny, Piero della Francesca, science fiction, TV Westerns, French sauces and American ice creams. A communicant of the Greek Orthodox Church, he is deeply religious. He patronizes only the best and costliest tailors, but the clothes

Preparing MOVEMENTS FOR PIANO AND ORCHESTRA, *in 1963.*

Two more moments from MOVEMENTS FOR PIANO AND ORCHESTRA.
Jacques d'Amboise watches intently
as Balanchine, working with Suzanne Farrell,
shows him how his part will go.

he wears are a sort of Russianized version of a Wild West dude's garb—bright, pearl-buttoned shirts, black string tie, gambler's plaid vest, frontier pants. On him, these surprising outfits appear natural and elegant. After some three decades in America, he is still enthusiastic about the country. He says he loves the way it looks, sounds and smells. A fervent Republican, he often talks about what a pleasure it is to pay taxes to support a country it is such a pleasure to live in—an enthusiasm which most of his fellow Republicans do not share. Most of the time, he would rather talk about politics, or almost anything else, than about ballet—ballet, he feels, being something you do, not discuss. He relishes luxury but does not give a hang for money. Gay, witty, and often playful, he is, however, fundamentally reserved about himself. Most people who have anything to do with him speak of him with great devotion and affection, but they also say that while he is a very easy person to be with, he is not an easy person to know.

Those who admire Balanchine's work are apt to rank him very high among the creative artists of the world. The word "genius" is used freely in referring to him. The poet W. H. Auden has been heard to remark that if he has ever known anyone who could be called a genius, it is Balanchine. The painter and stage designer Eugene Berman, in a memoir published in the *Saturday Review* in 1957, wrote that one of the privileges of his life had been the opportunity to work with Balanchine, whom he called "not only the greatest living choreographer, but in my view the greatest of all time, the Mozart of choreographers." The music critic B. H. Haggin wrote a few years ago that Balanchine was for him "an artist of the same magnitude as Picasso, and the only one I can think of now working in any of the arts," adding, "He is, it seems to me, even more disciplined in the exercise of his powers than Picasso: the originality, no matter how astounding, always remains part of the continuous development."

It is one of Balanchine's most pleasing traits, to those who know him, that he can never be heard speaking in such terms of himself or his work. He can seldom even be trapped into speaking of ballet as an art or himself as an artist. He prefers to view himself as an artisan, a professional maker of dances. When he talks of what he does, he often compares himself to a chef (he is, incidentally, a superb cook), whose job it is to prepare for an exacting clientele a variety of attractive dishes that will delight and surprise their palates, or to a carpenter, a good carpenter, with pride in his craft—

a cabinetmaker, say. Balanchine does not keep scrapbooks, programs or reviews of his work; in fact, he almost never bothers to read what critics and admirers write about him or about the ballet. If someone happens to tell him about an article propounding a theory in regard to his ballets, he is perfectly willing to listen politely. Then he will make his standard comment: "Too fancy!" He does not particularly blame writers for going on at length about ballet, if that is how they want to occupy themselves or make a living, but he thinks that what any of them, including his most ardent admirers, writes bears very little relation to what happens onstage while the music is playing. Though capable of expressing original and poetic insights himself in unguarded moments, he chooses—out of deep-seated principle, it would seem, or perhaps out of a canny intuition that so elusive an art cannot bear the burden of much theorizing or solemnity—to talk about his work as seldom as possible and then only casually, playfully or in matter-of-fact technical terms. The numerous people who see grave significance and profound portents in his ballets get no encouragement from him. "When you have a garden full of pretty flowers, you don't demand of them, 'What do you mean? What is your significance?' You just enjoy them," he says. "So why not just enjoy ballet in the same way?" Of people who insist on seeing explicit meaning in ballet, he has said, in a telling comparison, "People never seem to understand unless they can put their finger into things. Like touching dough —when people see bread rising, they smell something and they say, 'Oh, is it going up?' And they poke their finger in it. 'Ah,' they say, 'now I see.' But of course the dough then goes down. They spoil everything by insisting on touching."

Despite his lack of solemnity, there is no mistaking his own or his company's dedication to ballet. "He doesn't do it by talking," a member of the company has said, "but he implies at every moment that there is a great art of classical dancing that all of us, including him, are serving." An unforgettable impression of this concentrated dedication was once made on a friend of Balanchine's—a pianist—when he went backstage at the New York City Center during intermission one evening after a performance of Balanchine's early ballet *Apollo* to congratulate him and the dancers. It had been a triumphant performance, received by the audience with enthusiastic applause and repeated bravoes. The pianist had never gone backstage before, but on this occasion he had been so moved by the ballet that he felt impelled to offer his homage. When he got there, the scene that met his eyes surprised him. He had naturally assumed that, on the heels of such success, he would find dancers and choreographer standing amid a throng of admirers and graciously acknowledging their praise. Instead, he discovered them hard at work. They were, it seemed, going over aspects of *Apollo* that Balanchine wished to improve. They were grouped near the lowered curtain and must have begun this impromptu post-mortem rehearsal the instant the last curtain call was over. The visitor stood in the wings watching as Balanchine worked first with Patricia Wilde, who had danced the role of the Muse Polyhymnia, and then with Jacques d'Amboise, who had danced Apollo. He heard no harsh words spoken, no reproofs; when Balanchine finished making his point to Miss Wilde, the visitor saw her smile before she departed for her dressing room and heard her thank Balanchine warmly for his help, as if she were a mere beginner, rather than a distinguished ballerina who had just received a public ovation. From her, Balanchine turned to d'Amboise, and the visitor could see them going over various sequences together—facing each other, like one man looking in a mirror, while both of them danced. Occasionally, they would stop for a few words of comment. D'Amboise would nod vigorously. Balanchine would smile agreement at something d'Amboise said, and then they would spring into action again, face to face, about three feet apart. Time passed as they continued to work thus, and the backstage visitor watched them wonderingly. Dancers began to gather onstage for the next ballet, which was to be *Agon*. Bells could be heard ringing, announcing the imminent curtain. Stagehands hurried to their places. Totally preoccupied, Balanchine and d'Amboise ignored it all. When the pianist finally left, without having had a chance to congratulate anyone, they were still at it. They were gone from the stage, though, when the curtain went up on *Agon*. At the very last second, perhaps, the stage manager had taken each of them by an arm and led them off. The visitor, back in his seat, could not help wondering if they might not still be working away in the wings.

To visit the ballet company's studio while Balanchine is choreographing and to watch him get his "few ideas" and communicate them to a company of dancers is enjoyable and engrossing and can be salubrious as well. Balanchine has a businessman friend who, whenever he feels oppressed by the tangle of his own affairs or the confusion of the day's news, likes to close up his office early and spend an hour or two watching Balanchine at work on a new ballet. He says it is the best therapy he knows. The peaceful, assured, workmanlike way Balanchine creates his dances has become legendary in the ballet world. Anecdotes concerning other famous figures of that world often revolve around some pyrotechnical display of temperament. The characteristic Balanchine story, on the other hand, has to do with some crisis or other in which Balanchine was to be found calmly and productively carrying on with his choreography, apparently unaffected by the chaos and hysteria around him. There are people who have worked closely with Balanchine for ten years or more and have yet to see him lose his temper or hear him raise his voice in anger.

When Balanchine is choreographing a new ballet, quite a number of spectators are usually present—seated on a bench that runs along the mirrored wall, leaning against the practice bars on the other walls, or standing around the piano, which is off to one side of the room. They observe Balanchine, they talk among themselves, they come and go. He pays no attention. His tolerance of visitors is exceptional among choreographers; most of them detest being watched and exclude from the room not only outsiders but any members of the company who are not required at the moment. Even so, by the nature of his art, a choreographer can never fully enjoy the pleasure of creating in solitude; eventually he cannot escape the dancers who are the medium in which he works. If he gets stuck and runs out of ideas, there they are before him, waiting—"with patient, drawn faces," as the choreographer Agnes de Mille has ruefully written—for him to find inspiration. As yet, none of the systems of notation which have been developed have gained such widespread acceptance as to permit the choreographer to do as a playwright or a composer does—that is, prepare his work at leisure on paper and hand the script or score to his performers for them to study before assembling for rehearsal. (So far, dance notation has been employed principally as a way of making a record of an occasional ballet after its creation.) Before coming to the first rehearsal, the choreographer may work out in his mind a number of steps and patterns for his ballet and jot them down on paper in some shorthand of his own, or he may write out in words a detailed libretto of the action, but, ultimately, to create a new ballet, the choreographer must do what all the generations of ballet masters before him have done—get his dancers together in a large room and show them what he wants them to dance. The creation of a ballet has to be a public act. It is as if a composer had to assemble an orchestra (at a cost of hundreds of dollars an hour) and compose a symphony by standing in front of the musicians and making it up as he went along, first humming a snatch of music for the cellos to try, perhaps, and then turning to, say, the woodwinds and humming a theme they might play at the same time. For all its sophistication, ballet is really a prehistoric kind of art. Lacking a widely accepted written language, it has been able to preserve its masterpieces only by devoted, laborious effort, passing them on from one generation to the next by direct communication, like folk legends. And, like legends, few ballets survive this process unchanged.

These conditions of the craft, which many choreographers find extremely trying, do not disturb Balanchine; he takes them for granted. In advance of the first rehearsal, he makes no notes whatever. His way of creating a ballet is by extended improvisation under pressure. One of the fastest workers at his trade, he usually starts choreographing about three weeks before the date set for the première, though he has been known, in

A MIDSUMMER NIGHT'S DREAM.
*Above, as Oberon, Balanchine lulls the kneeling fairies
to sleep near the end of Act One.
At left, for Melissa Hayden's benefit, he becomes Titania,
enamoured of Bottom.*

an emergency, to choreograph a ballet in less than a week. By the time he begins, the forthcoming ballet will have been announced in the press, the season's performances will have been scheduled, and the costumes and sets will have been ordered. Balanchine's advance preparation consists chiefly in studying the music he is to use until he has soaked it up completely. Sometimes, as part of this process, he makes his own piano reduction of the orchestral score. The son of a composer and the product of several years of advanced conservatory training as a young man, Balanchine is unquestionably the most musical of all choreographers, and he analyzes an orchestral score the way a conductor does. At some point during his study of the music he has chosen for the ballet, he decides what dance quality is best suited to it—what palette of movement it calls for—settles on the size of the ensemble of dancers he will use and determines who his principal soloists will be. That is likely to be the sum of his preparations. All the rest must be done at rehearsal, with the dancers assembled and waiting and the large clock on the wall ticking away the costly minutes of rehearsal time and moving inexorably toward the production hour. When Tchaikovsky was asked, on one occasion, what conditions he required in order to be inspired to compose, he replied, "My Muse comes to me when I tell her to come." Asked the same question about his choreographing, Balanchine gives a paraphrase of this and says, "My Muse must come to me on 'union' time."

On the day rehearsals are to commence, Balanchine arrives at the studio shortly before the scheduled hour and changes into his working clothes— usually black pants, cut like sailor's pants, a T shirt, and soft-soled dancing shoes. Even in that garb, he does not lose his air of elegance. He has aplomb, in every sense of the word. ("Aplomb," as defined by the French ballet master Despréaux in 1806, is a specific kind of dynamic balance fundamental to every position and movement in classic ballet.) Promptly on the hour, he comes to the front of the rehearsal room and, standing with the mirrored wall at his back, claps his hands lightly. The dancers, who have been warming up or standing about in the spectacularly impossible attitudes ballet dancers naturally fall into in moments of repose, gather before him. He greets them with ceremonious courtesy. A minute or two of banter may follow, and then, rubbing his hands briskly, he will remark, like a journeyman carpenter about to knock together a tool shed, "All right. We begin."

Some choreographers, when beginning a new ballet, like to discuss their intentions at some length with the dancers, but Balanchine, who considers cerebration a deadly menace, prefers to engage in as little talk as possible. "You have to be vairy careful when you use your mind," he was once heard soberly cautioning a ballerina, "or you will get into trouble." In his cosmogony, dancers are like angels: they are celestial messengers who may communicate emotions but do not themselves experience the joys or griefs of which they bring tidings. The first thing he may do as he starts to work is arrange the dancers, in various poses, here and there about the room, in the pictorial composition they will form when the curtain rises. As they hold their places, he stands before them in silence, his hands clasped, head slightly bowed; he is listening to the first phrase of the music within him and summoning up in his mind's eye the dance phrase he will match to it—a phrase that may consist of five or six different movements by different soloists or groups at the same time. Standing there, he suggests a chess master planning a move. From the room next door, where other members of the company are rehearsing some other work, comes the sound of a piano thumping away, but it does not seem to penetrate Balanchine's concentration. As the dance ideas occur to him, his hands unclasp and his fingers come to life, as if they were dancing in the air. "All right," Balanchine says, stepping over to one of his soloists—the principal ballerina, perhaps—"you do like this." And he dances out for her the steps he has conceived, counting aloud each beat of the phrase as he does so. She immediately reproduces his movements while echoing his count. "And you," Balanchine says, turning next, perhaps, to the leading male dancer, "you do like *this*." In the same way, he produces sequences for the other soloists and the ensembles of the corps de ballet. When he has communicated in this way all the movements of the dance phrase, he will have the pianist play the few bars of music for it while the dancers put it together for his scrutiny. He may have them run through it several times more, and he may tinker with it or even discard it and try a fresh approach, but often it will be just the way he wants it from the start. With a brief nod, he murmurs, "Tha-at's right." The dancers store their steps away in their remarkable muscle memories, and Balanchine, in the same manner as before, takes up the next phrase.

So the work proceeds through the session. Every once in a while, Balanchine will make a quick foray to the piano to check something in the score—peering at the notes through a pair of glasses that he keeps in his pants pocket—or to show the pianist how a troublesome passage should

AGON — *with Diana Adams and Arthur Mitchell.*

go. Occasionally, some dance movement or sequence he has devised will make the dancers gasp with laughter or astonishment. Now and then, a dancer may say that he doubts whether he can master some particularly intricate or difficult passage. If Balanchine assures him that he'll be able to work it out with practice, he questions no more but says O.K., he'll try it. The dancer knows that later on, if the passage remains awkward for him, Balanchine will devise a variation to take its place—one probably no less intricate but in some way or other more congenial to that dancer's body conformation and dance style. Though Balanchine puts a continual challenge even to the most brilliant of the New York City Ballet's dancers, the choreography he ultimately provides is what each can dance best and most naturally. This is one of the things that Balanchine is noted for in the ballet world and that his dancers appreciate about him.

At the end of an hour of rehearsal, there is a five-minute break, which Balanchine spends either at the piano with the score or chatting with some of the dancers. As soon as the five minutes are up, he claps his hands and everybody is ready to continue. Once more, all goes forward with a kind of simple, serious, unself-conscious concentration on the task at' hand, as Balanchine serenely spins his web of dance, producing his delights and surprises as promised and on schedule. By the conclusion of the session, which usually lasts two hours, a measurable amount of progress will have been made—perhaps three minutes of ballet. The visitor who has sat in the studio while this was taking place often finds that a curious thing has happened to him. Whether or not he was familiar with the music before he arrived, he discovers that the steps and arrangements of movement that Balanchine has worked out already seem to him absolutely inevitable—as if the music itself had asserted a demand to be linked with just this pattern of dance and no other. Martha Graham, who is as eminent in the idiom of modern dance as Balanchine is in classical ballet, has said that she felt something of this sort when she visited Balanchine's studio one evening in 1959 and for the first time in her long career watched another choreographer at work.

As it happened, she and Balanchine were, in their separate studios, then engaged in a project that was to make dance history in its way. Miss Graham was doing the choreography for the opening part of the ballet *Episodes,* to the extremely difficult and atonal music of Anton Webern, while Balanchine was handling the rest; for once, those traditional foes, a classical-ballet choreographer and a modern-dance choreographer, were working together in amicable conjunction. The evening Miss Graham dropped in on Balanchine, his studio, as usual, held an assortment of spectators, among them the highly regarded composer Leon Kirchner; Hershy Kay, an arranger of orchestral works for ballet; and an old Russian-émigré friend of Balanchine's who had dropped in to see what Balanchine was up to. During the session, a brief mix-up occurred when Balanchine inadvertently skipped a couple of bars in putting two of his dance passages together. Upon discovering his lapse, Balanchine coolly took it in stride; there was no indication that it bothered him to be discovered in such an error by an audience containing a rival choreographer and a couple of

*As the night of a première approaches, Balanchine and Lincoln Kirstein
confer on production details.*

musicians. First he tried to see how it would go if he stretched out the preceding dance phrase to incorporate the missing bars. "No, that doesn't
work," Balanchine said. "I'll have to make something new to put in there."
And he did, forthwith. Miss Graham—whose own manner of choreographing is far more emotional and who, according to her friend Agnes de
Mille, sometimes dismisses all the dancers from the room when things are
not going well and communes with God and her soul—shook her head in
wonder at this manifestation of Balanchine's aplomb.

Throughout the rest of the session, she leaned forward intently, following every move. At the end, after Balanchine had had the dancers do a
run-through of what he had choreographed so far, she turned to the spectator beside her and said, "It's like watching light pass through a prism. The
music passes through him, and in the same natural yet marvelous way that
a prism refracts light, he refracts music into dance."

During the weeks just before the season opens, when Balanchine is not only choreographing new ballets but supervising the final polishing of old ones, he works in the rehearsal studio every day from noon to ten o'clock in the evening, with a little time off for dinner. Because of the complexity of the company's daily rehearsal schedule—its active repertoire during a given season consists of some thirty or forty ballets, which have to be worked on in various measure—Balanchine cannot count on having the full cast of any new ballet he is choreographing for more than a couple of hours at a time, so he is not able to work consecutively on a ballet from beginning to end. He has to make his ballets the way most directors make movies, working now on this section, now on that. As a further complication, he is often choreographing more than one new ballet at a time, so in alternate sessions during the day he may move back and forth between quite disparate works in progress—going, as he did in the memorably creative session of one recent season, from a complex, astringently witty, uncompromisingly avant-garde ballet like *Agon* to a sprightly, untroubled novelty like *Square Dance,* and from the romantic lyricism of the *Gounod Symphony* to the flashy brassiness of *Stars and Stripes.* The necessity of having to work in so disjointed a fashion provokes no complaint from him; he seems, if anything, to find the enforced variety refreshing to the spirit.

While Balanchine is working out his choreography and transmitting it to the dancers, he concerns himself little with nuances of performance. The last few days before the première, he usually concentrates on that aspect—on getting his ensemble to approach his idea of perfection. The style he has developed since coming to the United States is characterized by unusual precision and energy, and as he works on his dancers' performance techniques, he is constantly heard exhorting them to more vigor, to more clarity in their attack on every movement. "Audience must be made aware that leg is *your* leg and is going right *there!* Bam!" he will admonish them, slamming down his own leg to emphasize his words. The studio resounds, when he is engaged in this refining process, with "Bams!" and "Pows!" and similar exclamatory explosions, uttered in a voice that is charged with energy, though it does not go up many decibels in volume. If one were to hear these sounds and not see what was going on in the studio, one would hardly think that such a seemingly ethereal creation as a ballet was being prepared. Balanchine's intense vision of beauty as the end result of all this is always present, however, and no one is permitted to forget it. "Isn't it selfish of you," he

chided one girl, "to expect three thousand people to sit and watch you lift your leg if you're not going to do it beautifully?" From then on, though she was far back in the ranks of the corps de ballet, she danced as if she were going to be alone onstage the night of the performance.

To make a point, Balanchine is capable of producing an apt illustration or a vivid, often surprising metaphor. "Don't forget," he said to a ballerina who he thought was getting too dreamy in her style, "that Carpentier was the most lyrical boxer who ever lived, but Dempsey knocked him flat in no time." She nodded her pretty head, apparently discerning a vital truth for herself in this odd bit of information, and immediately attacked her dancing with as much vigor as if she herself were training for a match with Dempsey. To bring home to another dancer, one of the company's leading ballerinas, the reason her performance of a particular passage was not altogether satisfying, even though she was dancing it absolutely correctly and in tempo, he told her a little story about Louis XIV, who one day, it is said, emerged

from his palace with the intention of taking a ride somewhere and found that his carriage, instead of having long been drawn up awaiting his royal pleasure, was just arriving. It reached the palace door at the instant he came out. The King did not have to wait a second for it, or even slow down his stride, but he was nevertheless highly offended. As he swept into the carriage, he complained to the coachman, with majestic indignation, "You *almost* made us wait." The ballerina laughed at the story, and Balanchine said, "So you see, to be correct, to be perfectly on time is not enough. You must be *luxuriously* perfect if you want to satisfy."

On the whole, however, Balanchine's pedagogy, like his choreography, is essentially nonverbal. "You think, then," a dancer will ask him, "that it should go like this?" and she will perform the passage in question. "Ye-es," Balanchine will reply, "but maybe a bit more like this," and he will dance it himself the way it should be. In recent years, he has been suffering somewhat from an arthritic condition, which manifests itself in a slight stiffness in his

walk but, surprisingly, does not show up in his dancing or hinder him from dancing all day long at rehearsals. If this ailment ever got bad enough to prevent him from leaping about, or lifting a ballerina in the air when he wanted to show her partner how it is to be done, he would have to retire, he says, because he cannot imagine being a choreographer sitting down. When he performs a dance phrase for his company, he does not do the steps in full scale or finished form, but the effect is always astonishingly telling. He evokes an essence as easily as a master painter might with a hasty pencil sketch. Maria Tallchief says that when he was teaching her the role of the Swan Queen in his revised version of the second act of *Swan Lake,* she used to watch him do her part, and think, "I'll *never* look that beautiful." Similarly—though apropos of a very different kind of role—Jerome Robbins, who used to dance with the company as well as choreograph for it, and is at present its associate artistic director, recalls, "As a dancer, I got some of the best notices of my life for the role of Tyl in Balanchine's ballet *Tyl Ulenspiegel,* but I never came anywhere near the gusto and earthiness that he achieved when he was demonstrating it for me in rehearsal."

Eventually, in the course of preparing a new ballet, Balanchine will dance every step of all the parts—those of all the soloists and all the groupings of the corps de ballet. In a sense, when one witnesses a performance of the New York City Ballet, one is seeing a whole ensemble of Balanchines, in various sizes and shapes—and some critics consider this a fault or a limitation in the company. The matter is not so simple as this would suggest, however, for what a ballerina may pick up from watching Balanchine dance her part for her is a heightened awareness of her own special style and qualities, which his keen eye has perceived, and which he has rendered in clarified form for her. Still, there is no denying that all his dancers are acutely responsive in copying and appropriating the qualities he sketches out in dance for them. An instance of just how responsive they are occurred when he was choreographing *Bourrée Fantasque* a number of years ago. When he had the ensemble repeat for him a section that he had created the preceding week, he was perplexed to see that all the movements were being danced in a peculiarly cramped and agonized way. When he questioned the dancers, they insisted that this was the way he had shown the steps to them. He could not figure it out until he recalled that the week before he had been suffering from bursitis; the company had apparently picked up all his aches and pains and magnified them into a bursitic *Bourrée Fantasque.*

Last thoughts before the première.

Having done his best in the preparation of a work, Balanchine does not fret as the time for its première nears. "Somehow it will all work out all right," he says reassuringly when one of the usual emergencies arises shortly before curtain time, and, one way or another, it nearly always does. "Somehow" is one of Balanchine's favorite words. A recollection that Jerome Robbins sometimes summons up to help compose himself when he is getting jittery as an opening night approaches is that of Balanchine a few hours before the première, in 1954, of his version of *The Nutcracker*—the costliest work the New York City Ballet had ever put on till then. At five o'clock that afternoon, with the curtain due to go up at eight-thirty, it was learned that the costumes were still not ready. Balanchine and Robbins hastened over to the workshop of Karinska, the noted costume maker, to see what could be done about this crisis. When they got there, Balanchine, discerning at a glance that everybody in the shop was working feverishly to get the job finished, spoke not a word of exhortation or reproof. He simply sat down among the seamstresses, took up an unfinished costume, threaded a needle, and began deftly stitching a ruffle. Robbins found himself following Balanchine's example. "After a while, I looked over at him," Robbins recalls. "Here it was only about three hours before curtain and there sat Balanchine, sewing away as if he didn't have a care in the world. I said to him, 'How can you be so calm?' He just smiled and went on sewing."

When the curtain rises on one of his new works, Balanchine usually observes what he has created from the rear of the center aisle. Unnoticed by the audience, he slips into the auditorium after the lights have dimmed, and takes up a position just inside the door, where he stands among the ushers. As the curtain descends at the end of the ballet, he slips away backstage to his dancers, who, between curtain calls, are waiting to hear what he thinks of the way they danced. After everybody else has taken repeated bows—the conductor, the soloists, the corps de ballet—the audience may get a brief glimpse of Balanchine in the spotlight. Usually he emerges onstage in the grip of a couple of his dancers, like a culprit apprehended at the scene of his crime. His appearance always brings forth the most thunderous ovation of the evening, to which he responds with a quizzical smile, a shrug and a nod of acknowledgment. Then he quickly ducks back behind the curtain. People in the audience who do not know Balanchine have been heard to surmise that his diffident stage manner is a studied performance—like that of the nineteenth-century composer who, after the première of one of his

Taking a curtain call with Patricia Wilde after the first performance of NATIVE DANCERS.

operas, always had to be dragged bodily onto the stage, struggling valiantly to get away while muttering to his captors, "Pull harder!" Those who know Balanchine somewhat better disagree with this; the way he takes a curtain call, they say, accords with the engagingly modest, unpretentious manner in which he invariably comports himself when they meet him offstage. The few who know him very well, however, while agreeing that he does not put on an act and that his everyday behavior is delightfully unpretentious, say that modesty is not the explanation but just the reverse—a kind of monumental self-assurance. He is so sure of himself and his work that he does not need to boast or to bathe his ego in applause. "He seems as soft as silk, but he's as tough as steel," says Lincoln Kirstein, the general director of the New York City Ballet, who for some thirty years has been Balanchine's most devoted patron and partisan. "He's the most secure man I've ever met in my life. He has authority to the *n*th degree." It is Balanchine's feeling that in seeing his new ballet the audience has seen exactly what he wishes to show of himself and that it is irrelevant, and also not very interesting, to follow the ballet with a display of his own person onstage. He feels about this rather as Joseph Conrad felt when he was asked by the *Bookman* for a photograph of himself that it could publish; Conrad replied, "My face has nothing to do with my writing."

RUSSIA: CHILDHOOD
AND APPRENTICESHIP

Up until just a few years ago, a young ballet dancer, if not so fortunate as to be a Russian to start with, was expected as a matter of course to adopt a Russian stage name. (So Hilda Munnings became Lydia Sokolova, for instance.) Balanchine may be the only Russian in the dance world who has had to do the opposite. He was christened Georgi Melitonovitch Balanchivadze at his birth, which took place in St. Petersburg on January 22, 1904. The change to "Balanchine" was made twenty years later, at the request of Serge Diaghilev, when the young man joined that autocratic but inspired impresario's Ballets Russes in Paris. Diaghilev thought the name too difficult to pronounce. Strictly speaking, "Balanchivadze" is a name of Georgian, rather than Slavic, derivation. It was from his Georgian forebears that Balanchine inherited his physical characteristics—his black hair, intense dark eyes, hawklike features and wiry frame—and also, as he may be occasionally heard to assert nowadays, his type of artistic temperament. "We Georgians are not Russians in culture, not at all," he will sometimes vehemently declare, in his Russian-flavored accent. "We are Mediterranean people, like Italians."

Another important influence of a non-Slavic sort was that of the city in which he was born. In its fashions, its values, its style of thought, its very appearance, St. Petersburg was the most European of Russian cities—as it continues to be today, though bearing Lenin's rather than Peter's name. Italian architects—Rastrelli, Rossi, Guarenghi—worked here in the service of the Czars, creating great, baroque marble palaces, set amid carefully laid-out gardens and broad, handsome streets. Even the ordinary buildings along the streets, of brick or the local granite, were generally plastered and painted in Italian colors. Many a visitor to this city has found himself reminded by its appearance of Rome—but a Rome without the *dolce far niente,* a Rome icebound for months of the year, above whose Italianate palaces the strange lights of the aurora borealis glimmer of a bitter winter night.

Georgi, seated, during his second year at the ballet school, with his brother,
Andrei, who had begun attending a technical school.

Georgi's father and mother.

Of his mother's origins Balanchine knows very little in detail, and of his father's not much more. One thing he is sure of: neither of his parents was of aristocratic lineage. He has never heard tell of any princes among his ancestors, or even counts—and he finds this quite distinguishes him from nearly all the other Russians he has met in exile. His father, Meliton Balanchivadze, was born in Kutais. He was a composer and won a measure of fame, if little fortune, by collecting and arranging the folk songs of his native Caucasus region. "The Georgian Glinka," he was sometimes called. His compositions included an opera entitled *Tamara the Wily,* numerous choral works, a mass and other church services.

Meliton Balanchivadze was a convivial, elegant gentleman, something of a *bon vivant,* who on festive occasions was often called on to play the role of toastmaster because no one in his circle was as gifted as he at improvising flowery speeches of tribute. These were not hypocritical with him; he liked people very much, and with the aid of a little wine or vodka could readily believe that they were as distinguished and as delightful as he said they were. If his had been a less convivial nature, he might have left a more substantial body of achievements as a composer; but then, that is speculative. Cold sober, at some time early in his life, he may have taken the exact

measure of his talents and come to the conclusion that since he would never
be one of the immortals of music, it would be a pity to deprive himself,
during his mortal span, of such passing gratifications as the world had to
offer. His friends were mostly fellow Georgians. There would always be a
good deal of hearty drinking, for which the Georgians are renowned, whenever they got together, and much singing of Georgian folk songs. Among
his friends he numbered not merely fellow artists but people of varied
interests, including such political figures as Tseretelli and Chkheidze, who
were later to play leading roles in the brief-lived Kerensky regime. Balanchivadze very much enjoyed political discussions. He professed liberal,
antimonarchical tenets, but he was not a political activist himself. He
engaged in these discussions in the manner of a Chekhov character, as one
of the amiable and harmless distractions of a civilized man.

He was a man well into his forties at the time of his marriage to
Georgi's mother, Maria Nikolayevna Vassilyeva; he had been married once
before, had two grown-up offspring, and was a widower. Maria Nikolayevna
was a blond, petite, blue-eyed girl of less than half his age. A native of St.
Petersburg, where they met, she was of unpretentious background. Her
education, typical for a girl of her class, had not left her overly burdened
with erudition, but she was not insensitive to the arts and could play the
piano better than passably.

From this marriage three children resulted, each a little more than a
year apart in age. Georgi was the middle one; he had an elder sister, Tamara,
and a younger brother, Andrei. They lived in a modest, small apartment, for
Balanchivadze's music earned him very little in the way of financial reward.
Despite their straitened circumstances and the frequently expressed wish that
they could somehow get their hands on just a bit more money, the family
seems to have lived quite happily—happily, that is, until disaster struck,
in the way that in fairy tales disaster most loves to strike, disguised as
a fabulous piece of good fortune that bestows upon poor misguided mortals
everything they have wished for and more. Going gloomily to the bank one
day to cash in his last savings bond, Balanchivadze was informed by an
excited clerk that his bond's number had been drawn in the state savings
lottery and that he had won the top prize, a sum amounting, in present
terms, to perhaps as much as a hundred thousand dollars, tax free. Here
were riches far beyond the Balanchivadzes' dreams.

There followed, after the first delirious jubilation, such a series of ridiculous and distressing chastisements as the Brothers Grimm themselves might have plotted. First off, Balanchivadze alienated most of his friends by passing out presents. Those to whom he had given five hundred rubles were mortified at learning that others had received a thousand; those to whom he had given a thousand thought it curiously selfish of him not to have made it two thousand, or anyway fifteen hundred. A white carriage horse that a man with a luminously honest face sold to the Balanchivadzes (to go with an elegant carriage they had bought to go with their fine new twelve-room flat) turned out to be not a carriage horse at all but an old circus trouper. It danced and cavorted whenever it heard a band and kept trying bravely, despite the encumbering carriage behind it, to show how cleverly it could prance on its hind legs. One day, in the middle of the city, it threw over the whole equipage, itself and all, smashing the carriage and shaking up the occupants.

Surprised at how expensive life had suddenly become, Balanchivadze heeded the advice of people who urged him to put part of his new fortune into some sound business; he opened a handsomely decorated Georgian-style restaurant in a fashionable quarter of St. Petersburg. This venture soon proved to be a costly mistake, because the hospitable Balanchivadze could never bring himself to charge even the slightest of acquaintances for their meals, and they, in turn, never affronted him by offering to pay. To recoup his losses, Balanchivadze then invested in a factory that would produce foundry vats by a new process. This proved to be not merely a blunder, like the restaurant, but totally ruinous, and he was sent to prison for two years on a charge of willful bankruptcy. His wife did not tell the children where he was (they learned this only after they were grown), but gave them to understand that he was off in the Caucasus gathering folk songs. Balanchine well remembers the day his father returned. The boy, then about six or seven years old, was with his family on the porch of a house they had moved to in the country. Glancing up, he saw his father coming in at the garden gate, dressed as elegantly as ever and carrying a single red rose in his hand. "Oh, look!" Georgi's mother cried. "Here's your father back from—back from the Caucasus!" And they all rushed down the path to embrace him.

Balanchine retains few coherent memories from that first period of his life in St. Petersburg, the five years or so during which his family experienced unexpected affluence and impending doom. He recalls being

At about the age of four.

taken on walks by his nurse to a park not far from their flat, holding primly onto her hand as they crossed the broad street. One of his very earliest memories, dating from when he was about two years of age, is of being on a stage, with an audience staring at him. Taken by his mother to some holiday performance or fête, he happened to get separated from her in the crowd and wandered tearfully about until a stranger, perhaps an official of the fête, noticed his plight. The next thing he knew he had been carried onto the stage by the stranger and, wretched with embarrassment, was being held up to view, like an umbrella or hat that has been found about the premises, for the owner to come forward and claim. The interval that ensued before his mother rescued him from the stage, probably of the briefest duration, remains in his mind as an agonizing eternity. The episode could not be deemed an auspicious presage of a theatrical future.

An incident from his infancy which he does not remember but has often heard recalled was one that occurred in 1905, when he was little more than a year old. His mother had taken him and his sister to the park, where they played for an hour or so. Throughout that time his mother noticed a well-dressed, wealthy-looking man sitting on a bench close by, reading and enjoying the sunshine. He was still seated there when she gathered up her children and left, but no sooner had she done so, as she learned from the papers the next day, than revolutionaries threw a bomb which killed him. He was, the papers revealed, a high-ranking diplomat. The papers also quoted the assassins, who had been captured, as saying that they had waited in ambush in the park for a long time before throwing the bomb, because they had wanted to avoid harming some innocent people who were near their intended victim—a woman, they said, with two small children.

More vivid often than the serious or important events of childhood are those sensory impressions, usually slight or ordinary in character, which for some reason make an indelible mark. So, for Balanchine, the St. Petersburg of his childhood is a wispy cluster of such images: the rattle of droshkies' wheels on the wooden pavements, the cries of street vendors, the pealing of the church bells on High Easter; the mingled pleasurable aromas of coffee beans, spices and rope tar at a merchant's shop his mother sometimes took him to; the strangeness of waking up one night many hours after he had gone to bed and finding it still light as day outside—one of those midsummer nights it must have been when the sky scarcely darkens before dawn, what the St. Petersburgers call a "white night."

The country house to which his family moved when Georgi was small was about three hours ride by slow train to the northwest of St. Petersburg, in what is now Finland but in those days before World War I was part of the Russian empire. It was near the little village of Lounatiokki, in the vicinity of Viipuri, or Viborg, as it was then called. This property was all that remained to the Balanchivadzes from the fortune they had won. Built of logs in indigenous, rustic style, the house was roughhewn but spacious. It had ample grounds, in which the family raised most of the food required, and was surrounded by woods—pine, great white birches and mountain ash. Here Georgi had fewer restraints than in the St. Petersburg flat. He and his brother and sister could play outdoors all day. He was free, as he grew older, to roam in the woods. In season he would gather the mountain ash berries and bring them home, to be made into jam. Sometimes the family would go out into the woods and spend the entire day on a mushroom-gathering expedition; Georgi soon became expert at identifying all the edible varieties. He enjoyed also working in the family's vegetable garden, and in the large strawberry patch at the side of the house. It was an active, bucolic life for the boy, and on the whole a happy one, though the bucolic life has tragedies and bitter lessons of its own for a child. He had for a pet a little pig. A very smart animal and sweet-natured, it used to follow him about wherever he went, even accompanying him on walks in the woods. He was more fond of that pig than of any other pet he ever had as a boy. But the pig grew; the time came for it to fulfill its barnyard destiny and become bacon. Georgi's heart was broken as he was thus brought up against one of the basic facts of life: man's inhumanity to pig. It made a vegetarian of him for a while.

Reading and writing, arithmetic, the Bible and a little history were taught him by a tutor. When he was five, he was started on the piano, taught at first by his mother and then by an imposing, bespectacled German lady who, when satisfied with his efforts, would at the end of a lesson ceremoniously open her handbag and take out a piece of chocolate, smelling

The house near Lounatiokki.

of face powder, which she would confer on him as if it were the Iron Cross, First Class. He did not at all want to learn the piano at first; practicing was a bore; but his mother was firm with him, and put him to bed without supper when he balked at his task. Then one day, as he was thumping mechanically at a movement of a Beethoven sonata, something of the potential beauty and grandeur of the music suddenly came glimmering through to him. It brought tears to his eyes. He could not fathom what it was all about, but he felt it. From then on, though he still often preferred romping outside to sitting down to practice, the most deadly element of boredom—that of meaninglessness—had been removed for him. Before long, he began to show considerable aptitude for the instrument. In the evenings, he and his mother would often play four-hand music together. His younger brother, Andrei, who later in life would become a composer, early showed talent for the piano also, and soon joined in this family music-making. One might have expected that it would be the composer father rather than the mother who would serve as the boys' mentor and companion in music; but the father was not at home much; aside from his spell in prison, he was often on tour with a choral group he had organized. Nor would he have had the necessary patience. Nearly fifty when Georgi was born, he remained a rather distant figure to his children, one who, despite his amiability and his kindness to them, inspired them more with awe than spontaneous affection.

Even as a young boy, Georgi possessed a keen eye for feminine beauty. There is no way of measuring such a faculty, but it is probably as much a part of the precocious endowment of a future ballet master as an ear with absolute pitch is for the future composer. Lounatiokki had not much to offer in the way of pulchritude, but it was not wholly a wasteland; there was, glory be, the village dentist. A blonde in her twenties, she was the first woman he ever thought beautiful. Even when she was causing him agony, he could not help appreciating her charms. The arch of her neck, as she bent to inspect an aching molar, seemed to his already discriminating judgment near perfection; the line of her arm, as she reached for the forceps, was exquisite; the serene imperturbability with which she endured his groans was the expression of a goddess, no ordinary mortal. Going to the dentist was thus an even more acutely ambivalent experience for him than it is for most people.

Little diversion of a cultural nature was available in that remote region of the country. In the woods near the village was a rustic theatre, where

*In motley — Georgi,
at about the age of five, with
his sister and brother.*

an occasional troupe of players would perform. Georgi was taken to the
theatre by his mother a few times, but the performances made little impression on him. Once, though, while taking a walk alone through the woods
at the age of about eight he came by chance upon the empty theatre and,
on impulse, made his way into it through a trap door he found underneath
the stage. He wandered through the dressing rooms, intrigued by the props
and costumes and makeup boxes. And he stood on the stage, looking about
him in the gloom of the unlighted theatre, strangely excited. He was aware
of a curious sense of wonder and mystery now such as he had never known
when he had been there before as a regular part of the audience.

A moment of strange wonder it was for the boy but no epiphany, no
revelation that the theatre was to be his destiny and the stage the place
where he would someday work a magic of his own. His parents had it all
settled by that time that Georgi would have a military or naval career, as
had several of his relatives. His half-brother, Apollon, was a captain in the

Army, and one uncle was a colonel. Throughout his early boyhood be-whiskered uncles and uncle types would eye him appreciatively, appraising his military potentialities. "Look at that back!" one of them used to roar admiringly. "Just look at that back, would you! The boy's a born officer, I tell you. He'll wear a uniform beautifully."

Georgi found the idea of becoming an officer agreeable enough. At times, though, he thought it would be even more splendid to be a priest, as were a number of his father's kin—most notably an uncle who was the Bishop of Gori, in Georgia (from whence, incidentally, also came Joseph Stalin—a stray from the Bishop's pastoral flock). To the boy's mind no field marshal could equal a bishop when it came to sheer pomp and display. The Orthodox Church, with its antique ritual, its Byzantine panoply and sublime music, appealed strongly to both the mystical and the theatrical sides of his nature, and one of his favorite childhood pastimes was to play bishop. Dressed in such ecclesiastical costume as his fancy could improvise, he would spend hours in his room before an altar composed of a stack of chairs, pretending, with portentous gestures, that he was presiding over High Mass. More thrilling to him than any visits to the theatre were the occasions when, in St. Petersburg, he and his family would attend services at the great Cathedral of Our Lady of Kazan. Modeled in architectural style after St. Peter's of Rome, the cathedral was noted for its superb choir of two hundred boys' voices; the pianissimo they could produce, seeming to float in the heavens, always sent chills along Georgi's spine. Sometimes, adding to the emotions he was experiencing, would be the awareness that the choir was singing music composed by his own father. It was in this cathedral that Georgi witnessed the most impressive scene of his early child-hood when he was present at his uncle's investiture. It was a ceremony of burial and resurrection. He heard a solemn requiem being intoned and saw a great black cloth being draped over his uncle, who lay face down, arms spread, before the altar. The secular man was being interred. Then the boy saw his uncle emerge—transformed, as it were, and saw him clothed in his new vestments until at last the priest stood before them in all his new glory.

When Georgi was ten, he and his mother and sister took the train for St. Petersburg one day. His mother was planning to enroll him in the Imperial Naval Academy. The sister, Tamara, was to try out for admittance to the Imperial School of Theatre and Ballet. At the naval academy,

Georgi's mother was given the disappointing news that the rolls were full and that he would have to wait a year before his application could be considered. The three then went over to the ballet school, hoping that Tamara would meet with better luck. Both she and her mother had their hearts set on the girl becoming a ballerina—another Pavlova or Karsavina, rich and famous, dazzling the whole world with her art and beauty. In the St. Petersburg region, and for miles around, many of the parents of young girls were infected with this dream in those days—much as in Odessa, as Isaac Babel tells it in his story "Awakening," the parents of little Yiddish boys all dreamed of making violin prodigies out of them. Some caught lasting cases of the contagion, others got over it.

This was to be Tamara's second try for the ballet school. She had been turned down the previous year. Without *protektsia*—some influential sponsor—it was difficult to gain consideration, for there were so many seeking admittance. At the academy, when they arrived there this day, they found about a hundred and fifty girls and fifty boys trying out for the twenty or so openings. As the Balanchivadzes were waiting on a hall bench, one of the school officials, who was acquainted with Georgi's mother, stopped to chat and, in the course of the conversation, suggested that Georgi might as well audition, too, since he wasn't doing anything else that day. He did not need to point out that a career in ballet was considered in the Russia of that time (as in the Soviet Union today) an honored and respected one for a man to pursue; but he did remark that there was nothing to lose, for if it did not work out the boy could still go ahead and apply once more for admission to the naval academy the following year.

Georgi's mother agreed. Times were hard for the Balanchivadzes now, and here at least was a chance for a free education for the boy. So Georgi, unaware that the decisive moment of his life was at hand, joined the other boys in line.

The audition was a lengthy but not demanding procedure. The young candidates were not expected to demonstrate any abilities in the dance; they were assayed in terms of health, physique, carriage, general air and appearance and such other subtle considerations as the examining board had evolved through the years. First each child was given a medical examination. Then each one in turn had to walk back and forth across a large room under the penetrating scrutiny of the judges. Among the judges was the famed prima ballerina Olga Preobrajenska, then nearing the end of her long, glorious dancing career. Ignorant though he was of ballet, Georgi had nevertheless heard enough about Preobrajenska to be awed at finding himself in her presence. He had never felt more awkward than he did that day whenever he was called back into the large room and requested once more to walk back and forth in a natural manner. Yet something about his looks—his vitality, the elegance and strength of his slim young body—caught the discerning eye of the ballet-school judges. Preobrajenska, in particular, seemed interested in him and spoke to him in friendly fashion when he made his last appearance in the auditioning room.

At the end of the day it was announced that he was one of the eight or nine boys chosen. His sister, to her grievous disappointment, was again turned down. Though pleased for her brother, she might well have been piqued enough at the ironic turn of events to wish she could show him up by trying out for the naval academy. Thus it was, at any rate, through a whimsical combination of circumstances, that Russia lost a naval officer and the world gained a master of the dance.

CHAPTER THREE

So Georgi's feet were set on the path of his destiny. He took one frightened look down it and turned tail. He promptly ran away from the ballet school.

In the light of history, we may savor now the irony of this action on the part of one who was to prove himself so devoted to the art of the dance and so consequential a figure in it. A child is not impelled by historical perspective, however, but by his immediate feelings and impulses. Georgi had never seen a ballet in his life and had only a dim idea what the word even meant. The whole thing had happened so suddenly and without transition; his mother had left him at the school the very day he had been accepted and, with Tamara, had gone off back to their home. He felt as miserable and bewildered as a dog whose master has taken it to some strange city and then abandoned it.

Fleeing the school, he ran through the streets of St. Petersburg until he managed to make his way to the apartment of a maiden aunt—his Aunt Nadia. "What's this?" she exclaimed on opening the door, alarmed at the sight of the boy's forlorn, desperate appearance. "What's this?" She took him in, made him tea and listened to his plaint. She was kind but firm. He would have to go back to the school, if the authorities would take him back after this misdeed. There was no question of acceding to his wishes, no matter how strongly he felt; his elders knew best what was good for him (as, indeed, they did—at least in this case). For such a breach of discipline Georgi could well have been expelled forthwith. The first year at the school was a probationary one. With so many seeking admittance, only those who showed themselves eager as well as apt were retained. But the authorities heeded the pleas of Georgi's aunt and agreed to give him another chance.

Georgi was not grateful to his aunt for her intervention—not then, at any rate. The whole first year he was intensely miserable. The postures and movements which he was spending grueling hours trying to learn seemed to him useless and absurd; he would never master them, he was sure, and did not want to even if he could. In most of his academic subjects—French, arithmetic, Russian grammar and literature—he did poorly also, excelling only in the classes in music and religion. On top of that, he did not get along with the other students. He had a trait, when nervous, of sniffing perceptibly, a twitch of his upper lip which showed his front teeth; his classmates promptly seized on this to nickname him "Rat."

Nevertheless, he somehow survived the probationary period and was promoted to permanent status. Then, in his second year, when he was eleven, something happened to him that had the force of a revelation, transforming everything for him and causing him to view his school experience in a new light. He appeared in his first performance.

It was the custom that students from the school, from the second year on, were used in some of the ballets put on by the Imperial Ballet Company at the famous Maryinsky Theatre. This provided the youngsters with invaluable professional apprenticeship while also making for a piquant supplement to the already vast resources of a company numbering some two hundred dancers. Court coaches, emblazoned with the Czar's double-eagle emblem and each with a liveried coachman in front and behind, transported the children on those occasions from the school to the Maryinsky stage door. Six children rode in each coach. The night Georgi took his first part the carriage he rode in was one of a cavalcade of ten. The ballet that evening was *The Sleeping Beauty*. Georgi appeared as a cupid in the last act. When he was not onstage he stood wide-eyed in the wings. The lush, poignant Tchaikovsky music; the fairy-tale story; the miraculous stage effects, of cascading fountains, walls of flame that suddenly sprang up from nowhere, a boat that seemed to sail forever across the lake of an enchanted forest, and great trees and shrubbery that grew before one's very eyes, until the bewitched palace, so full of life and gaiety a few moments before, was all overgrown and the garden colonnades entwined about with vines; the dancing, such as he could hardly believe possible even as he watched; the sumptuous theatre itself, with its glittering chandeliers and gold, white and peacock-blue decor—all worked magic on the boy's imagination. So this was what ballet was! This was what it was all for, the rigors and demands of the school! The sudden light of insight was like that he had experienced on that occasion a few years before when he had first apprehended the beauty of the Beethoven sonata he was practicing—but magnified now by all the circumstances.

That night, as he watched the dancers—Karsavina, Andreyanov and all

the others in the great company—the boy was stirred by the realization that
every one of them had gone through the very same schooling as he, in the
same building and with many of the same teachers. He admired these
dancers and wanted to emulate them. In his mind at that time there was no
soaring ambition to become someday a great choreographer, with an academy and a company of his own. Even in fantasy he would not then have
been so bold. For the moment, all he could think of was that if he worked
with all his might and tried his very best, perhaps he could earn the chance
to dance with the Imperial company as often as it put on a ballet that called
for children from the school.

It had been August, 1914, when Georgi Balanchivadze was enrolled in
the ballet school. Throughout Europe the guns were beginning to thunder.
Surprisingly, ballet, theatre and opera continued to flourish in Russia
throughout the war. At the ballet school, the children devotedly sweated
away at their exercises—striving to perfect their *arabesques* and *entrechats*,
their fifth-position turnout and *rond de jambe en l'air*, their courtly bows
or curtsies—as deeply absorbed in their own cosmos as novices in a Tibetan
monastery, and just about as remote from everyday reality. One day a week
they did without sugar, as a contribution for the soldiers at the front.
Beyond that, as some of them have since wonderingly recalled, they were
scarcely aware that the war was going on at all.

The design and location of the school building served to foster this
atmosphere of remoteness and self-absorption. Theatre Street, on which it
was situated, was actually not far from the busy Nevsky Prospect, but it was
a short, spacious and tranquil cul-de-sac of a street. The width of the street
at one end was taken up by the Alexandrinsky Theatre, the great imperial
theatre for classic drama. One side of the street was occupied by a building
housing the ministry of culture, where the Lord Chamberlain had his offices.
The school building occupied the entire other side. Designed in baroque
style by the Italian architect Rossi, its proportions were palatial—with spacious, high-ceilinged, elegant rooms. This whole palace of a building housed
in all perhaps sixty girls and forty boys. One lived amid an atmosphere of
space and grandeur, with an abiding sense of being especially privileged.

There were two floors to the building. The girls had their quarters on
the first floor, the boys on the second. Boys and girls attended the academic
classes together, but their dancing classes, with the exception of those in

adagio and in ballroom dancing, were held separately. The academic class-rooms were on the second floor, as was also a small jewel of a church. Down-stairs was a splendid, completely equipped little theatre just for student use, where concerts, plays and dance performances were frequently put on. On this floor were also two huge rehearsal rooms and a smaller one. When ballets were being prepared for production, the distinguished artists of the Maryinsky would rehearse in the largest of the rehearsal rooms. The students were not supposed to loiter about the hall then and peer in, but most of them, including Georgi, could not resist doing so whenever they found the opportunity. Peering through the crack in the door at these glamorous and superbly proficient beings, they were in a sense spying on their own future and wondering if it was really possible that they would ever attain it. It was on one of those occasions that Felia Doubrovska, who was a promis-ing young soloist with the Maryinsky company at the time, having graduated from the school the year that Georgi Balanchivadze entered it, first re-members seeing him. She noticed him watching her and the other dancers at rehearsal. It was his eyes she noticed—the intense, searching scrutiny of his gaze, perfectly polite but completely merciless. "There's a little boy," she thought, "who doesn't miss a thing."

As a student at the ballet school, young Balanchivadze wore the same sort of uniform that would have been issued to him if he had qualified for one of the imperial military academies, dark blue with a velvet collar. The chief distinguishing mark was the collar insignia, that of the ballet student being a silver lyre—the symbol of Apollo, leader of the Muses. The regimen of the school was in many ways as firmly regulated as a military academy as well. Corporal punishment was not administered, but an occasional cuff might be given by way of pedagogical emphasis or as a mnemonic aid—a more direct and efficacious communication than words in this wordless art with which they were concerned. One ballet teacher used to rap the children with his knuckles on offending parts of their anatomy when correcting their postures. He wore a couple of heavy rings on the hand he taught with, and there was seldom a time during his first years at school when Georgi did not have a bruise somewhere on his body.

Despite this, he did not feel abused. He considers himself to have been extremely fortunate in his teachers. For his classes in mime, acting and makeup he had as his teacher the remarkable Pavel Gerdt, whom the *Dance Encyclopedia* describes as "probably the greatest classic dancer and

partner of all time on the Russian Imperial stage." In 1914, when Georgi
entered the school, Gerdt was seventy years old and still making memorable
appearances in character roles on the Maryinsky stage. His mime classes
were, for Georgi, a significant and fascinating experience. Under Gerdt he
learned how one can transform oneself to fit the role being played, and he
became very adept at this. In the student plays that were performed in the
school theatre—such plays as Chekhov's *The Bear,* Ostrovski's *The Storm*
and Griboyedov's *Woe from Wit*—he was often cast to play the roles of
old men, because none of the other boys could carry the parts off so con-
vincingly.

For the classic dance, Georgi's main teacher throughout most of his
years at the school, and the one he admired most of all his teachers, was
Samuel Constantinovitch Andreyanov. A tall, blond man in whom grace and
elegance were combined with strength and indubitable but unostentatious
virility, Andreyanov was then in his thirties and at the height of his powers
as a dancer. As a teacher, he had a reputation for bringing out the best in
his pupils, of whom he was considerate without ever being condescending.
He never sought to woo their friendship. There was no chumminess between students and teacher, but they felt, nevertheless, great affection for
him—an affection that was founded on a profound respect for him as a
person, as a dancer, as an authority.

In some other fields of endeavor, we are accustomed to seeing youngsters of talent asserting their independence from an early age and rejecting
their mentors as ridiculous or tyrannical fuddy-duddies, from whom they
must escape if they are to fulfill themselves. That is the standard early-
chapter theme in the biographies of certain kinds of artists. But the situation
is very different in a specialized, difficult craft like ballet, in which, no
matter how sublime a soul a student may feel himself to possess, he must
manifest his achievements in terms of specific details. A young ballet student
is not likely for a moment to think himself better than his teachers, for he
can readily see by a glance in the mirror how vain that notion would be.
At the school on Theatre Street in St. Petersburg the students knew that
they were not being taught by mere theoreticians; those who were showing
them what to do were, the youngsters were aware, the best in the world at
it. A bond of tradition linked students and teachers together as those of the
older generation passed on to the younger, as if in apostolic succession, the
mysteries and subtleties of their ancient art. It is probably not amiss to say,

Andreyanov,
Georgi's teacher, as he appeared
in SWAN LAKE.

as one writer has observed, that a ballet student's relations with his teacher, at an academy like that in St. Petersburg, has in it something of the quality to be found in the relationship between a Hindu disciple and his *guru.*

In his early years at the school Georgi was lonely, even though in the midst of so many other children and with his days so occupied. He had no close friends among the others for some time. Alexandra Danilova, who was in the class just above his, recalls that her first impression of him was of a shy boy who kept himself rather aloof from the others. She thought there was something very distinctive and mysterious about him and says she promptly fell in love with him, though she wouldn't have dreamed of letting him know it then. Even as a boy he had an extraordinary self-control and calm of manner. He did not show his feelings. His slim Georgian body was possessed of great energy and of more strength than one might have guessed; he loved to run and jump and to dance, but he did not much care for the boisterous horseplay some of the other boys enjoyed. Some of them made him a butt because of this. One boy in particular set himself the task of trying to provoke him into losing his temper. Eventually he succeeded, to his regret. When at last Georgi lost his patience, he threw himself on his adversary so violently that he broke the other boy's collarbone. It was the only fight he had in his school years, and was the only time his schoolmates ever saw his temper out of control. There have not been many such times in his life. It may well be that the extraordinary outward calm of manner he has culti-vated throughout his life stems from the intuition that his nature may be too turbulent to go unleashed.

Music was his greatest source of satisfaction. Throughout the school building there were a number of pianos; wherever he happened to be, when he had a few spare moments, he would sit down and play. Music was a compulsory subject at the academy. Each student was expected to learn to perform passably on the piano or the violin, but there were none, not even in the higher grades, who could play so well as he. Soon he was being chosen by senior students to be their accompanist at the dance performances each had to give in order to graduate; this was considered a signal honor for so young a lad as Georgi and brought him to the attention of the faculty and influential personages who attended these graduation examinations. It also gained him respect and admiration from the younger fellow students who had been at first puzzled by him and therefore, in the way of children and other primitive tribes, hostile to him.

In his third year at the school he performed his first ballet role at the Maryinsky that was considered worthy of mention in the program's cast of characters. The part was that of a monkey in the ballet *Pharaoh's Daughter;* he had to clamber about in the treetops while Kchessinska, *prima ballerina assoluta* of the Maryinsky, tried to shoot him down with bow and arrow. His billing on the program read: "Monkey—A Student." This ballet was his favorite work for a time. He enjoyed immensely scrambling about high above the stage and leaping from branch to branch; here was a part, he

The exterior of the Maryinsky (now the Kirov) Theatre.

felt, for which he had a special affinity. Even though just a monkey, he considered himself privileged to be on the same stage as Kchessinska, whose technical abilities were extraordinary and whose presence was regal—as well it might be, since she had been the mistress of Czar Nicholas II himself, before his accession to the throne, and was then the consort of the Grand Duke André. Kchessinska was not Georgi's favorite of the Maryinsky ballerinas, though. Best of all he liked Karsavina and Elizaveta Gerdt, the wife of his teacher, Andreyanov, and daughter of Pavel Gerdt. Some critics thought Elizaveta Gerdt's dancing too cool—too "vegetarian," as the critic Volynsky put it—but to Georgi's eye it possessed a crystalline purity that was near perfection. Of the male dancers he saw at the Maryinsky, he most

The Maryinsky's interior.

admired Andreyanov and Vladimirov; both seemed to him truly noble figures.

As time went on, Georgi was given a variety of opportunities. He danced in a mazurka in *Paquita,* a part, incidentally, in which Nijinsky, as a boy, had made his first appearance on the Maryinsky stage a decade or so before this; he was one of a group of boys who performed a delightful Spanish character dance in Fokine's *La Jota Aragonese,* which that choreographer staged at the Maryinsky in 1916; with broad dramatic flair he played the role of the child prince in *The Nutcracker.* Whether he was onstage or watching from the wings, those ballet evenings enthralled him. The plots of the ballets in the repertory—*Paquita, Esmeralda, The Corsair,*

Swan Lake, Pharaoh's Daughter, and the rest—may have been unbelievable and absurd but, as performed at the Maryinsky, with the lavish resources the Czar provided at its command, there was nothing to compare with them for sheer spectacle. They were, as they were intended to be, a distraction fit for a king.

All this—the theatre, the school, the ballet company—existed, Georgi was brought up to think in those years, to gratify and glorify the Czar. Without the Czar, he could not imagine that there would be any ballet in Russia, but then he was not able to imagine Russia without the Czar. Georgi himself, as a student at the Imperial School of Theatre and Ballet, was considered a member of the Czar's own household. Once he, along with other students who were appearing in the ballet that evening, were conducted, after the performance, to the royal box and presented to the Czar and to the other members of the Czar's family who were there. It was in 1916, on December 6—Czar's Day. The Czar patted Georgi on the shoulder, bestowed a vague, gentle smile on him and gave him a silver box, ornamented with the imperial crest, and filled with chocolates. Some children were so awed that they almost swooned; they kept their chocolates as sacred relics, until they crumbled moldily away. Young Georgi Balanchivadze was thrilled too, but he ate his chocolates. It was just as well he did—there were to be not many sweets in the years ahead.

If Georgi Balanchivadze was not aware then that a great revolution was brewing, he was not the only one. Most of those whose profession it was to keep informed about political and social matters did not anticipate that upheaval. Even after it began, most people were slow to recognize the significance of what was happening. On March 8, 1917, that historic day when the Russian Revolution broke out, the chief topic of conversation among guests at a dinner party at the French Embassy in St. Petersburg, the topic that aroused the most fervor and debate, according to the memoirs of the French Ambassador, Maurice Paléologue, was which of the exquisite ballerinas who had graced the Maryinsky stage could be considered the very finest —Pavlova, Karsavina or Kchessinska. And in November of that year, a friend of Kerensky's recalls standing on the Troitsky bridge late one night, as Bolshevik troops bombarded the nearby Winter Palace in the crucial action that was to topple the Kerensky provisional government and bring the Bolsheviks to power, and being told by a passing acquaintance that it was a

shame he had missed Chaliapin in *Don Carlos* at the Maryinsky that night—
the basso had been in glorious voice.

With the triumph of the Bolsheviks, the ballet school's Tibetan isolation
from the harsh realities of the world outside came to an end. One day Red
sailors came through the dormitories looking for Czarist agents and counter-
revolutionaries. Not long afterward the school itself was shut down, and the
ballet company disbanded, as a decadent, counterrevolutionary institution,
a vain burden on the honest masses, an unwanted luxury, and an offensive
symbol of the despised old regime. The students were turned out to get
along as best they could.

Georgi was then not quite fourteen. For a short while he lived with his
mother, brother and sister in an apartment on Bolshoi Moskovska
Street, next to the lodgings his Aunt Nadia occupied. His father had gone
to Tiflis, where he became the minister of culture in the brief-lived Georgian
Republic that was established in the spring of 1918. Early that year all of
the family except Georgi managed to make their way to Tiflis to join him.
Georgi was left with his Aunt Nadia to be available in case the school should
reopen. Though he did not suspect it then, he would never see his parents
or his sister again.

To help support himself and his aunt during the times of terrible
privation that were now being endured, Georgi put his hand to whatever he
could. He worked as a messenger and then as a saddler's assistant, his job
being to stitch the canvas pieces of horses' girths and bellybands. Evenings,
for a while, he worked as the house pianist for a small, shabby movie
house in a remote part of the city, improvising appropriately banal passages
of musical noise to accompany the flickery, silent fare on the screen, mostly
the one-reelers of the German comic dandy Max Linder, the best-known
predecessor of Charlie Chaplin. These labors of Georgi's were not for money,
money having become meaningless, but for whatever scraps of food his
employers could spare or for whatever he might be able to trade for something to eat—some matches or some soap, perhaps, that might be bartered
for a crust of bread; or some coffee grounds that he might succeed in
trading for potato peels with which to thicken a watery soup.

His plight was not unique. Nearly everyone about him was desperate
from hunger. One day Georgi witnessed a sight he never forgot. A mere
skeleton of a horse, drawing a wagon, dropped dead in the street—perhaps
from exhaustion, possibly from some disease. Nobody stopped to inquire

From all the houses on the street people rushed out with knives and began hacking up the corpse, for meat. Within a few minutes there was nothing left of it. Balanchine remembers also how few cats were to be seen in St. Petersburg—or rather Petrograd, as it had become—by the middle of 1918; by then most pets had gone into the stew pot. Rats were abundant, though; for them conditions were ideal.

Sometimes Georgi, along with one or another of his friends from the school, would creep under cover of darkness to the Army barges docked along the Neva to pilfer such rations as they could put their hands on. Once Georgi and a companion stole a large fish, which the other boy hid in his blouse. As they left, strolling past the Red Army sentry with careful casualness, the fish suddenly revived and began flopping about inside the blouse. They took to their heels, the other boy beating his bosom with his fist to stun his plunder, and Georgi's heart leaping in his own breast, like the fish, as he ran.

It was ludicrous but it was no game. Martial law was in effect and they could have been shot as looters. Civil war raged. There were barricades in the streets. More than once Georgi, as he went about the city, had hastily to duck into a doorway to avoid being riddled by stray bullets from some skirmish or riot. At one time, when it looked as if the White forces, supported by a British gunboat on the Neva just outside of Petrograd, were about to launch a full-scale attack on the city, Georgi and other boys his age were marched out to one of the city squares, given a rudimentary training in the use of arms and told where to report if the attack materialized. Fortunately for him, he never had to put this hastily acquired knowledge to use.

One wonders what effect his experiences during this period must have had in the shaping of his character. Undoubtedly, self-sufficiency, resourcefulness and adaptability were fostered in him then, and the lesson that most people never have to learn: that simply to survive can be a considerable achievement. It is likely that a strong strain of fatalism to be found in Balanchine's character was reinforced during those years, and a kind of ultimate aloofness and untouchability which one senses despite his good humor—an emotional independence from others which, in the opinion of some who have known him, amounts to an indifference so fundamental as to be cruel. But that may be the Georgian in him.

Whenever he could during those days, Georgi would go over to

Theatre Street. An Army unit was stationed in the school, but the street was the meeting place where he could expect to find his friends and former schoolmates, among them such as Leonid Lavrovsky, who in later life was to become chief choreographer of the Bolshoi Ballet, and Pyotr Gusev, who became head of the Bolshoi's choreographic school. They would look to see if any notices had been put up regarding the reopening of the school and would share with each other rumors they had heard. From there they might then go off together through the city to scrounge for scraps of food. One day, when they had begun to give up hope of ever seeing it, they found posted on the wall the notice they had been looking for: the announcement that the school was to reopen. This had been brought about through the efforts of Anatole Lunacharsky, the Bolshevik Commissar for Education, who was a man of considerable culture and who happened to be something of a balletomane. Lunacharsky managed to convince Lenin that such arts as ballet and opera were not *inherently* decadent or all the other contemptuous things the Bolsheviks had said they were, but rather could be considered a sublime heritage of the Russian proletariat which the aristocracy had stolen from the people and perverted, and that, when properly used—that is, for propaganda purposes—these arts could be as valuable to society as a pig-iron factory. This interesting conversation may well have occurred amid the gilt and fluted splendors of a palace that the Grand Duke André had built for Kchessinska, for the Bolsheviks had taken the ballerina's palace over and made it their party headquarters. It had been from Kchessinska's balcony that Lenin, upon winning power, had made his first important address to the public. Among the crowd in the street below on that momentous occasion had been young Georgi Balanchivadze, thoroughly bewildered by the changes that were taking place.

His bewilderment continued during the first performances he appeared in after the school and theatre were reopened. For a time the dancers—these former members of the Czar's household whose education had included such refinements as how much more profound a bow one makes to a grand duke than to a simple duke—were called on to perform only at Communist Party meetings, some of which were held in the Maryinsky Theatre, with the functionaries at a long table on the stage and the rest of the delegates seated in the auditorium. Bits of ballet—the hoop dance from *The Nutcracker,* perhaps, or the Hindu dance from *Bayaderka*—would be served up as postludes to four or five hours of debate on, say, the menace of Men-

shevik deviationism. It was all very strange. While waiting to dance, Georgi
would stand in the wings intently observing what was going on, just as in
the very same place a few years before he had stood watching *The Sleeping
Beauty*. The debates—grim, involved, devious, tedious—scarcely worked
the same magic on him; but they made an impression. To this day he can
give a telling imitation, both ludicrous and frightening, of a Trotsky har-
angue he once heard from the Maryinsky wings.

Eventually regular performances were resumed at the Maryinsky.
Under the circumstances, one must consider it remarkable that the Bolshevik
government was willing to allot any portion of its meager budget for such
activities. There was no fuel to heat the theatre, even when the temperature
dropped below zero. The audience sat bundled in fur and sheepskin coats,
stamping their booted feet to warm them; the dancers, in their flimsy costumes, were in constant danger of being frozen to the spot whenever they
held a pose, and, as they moved about, clouds of steam puffed from their
mouths and nostrils. At the school, the boys were sometimes given the day
off to go out and hunt for wood to burn. They made shirts out of the velvet
draperies as their clothes wore out. For food, it was a feast to celebrate
when they could get horse lungs, neck or heart for a stew. "Everything was
free in those days—streetcar rides, food, goods—because the millennium was
here, the ideal society had been achieved," Balanchine later wryly recalled,
in summary of that epoch. "The only trouble was that there wasn't anything.
No streetcars, no food, no nothing."

Instead of being transported luxuriously to the theatre in court coaches
on performance nights, the children were expected to walk now. It was
good revolutionary discipline for them. In time, the authorities relented—
this may have been Lunacharsky's doing again, or that of the new theatre
director, a scholarly Communist with the apologetic-sounding name of
Excusovitch—and the old court coaches came back, but stripped of the
double-eagle emblem. One day, Lunacharsky himself took a hand in the
process of helping these former protégés of the Czar adjust to the new
conceptions of society. He took the children to a showing of D. W. Griffith's
Intolerance, translating the subtitles into Russian for them as the film went
along. Thus, in an environment that was an incongruous and unresolved
mixture of the old and the new—of royal modes and revolutionary ferment,
of classes in the elegant, aristocratic and thoroughly artificial conception of
movement known as ballet carried on amid near-starvation conditions on

*At sixteen, with Lydia Ivanova —
a classmate with whom
he often danced.*

behalf now of Marxist materialism and the proletarian masses—Georgi
Balanchivadze pursued his last years at the school.

A reminiscence of him as an upper-grade student during those curious
years after the Revolution has been written recently by V. Kostrovitskaya,
presently the senior instructor of classical ballet at the school, who was a
student there then, in a class three years below Balanchivadze's. It is interesting that prominent among the things that come to her mind as she
recollects him after an interval of some forty years should be his courtesy
and consideration; one is a little surprised, though perhaps one has no right
to be, at finding these traits cherished in a memoir from the Soviet Union.

*I remember [she writes] a slender youth with a fine, pale Georgian
face, straight dark hair and irreproachably polite and modest manners. He
never teased us "little ones" nor despised us but acted as if we were equals
and of the same age, although in those early years a difference of three
classes was enormous. Among the students he was noted for his extraor-*

dinary understanding of music. He could never pass with indifference by any musical instrument. The minute he came down to our floor of the school the sounds of a piano would be heard from one of the big rehearsal halls—that would be Balanchivadze improvising or playing the most difficult compositions while waiting for the rehearsal to begin. Sometimes, in the evening, we would secretly climb the stairs to listen to Balanchivadze playing Liszt, Chopin or Beethoven in the boys' quarters above us. Whatever he played, one could always feel a sort of special, exciting inspiration. There was no doubt that Balanchivadze was a young man of many talents, though it was not yet clear how his talents would further develop.

To Georgi Balanchivadze himself it was not yet clear either how his talents would develop or how he wanted them to. Upon graduation from the school, with honors, in 1921, he was taken into the ballet company as a member of the corps de ballet; but at the same time he enrolled in the Petrograd conservatory of music—which happened to be located just across the street from the theatre—and for the next three years, while carrying on his dance activities, studied musical theory and piano. He was at the time strongly tempted to become a musician rather than a dancer. Such hesitation on the part of a young man on the threshold of his career, before finally committing himself to what later will seem to have been inevitable all along, is not at all unusual. Fokine, it will be remembered, at the same point in his life, studied painting for a year, feeling that the dance, as institutionalized in the Russian ballet, was not taken seriously enough to be thought of as a career for one who wished to be a true artist. He had solemnly circulated a questionnaire among the members of the ballet company asking them for their definition of what ballet was, and was much discouraged by their responses. "Pornography, pure and simple," replied one dancer.

If Fokine could have his doubts about a ballet career at a period in Russian ballet history when the institution was so securely established, how much more reason did Balanchivadze have to be doubtful, graduating as he did at a time when all was in a state of upheaval, in which old forms of thought and behavior were being replaced by new. In the state of flux which then prevailed, the direction of the theatre and school was lax and irresolute as to policy; rehearsals were irregular; remuneration for the dancers was scant. Occasionally, Balanchine remembers, some of the members of the company would get together to talk about the situation, saying to each other, "We must all do what we can to preserve ballet," but not all of them were so certain, when they thought of it, that there really ought to be any place for so antiquated a form as ballet in a revolutionary new society. Balanchine himself was by no means sure, his own dance ideas at the time of his graduation being also of a revolutionary nature, far from the classical ideal.

All that aside, if Balanchine could have become a worthwhile composer, that is what he would rather have been than anything else in the world. Composition has always been in his mind the noblest of the arts; he is sure that the highest seats in heaven are set aside for the great composers. At the conservatory, he tried his hand at composition, urged on by encouraging letters from his composer father, but he was dispassionately perceptive enough to recognize that he would never be of significance as a composer. All this intensive musical training, such as no other choreographer has ever had, was to prove invaluable to him when the dance reclaimed his undivided allegiance. Musically, he might, if he had chosen, have become a conductor or a pianist, once he had given up his dream of composing, for he possessed talent enough. One may be grateful that he did not. As Igor Stravinsky has said on this point, "The world is full of pretty good concert pianists but a choreographer such as Balanchine is, after all, the rarest of beings."

CHAPTER FOUR

Balanchine does not remember when he first actually decided that he would become a choreographer or that, in fact, he ever consciously made such a decision. The deed preceded the wish. "In the old days," he says, "you first were a choreographer and then you became one"—meaning that you made up dances long before thinking of yourself as destined to be anything special, whereas nowadays artistically inclined youths have been known to announce themselves as would-be choreographers before they have taken a single dancing lesson. He was perhaps sixteen when, on the occasion of one of the school concerts in the little theatre there, he made his first serious choreographic essay. Set to Anton Rubinstein's music "La Nuit," it was a love duet, danced by himself and a girl from his class. It created a minor furor. One strait-laced staff member condemned it as a "scandal of eroticism" and favored dismissing Georgi from the school forthwith. Of this work, Balanchine commented to the British ballet devotee and critic Arnold Haskell, during an interview some thirty years later, "As I remember it today, it would be perfectly suitable for presentation in a young ladies' seminary. I thought it very daring at the time." The outraged Puritanism of the staff member who wished Georgi disciplined was not shared by the head of the school, Grigory Isseyenko, who was taken by the work and was strongly impressed, not only by the abilities the dance revealed but also by the initiative Georgi had shown in conceiving and carrying out this project all on his own. Such creative enterprise on the part of a student was a rarity in that academy, organized as it was along such hierarchical lines and with so carefully planned a regime. Isseyenko told the other upper-grade students that he hoped Balanchivadze's example would inspire some of them to creative efforts of their own.

Whether others were inspired by his example or not, Balanchivadze himself continued to make up dances now at every opportunity. His second effort, another romantic duet, danced this time with Danilova, was called *A Poem,* to music by Fibich. Balanchivadze himself designed the costumes, that of Danilova being of a transparent material of a light blue shade. One of Balanchivadze's schoolmates who saw this duet danced—Marietta Frangopulo, who is now the curator of the academy's museum and library in Leningrad—recently wrote: "There are some themes and impressions which are remembered throughout one's life. The dance to Fibich's 'Poem' is one of those—it remains in my memory as something beautiful and poetic." Kostrovitskaya also speaks of it in her reminiscence of Balanchivadze. "The choreography of the beginning of this piece," she writes, "was extraordinary for that epoch: Balanchivadze came out on stage carrying Danilova, who was weightlessly reclining on his shoulder and arms. The success among the public and artistic young circles was tremendous. The piece was performed at numerous town concerts and always had to be repeated as an encore."

Another of his early essays was a duet to a waltz he had composed. A performance of this piece, incidentally, received a mention in a Leningrad periodical, *Theatre and Art News,* June 11, 1922. This is the first review to be found in print of a Balanchine ballet. ". . . on the last night, a special attraction was *Valse,* music and choreography by G. M. Balanchivadze, executed by A. D. Danilova and the author. The first name speaks for itself; G. M. Balanchivadze proved to be a talented composer, choreographer and dancer. Such a combination is a rare one, promising him much in the future." The performance mentioned here took place at one of the pavilions in the suburbs where concerts and dance programs were often given during the summer. In addition to their appearances at the Maryinsky, the company's dancers frequently performed at various benefits and other entertainments. There was one Red Army charity performance around that time at which the former prima ballerina of the Maryinsky, Olga Preobrajenska, was the featured artist. A great favorite with the populace, she was then over fifty but still full of her inimitable verve and gaiety. For her partner on this occasion, she chose the young Balanchivadze—a great honor for him—and the two of them whirled through a tarantella, while the audience cheered.

A year or so after his graduation, Balanchivadze gathered a group of about fifteen young dancers and began preparing a program which was supposed to be the first in a series called "Evenings of the Young Ballet." The performers included such youthful talent as Danilova, Ivanova, Lavrovsky, Gusev, Kostrovitskaya, Stoukolkine, and Tamara Gevergeva—most of them fledgling members of the Maryinsky company, a few still students at the academy. He was aided in organizing this project by a gifted young painter named Dimitriev. Another who assisted was Yuri Slonimsky, the present eminent Soviet ballet critic, who was in those years one of Georgi's closest friends. His friendship brought Georgi not only companionship, encouragement and advice but also an occasional and most welcome meal at the home of Slonimsky's parents, including—the Slonimskys being Jewish— one memorable Purim feast (recollections of food are among Balanchine's most intense memories of the postrevolution years; he says that, alas, he can remember in detail just about every decent meal he ate then).

For the forthcoming ballet program, the young dancers sewed their own costumes, from designs made for them by Boris Eronstein, who was later to become a well-known theatrical designer. They met in their spare time, whenever they were free from performances or rehearsals at the state theatre, and worked enthusiastically till late into the night on the new dances Balanchivadze was choreographing. "We had confidence in Balanchivadze," one of them later said. "Gentle and shy as he was, he yet had authority among us." They felt they were creating something such as had never been seen before.

One tends nowadays to forget what this period of time was like and to think of the Soviet Union's arts as having been from the beginning in the grip of a rigid, stultifying bureaucratic ideology. In actuality, there were a number of years, before Stalin consolidated his power, when the arts were uncensored and experimentation was applauded. Mayakovsky, Essenin, Pasternak, Babel and others were expressing themselves spontaneously in new literary forms; Malevitch and Kandinsky were developing the conceptions of abstract painting they had asserted, and, indeed, it was in Petrograd in 1919 that the very first abstract expressionist canvas—Malevitch's "White on White"—was exhibited; Prokofiev was composing some of his freshest scores; stage designers were experimenting with constructivism and other unusual approaches to theatre decor; Eisenstein was making *Potemkin*. Later Soviet histories invariably deal with this period in solemnly patronizing terms: "a rash and turbulent era . . . novelty for its own sake . . . individualist self-indulgence . . . deformations of natural beauty, distortions of reality," and so on. Yuri Slonimsky—an older and safer Slonimsky than the one who collaborated so eagerly with Balanchine on the "Evenings of the Young Ballet"—strikes the conventional note in his work *Bolshoi*

Theatre Ballet, published in 1952: "In the 1920's Soviet Ballet went through all the phases of barefoot naturalism, strident constructivism, unnatural plastic expressionism and erotic orientalism. But time and reality, as usual, exposed the fallacy of the then prevailing conceptions."

Among young artists, particularly, the Revolution seemed to generate a great release of energy, an innocent sense of unlimited possibilities. Frangopulo's reminiscence of her contemporary, Balanchivadze—a reminiscence by one who stayed in the Soviet Union—is fascinating in its mixture of conventional moralizing about that bygone epoch and acute nostalgia for it.

I remember Georgi Balanchivadze [she writes] in the years when we were all very young, that is after the great October Socialistic Revolution, when we were starting independent lives. It was, in its novelty, an extremely interesting period, full of a strong will for creation—the time of experiments, of daring, the time out of which came the creation of the new Socialistic art, now belonging to the Soviet people. Naturally the interest of the young people in these new trends was extremely lively and sharp, and they were burning with the desire to change a great deal—sometimes to destroy, but also to create. In many cases this was a matter of principle and it was right, but sometimes, as youth will have it, not well thought through and rash. Still and all, life was like a bubbling spring, fervent and intense, and young people were full of enthusiasm to perform new and great deeds in art.

The first program of the "Evenings of the Young Ballet" was to be in the form of a demonstration in three parts, the last and longest part of the evening being devoted to Balanchivadze's works—among the new ones being dances to some of Ravel's *Valses Nobles et Sentimentales;* a composition of Balanchivadze's own entitled *Extase;* and, as the young choreographer's major opus to date, *Marche Funèbre,* to the music of Chopin. The program was grandly entitled "The Evolution of Ballet: From Petipa through Fokine to Balanchivadze." Pretentious titles of that sort, treating the new epoch as the culmination of all history, were standard fare in those days. Anyway, such presumption in this instance may be palliated for those who read of it now by the awareness that the main line of ballet choreography during the past hundred years or so has, indeed, actually followed such an evolution, or rather, let us take care to say, such a "course," since art changes from era to era but does not necessarily improve: from the

Two moments from MARCHE FUNÈBRE — *Stoukolkine kneeling,
Kostrovitskaya on points. These pictures, taken in 1923, are the earliest
photographs of Balanchine choreography extant.*

spectacular, spacious classicism of Marius Petipa, the choreographer of
The Sleeping Beauty and some fifty other full-length ballets during the
forty-one years of his career as ballet master of the Maryinsky Theater;
through the romanticism of Michel Fokine, who in the peak period
of his creativity before the First World War realized such masterly
evocations of mood as *Les Sylphides, Le Spectre de la Rose* and *Prince
Igor;* to Balanchine's neoclassicism, the most notable choreographic expression of our day. (The conscientious ballet historian would, of course,
add to the above list the name of Leonid Massine, as belonging temporally
between Fokine and Balanchine in any survey of the art. Balanchivadze
and his young associates could not be blamed for omitting this name from
their grand, evolutionary overview, however, for they had had no opportu-

nity to see *Parade, Le Tricorne, La Boutique Fantasque* or the other works with which Massine, as ballet master for Serge de Diaghilev's Ballets Russes, had in recent years been delighting and amazing Europe's taste. Anyway, Massine had not come from St. Petersburg but from Moscow, and how could they take seriously anyone from Moscow?)

Of the influences which have formed Balanchine choreographically, that of Petipa, it can be clearly seen now, has undoubtedly been the most significant. From Petipa have been derived such characteristics of Balanchine's mature work as the frank delight in the classic dance for its own sake, the elegant grace of deportment of the dancers, the conception of ballet primarily as a means of giving pleasure and not as a vehicle for transmitting a portentous message. As manifested in Balanchine's ballets, however, these characteristics are presented in a distinctly contemporary manner, without the framework of the elaborate story or spectacle in which Petipa embedded his moments of dance. The aspects derived from Petipa have been, in Balanchine's work, transformed, concentrated, intensified, accelerated, modernized. He gives you, one might say, a transmuted quintessence of Petipa (or, if one does not care for the effect, one might call it Instant Petipa), but in a way which reflects Balanchine's own distinctive outlook and attitude.

It was to be some years before Balanchine developed to the point of acknowledging or revealing these traits or the influence of Petipa, or to recognize Petipa's ideals as, in part, his own. Virtually nothing of Petipa showed in *Marche Funèbre, Extase* or the other dances the young choreographer was devising for his first program of the Young Ballet. The Petipa material was then present within him, but buried. He had stored Petipa up in his very muscles, having danced in nearly all the Petipa ballets, since they constituted virtually the entire Maryinsky repertory. Though in time he would draw on this glittering heritage for his own purposes, it was only natural that, as a youth demonstrating his capabilities for the first time and during an epoch of revolution, he should seek to assert himself in other wise.

Of other influences under which he had passed, that of Fokine should be mentioned. A number of Fokine ballets were in the Maryinsky repertory, and Fokine himself, after breaking with Diaghilev, returned to the Maryinsky, where he worked from 1914 to 1918, when he left Russia for the last time. It was during that time that Balanchivadze, aged thirteen, had the opportunity to work under Fokine's direction in *La Jota Aragonese.* The Fokine ballet which affected young Balanchivadze most, though, and planted a seed in him, was *Chopiniana* (or *Les Sylphides,* as it is known outside of Russia). Seeing this ballet as a youth, Balanchivadze was captivated and intrigued. He had never before seen a ballet which evoked a mood just by dancing, without any story, and he kept puzzling over it, trying to figure out what it meant and, in accordance with his training and experience, supply a more literal reading of it than was intended. At that time, as a boy, he took it for granted that all ballets were required to tell a story; later in life he was to make the storyless ballet his most characteristic medium. Indeed, *Chopiniana,* in this respect, is more characteristic of Balanchine's own main line of development than of Fokine's. For this was one of the few storyless ballets Fokine made in his life; he did it, as he has said, just to show that he could if he wanted to; the rest of his career was devoted to his efforts to give ballet *more* explicit content and meaning, not less.

For Fokine, and for his generation, one of the most powerful of experiences had been that of seeing Isadora Duncan dance, when she first visited St. Petersburg in 1905. She left Fokine and other members of the ballet company questioning their own approach to the dance. They had learned to be cool, formal, professional. Isadora, in her filmy drapes and rapt air, offered the virtues of inspiration, improvisation, freedom, soul. For them the dance was theatre, for her ritual. They regarded the dancer as an entertainer, she as a high priestess. They found her very convincing. Balanchivadze too saw Duncan, but she did not make that sort of impression on him. It was 1922 when he saw her. She had come to Russia at the invitation of Commissar Lunacharsky to establish a Duncan school of the dance, for which Lunacharsky had promised in a rash moment to put a thousand children at her disposal, a promise he did not find it convenient to keep. In 1922, at the age of forty-four, she was still an extraordinary personality, with a fervor for complete revolution that none of the Bolshivek leaders could match. Swathed in her red Marseillaise scarf, she went about Moscow and Petrograd, accosting the Bolshevik leaders and calling them bourgeoisie in disguise because she found them listening to operas and giving receptions amid elegant salons, such as Kchessinska's palace. "Give me your children," she would cry to the astonished Bolsheviks, "and I will teach them to dance like gods—or you may assassinate me!"

Nevertheless, despite the vividness of her personality, she was past

her peak as a dancer. To Balanchivadze's eyes she was unbelievably ludicrous and incompetent. In an interview printed in *Horizon* magazine many
years later, he cruelly summarized how she had appeared to him: "To
me it was absolutely unbelievable—a drunken, fat woman who for hours
was rolling around like a pig. It was the most awful thing." Balanchivadze could not believe that she had ever been a good dancer. For him
inspiration has never been a satisfactory substitute for technique.

If there was an avowed and discernible influence on the choreography
of the youthful Balanchivadze then, it was that of Kasyan Goleizovsky—
a name little known in the Western world, and not much better known in
the Soviet Union of today, though he still lives and carries on his craft, but
who attained both fame and notoriety during the turbulent twenties. A
product of the St. Petersburg Imperial Ballet academy, from which he graduated in 1909, Goleizovsky served as *premier danseur* of the Bolshoi Ballet
until, becoming dissatisfied with the aesthetics of classical ballet, he resigned
to establish his own school in Moscow and found a chamber dance group
to put his dance conceptions into practice. Like Fokine, he had felt acutely
that the classic ballet, as it was then institutionalized in Russia's major
theatres, had become superficial and devoid of any significant creative impulse—sustaining itself only by the technical excellence of the performers,
the sumptuousness of decor and spectacle, and the chic unconcern of the
kind of languid, aristocratic audience it attracted. He preached—and with
all the fervor of a gospel preacher—the development of an art of pure dance,
one exalting the human body and revealing itself not in a chain of stereotyped steps but in fluid, unfolding motion. To this end, he chose for his
dances not the kind of banal, rhythmically obvious music which classical
ballet had almost always preferred but subtle, sensuous music of a complicated rhythmical nature—Scriabin, Debussy, Richard Strauss, Prokofiev.
His troupe danced barefoot and scantily clad; in an art form in which the
human body is the expressive medium there should be as little costume
hiding and encumbering it as possible, he felt. The choreography utilized
fluid, plastic, sometimes acrobatic movements. The effects achieved were
strange, startling and according to many contemporary accounts, including
Balanchine's, sometimes extraordinarily beautiful. Goleizovsky himself was
a strange, powerful figure—romantic, temperamental, iconoclastic. It was
undoubtedly he who was most in the critic Slonimsky's mind when he
damned in retrospect the dance directions of the twenties, for he was cer-

tainly the most prominent innovator of the times. A work of his, *The Legend of Joseph the Beautiful,* was produced at the Bolshoi in 1925, creating a great sensation; but not long after that the heavy hand of Soviet conformism began to make itself felt, and Goleizovsky was pushed from the great state stages into obscurity.

Balanchivadze saw a performance in Petrograd, at the old Hall of the Nobles, by Goleizovsky's group in 1921, when he was just graduating from the ballet school. Some of the older members of the audience were scandalized by what they saw that evening, but on Balanchivadze an immediate and overwhelming impression was made. After the performance he rushed backstage to congratulate Goleizovsky and tell him how moved he had been. It was this occasion which gave Balanchivadze the impetus to found his own chamber group of the Young Ballet some months later, and the images of Goleizovsky's dances were very much in his mind as he worked on his own choreography for the forthcoming performance. It is doubtful if any traces of Goleizovsky's style are to be found in the Balanchine choreography that the Western world knows, but Balanchine has no doubt that he owes Goleizovsky a great debt. "Seing Goleizovsky was what first gave me the courage to try something different on my own," he has said.

As the date approached for the "Evenings of the Young Ballet" program, the youthful participants scarcely took time out to sleep, so engrossed had they become in this adventure. For their theatre, they somehow obtained the hall of the Duma, or city parliament, on the Nevsky Prospect—an enormous round hall with steep banks of seats entirely surrounding the space used for the stage. It had been turned, after the Revolution, into a hall for conferences and lectures; Mayakovsky, Essenin and Blok had appeared there, and read their poems to the public. In their innocence, Balanchivadze and his associates had neglected to advertise the performance or send out invitations to it; they consequently did not expect much of an audience. But word of it somehow got around. To the astonishment of Balanchivadze and the others, the hall was filled with spectators, even to the very top. A great many young people were present—students, actors, artists, even young workers. "The success was so great that we could hardly believe it," recalls Kostrovitskaya. As the performance went on from one new work to the next, the audience's excitement grew. None of the spectators seemed able to watch with calm indifference. From some of the older, conservative members of the audience came whistles of disapproval.

The younger people cheered vociferously, cried out for encores and demanded a bow from the choreographer.

As an event in the life of the city, this performance created a sensation
such as nobody had anticipated. "The whole town started talking of Balanchivadze," writes Kostrovitskaya in her memoir of him. The attention being
paid him was additionally stimulated now by a severe condemnation of him
and his works, which was penned by Akim Volynsky, the most learned and
distinguished ballet historian and authority in all of Russia. As a critic,
Volynsky was consistent. He had witnessed Fokine's first effort in 1905
and had hated that too.

Instead of accepting this rebuke like a chastised schoolboy, as he was
supposed to, Balanchivadze penned a counterattack of his own—one of his
rare written effusions, and also one of the few times in his life he has ever
bothered to respond to a critic's words. This article was not a defense of his
own choreographic works, but a scathing discussion of Volynsky's—for the
critic had made the mistake recently of opening up a choreographic school
of his own and thus laid himself wide open to the kind of treatment he had
been accustomed to meting out to others. Balanchivadze called his article
"How Mr. Volynsky Flogged Himself," parodying a phrase from Gogol's
The Inspector General. It appeared in the magazine *Teatr* (*Theatre*), and
the cover of that issue, December 11, 1923, consisted of a photograph of
Balanchivadze.

The face that gazed from the cover of *Teatr,* intense, poetic, with
brooding dark eyes and disheveled hair, was that of a young Byron or
Chopin. It was a look assiduously cultivated by the nineteen-year-old Balanchivadze, as well as by many of his artistic contemporaries—particularly
those of a group he belonged to who liked to call themselves The Feks, an
abbreviation standing for The Fabricators of Eccentricities, Incorporated.
Balanchivadze carried the Chopinesque style through by dressing in black
garb, letting his hair grow long and cultivating dark, mournful circles
under his eyes. With the pervasive hunger and physical deprivation of the
era, it was not difficult to acquire dark circles under one's eyes, but some of
Balanchivadze's friends thought he was not above using the makeup pot
to add to the effect on dramatic occasions. He was seen alone a great deal,
stalking through the streets, brooding publicly in all the best places for
public brooding.

One problem he had, though, was that his natural gaiety, liveliness and

G. M. Balanchivadze,
as he appeared on the cover of TEATR
for December 11, 1923.

risibility kept asserting themselves just at a time when your true Byron would have been a very model of romantic melancholy. It wasn't so easy to be gloomy, try as one might. Among his friends he was as cherished for his spontaneous flights of humor and fantasy as he was for his more serious activities. One fanciful exploit of his, which caused delighted amusement among all who were aware of it, was an episode that took place at the Maryinsky Theatre, where he was then a corps de ballet member with an occasional small solo role from time to time. In the ballet *Esmeralda* he was given the part of a tramp to play. When he appeared onstage, it was to be seen at a glance that he had made himself up to look exactly like the artistic director of the theatre, one V. P. Rapoport, who happened to be something of a caricaturable figure, being a short man with a large head, adorned on the pate with long hair and at the chin with a dapper goatee—

someone who in appearance and mannerisms very much resembled a
Spanish grandee in an operetta. Balanchivadze had not merely managed
to look like Rapoport but while doing his dance succeeded, with inspired
mimicry, in suggesting Rapoport's mannerisms, incorporating them into the
movements of his dance. Throughout this impersonation stifled sobs of
laughter could be heard from what had been the Czar's box in the theatre
but which after the Revolution had become the box assigned for the use of
performers on their nights off and other artists of the opera and ballet companies. Fortunately for Balanchivadze, Rapoport had enough of a sense of
humor not to punish him for his impertinent joke.

As behooves a romantic figure of a youth, Balanchivadze was passionately in love in those days. The object of his ardor was a flaxen-haired
girl, nearly three years younger than he, whom he had met at the ballet
school, where she was taking evening classes, having before that studied
dance with a private tutor. Her name was Tamara Gevergeva (a name
that was eventually changed, for professional purposes, to Geva). Only
fifteen when they met, she was a beauty. Tartar blood on her father's side
and Swedish on her mother's mingled in Tamara to most striking effect.
She was tall and had a breath-taking figure; her face was Nordic in its
features but with an exotic hint of the Tartar about the cheekbones and
eyes. Her personality was vivacious, and she was interested not just in
dance but in other arts as well—poetry, drama, music, painting.

They began filling small dancing engagements together at one or another of the little night clubs that had sprung up about the city during the
past year, since the proclamation of N.E.P.—the New Economic Policy per-
mitting a temporary return to private enterprise in modest form. Tamara
had a pleasant singing voice, of the German cabaret type; at some of the
clubs she would sing and Balanchivadze would accompany her at the piano.
These engagements brought them in a little much-needed income.

At Tamara's home, when he called on her, Balanchivadze found a welcome and stimulating environment. Her father, Levko Gevergeyev, was an
interesting figure. He had made a fortune in Czarist days from the manu-
facture of gold lamé for ecclesiastical vestments and from the sale of other
religious items; it was not the sort of trade that could be expected to survive
a materialistic revolution. Gevergeyev's interest in these religious objects had
always been pecuniary and aesthetic, for his own father had been a Moham-
medan and he himself was a freethinker. A leading authority on the theatre,

he had assembled during his lifetime one of the world's finest collections of
theatrical memorabilia and had built an experimental theatre next door to
the nine-story building on the Grafsky Pereulok, where he lived and had his
factory. He had long been a patron of the arts. After the Revolution, when
the state confiscated his property, Gevergeyev—as a result of a petition on his
behalf by a long list of young intellectuals whom he had befriended and
aided—was allowed to remain in it and was appointed (without salary, of
course) director of the museum he had once owned. His home continued
to be, after the Revolution, a center of the arts and a meeting place for the
avant-garde. Here Balanchivadze first met Mayakovsky one evening and
many others of the artistic world of the day.

Gevergeyev took to young Balanchivadze from the start, thinking him
gifted and very promising. Sometimes when Balanchivadze came to the
house for Tamara, her father would meet him in the living room and suggest he play a little of Wagner on the piano for him before Tamara was
summoned from her room. Gevergeyev adored Wagner and considered himself, by this means, to be correcting a deficiency in the youth's education,
Balanchivadze having heard very little of Wagner's music up till then.
Gevergeyev would seat the young man at the piano, set before him the score
of *Tristan und Isolde* or *Parsifal* or *Tannhäuser* and say, "Come on, my
boy, let's hear those sublime opening chords." Balanchivadze would commence, while Gevergeyev, with eyes closed, would settle back in rapture.
When, after a time, Balanchivadze would stop, Gevergeyev would open his
eyes in surprise and say, "But how can you break off at *that* point, with
every chord and tension unresolved?" Or he'd say, "Go on just a little
further, will you. I want you to see what a marvelous thing Wagner is about
to do here."

With a discreetly concealed sigh, the young suitor would play on and
on, while elsewhere in the house waited the fair, white Tamara. One evening
he had to play through the whole of *Siegfried* before Tamara's father would
let him go. It was an ordeal like that of Jacob, who had to labor twice
seven years before being rewarded with Rachel. For Balanchivadze each of
these evenings with Wagner were at least seven years long. The ordeal left
its mark. He has never been able to stand Wagner since.

As for young Balanchivadze's intentions toward Tamara in those days,
they were probably—shall we say?—dishonorable. After all, what other intentions could a self-respecting Bohemian have in the revolutionary new

society where bourgeois conventions had been cast off. One day, though, Gevergeyev detained him and Tamara as they were going off, hand in hand, to a dancing engagement and said to them, "Look here, you children, why don't you two get married?" They stared at him in astonishment. "Oh, I know you're both much too young," Gevergeyev went on, "and if the times were different, I wouldn't even permit such a thing, let alone suggest it. But these are very strange times. One must adjust as best one can. I can see how you feel about each other, and I think that if you don't watch out, you're going to get into trouble and make each other unhappy. I could forbid my daughter to see you any more, Georgi, but I'm not that kind of father—besides, Tamara wouldn't pay any attention. No, really, marriage would be the best, I think. You can have a room here and be comfortable, and not have to be furtive about meeting. What do you say?"

The two young people looked at each other, trying to keep a straight face. To have this solemn idea popped at them like that, so suddenly—it was really very funny! "Well," said Balanchivadze after a moment, with an impulsive gesture, "why not?"

"Yes," echoed Tamara, "why not?"

The next day they went out and found a dingy, cluttered bureau where a bored Soviet functionary scribbled a few words on a piece of paper for them. And so the two "children," as Gevergeyev had called them, Tamara not yet sixteen and Balanchivadze all of eighteen, became man and wife.

Meanwhile Balanchivadze was continuing his choreographic efforts in a variety of forms and for whatever stages he could find. He staged the Milhaud-Cocteau *Boeuf sur le Toit* as a pantomime for the Petrograd Free Theatre. For the Alexandrinsky Theatre he created dances for Toller's *Broken Bow* and for Shaw's *Caesar and Cleopatra*. He choreographed another duet, *Enigma*—to music by Arensky—which was put on at the Maryinsky as part of a concert for charity, and he sought permission from the Maryinsky authorities to choreograph Stravinsky's *Sacre du Printemps* as a major work for the theatre but received no encouragement. Late in 1923 he put on another of the "Evenings of the Young Ballet" at the Duma hall, this one even more experimental than the first. No music was used on this program. Instead Balanchivadze created patterns of mimed action for the dancers to perform while a chorus chanted the lines of Blok's *The Twelve* and other poems. For the dancers this was an extremely difficult problem but, as one of them—H. Stoukolkine—later wrote, "We young people believed in Balanchivadze's talent and were ready to perform any and every one of his conceptions as a ballet master."

The authorities of the Maryinsky were less enthusiastic, however, as were the city's conservative balletomanes and critics such as Volynsky. To them, such work as Balanchivadze's and that of his mentor, Goleizovsky, represented a kind of heresy, a dangerous threat to the precious traditions they were desperately trying to preserve amid the chaos of the Revolution. After the second of the "Evenings of the Young Ballet," the directors of the Maryinsky turned decidedly against Balanchivadze. They announced that any dancers in the company who took part in such programs outside of the theatre would be fired, unless special permission had been granted. Balanchivadze was thus, if not checkmated, at least in check. It is possible that despite the extreme physical hardships of life in Russia at that period and the increasingly baleful political atmosphere, he might not have chosen to become an exile from his homeland if only he had been able to work to the full extent of his powers there, but one can only speculate about this, for leave Russia he did, within a year of his official rebuff by the Maryinsky directors.

The opportunity to depart presented itself in the summer of 1924. Vladimir Dimitriev (no relation to the young painter mentioned earlier), a baritone in the Maryinsky opera company who admired Balanchivadze's abilities, managed to get permission to organize and take abroad for the summer-vacation period a small group from the Maryinsky, who would be known as the Soviet State Dancers. The group was to include three singers, a conductor and five dancers, the latter being, beside Balanchivadze, Tamara Geva, Alexandra Danilova, Lydia Ivanova and Nicholas Efimov. Lydia Ivanova was considered as promising a future ballerina as any young dancer to have appeared in many years. She and Danilova were rivals. Just before the permission for the group to depart was received, she was drowned in a mysterious accident when a boat in which she was paddling on Lake Ladoga was run down by a lake steamer. It was a great loss and cast a pall over the joy the others felt at learning that, after many delays, their exit permits had at last been granted.

The group hurriedly packed to leave before the authorities could change their minds; the packing consisted of putting their costumes into wicker baskets and wrapping their meager personal belongings in brown paper to carry as bundles under their arms. None of the young performers talked openly of this trip as a chance to get out of Russia for good. Quite likely, Dimitriev knew full well what he was going to do from the time he devised the scheme, but the dancers—young and ignorant of the world as they were, and accustomed to living from day to day without trying to shape the future—may not have admitted even to themselves that they harbored such a thought. Nevertheless, as they went to board the ship—a German steamer that was to carry them across the Baltic Sea to the East Prussian port of Stettin—there was more tension among them than a mere vacation tour would warrant. A petty immigration official caused them anxiety at the dock by examining their papers with such leisurely skepticism that they were certain the ship would go off without them. Even when they were

Shortly after his departure from Russia.

aboard and under way, it was a while before they felt secure enough to relax. Danilova, the daughter of an artillery colonel, remembers that she did not breathe easy until the ship had got well beyond the range of the guns at the Russian naval bastion at Kronstadt.

After seven years of semistarvation in revolutionary Russia, the travelers could scarcely believe their eyes when they went down to supper and saw on every table baskets of bread and rolls, accompanied by dishes of butter. "It was such a beautiful sight—all that beautiful bread just sitting there like that, so casually, with nobody guarding it—that I almost wept," Balanchine recalls. For the next two and a half days, the group gorged its way across the Baltic Sea. Even in normal times, dancers are among the most voracious of God's creatures; a ballerina, her appetite whetted by her exertions in some ethereal role like Giselle or the Swan Queen, can stow away as much food at a sitting as a stevedore. So it is not surprising that the young Russian dancers devoted that voyage to an attempt to make up for all the meals they had missed. By the time they reached Germany their abiding hunger was somewhat appeased. At least, they had taken the edge off it.

No advance bookings had been made for them. They had not much money and knew nobody, and none of them could speak German. Berlin was quite deserted, since many people were away on vacation. Still the Russians were delighted with everything they saw. To the rest of Europe Berlin was then a drab city, still impoverished from the war. To Balanchivadze and the others, though, it looked dazzlingly prosperous, and to their eyes the dowdy Berliners appeared incredibly chic. They shopped for some clothes here. Balanchivadze tried to buy a hat, but before he was able to find one to fit him he had to go a barber to get his long mop of hair shorn. Such money as they had brought quickly disappeared. While they were pondering how one went about obtaining a dance engagement in Germany, a telegram arrived from the Soviet Union, brusquely ordering the group to return at once. It was a fateful moment of decision. The conductor and the three singers chose dutifully to go home; the young dancers and Dimitriev chose at that point to defect. The Soviet State Dancers company, as they still called themselves, were now down to four; it was a grandiloquent title for a troupe consisting of four youngsters, no scenery and only a few sleazy homemade costumes.

The resourceful Dimitriev managed to arrange a tour of Rhineland resorts, which went off congenially enough, and in the autumn got them booked into the Empire Theatre in London, a variety music hall. Among the variety acts they did not make a great hit; they had not learned anything about vaudeville house tempo and their costume changes between dance numbers were too slow. While they were there, an American impresario who was considering booking them wired his British agent and asked him to take a gander at their program and see what they were like; the British agent did so and wired back that they weren't worth bothering with.

Another who had heard of them was Serge Diaghilev, who was ever seeking replenishments for his Ballets Russes. He sent them a telegram and transportation money and asked them to come to Paris for an audition. Diaghilev was particularly interested at the prospect of finding choreographic talent among them, being then at odds with his current choreographer, Bronislava Nijinska.

The audition was held in Misia Sert's famous salon—a room swimming in green light reflected from the Seine on one side and on the other glowing with the orange hues of the mural which Bonnard had painted for Mme. Sert and which she, on impulse, had trimmed with her scissors so that it would follow the line of her walls. It was Balanchine's introduction to that *haut monde* of exquisite taste, willfulness and wealth which provided Diaghilev's Ballets Russes with its coterie, its patrons and its claque.

In the salon, waiting majestically for the young Russian dancers, sat Serge Diaghilev, that extraordinary figure who had made a unique impact on the cultural life of Europe and who, as a personality, has been an endless source of speculation and fascination. "His dancers called him Chinchilla" [so wrote Jean Cocteau] "because of a white streak in his hair, which was dyed deep black. He wrapped himself in a pelisse with an opossum collar and sometimes fastened it with safety-pins. He had the face of a bulldog and the smile of a baby crocodile, with one tooth sticking outside. If he ground his teeth, it was a sign of pleasure, fear or anger. . . . And his moist eyes as they looked downwards were curved like Portuguese oysters."

On Balanchivadze at that first meeting Diaghilev did not impose himself in quite such vivid detail. Balanchivadze noted then simply an impressive-looking gentleman with a perfume or hair tonic that was scented with almond blossoms. To tell the truth, the young man was not aware of how awed he should be at this encounter. He had not heard a great deal about Diaghilev or his company while in Russia and assumed as a matter of course that Diaghilev's company was bound to be inferior to the great Maryinsky company in which he had been trained. Danilova was of rather the same mind. She was quite huffy at being asked to dance for an audition —she, a Maryinsky soloist! Still, they complied, and Diaghilev was pleased with what he saw. He asked Balanchivadze if he could make opera ballets very fast—a question that stemmed from the fact that the Ballets Russes had recently been taken under the patronage of the Princess of Monaco, with the company dancing in the opera performances at Monte Carlo as well as giving evenings of ballet there. Balanchivadze had never created an opera ballet in his life, but he replied yes, he could—*very* fast. "Good!" Diaghilev said.

A few days later, in London, where the Ballets Russes was having a season at the Coliseum, Diaghilev put a part of the company at Balanchivadze's disposal for the day and, as a test of his abilities, asked him to prepare a demonstration of one of his works. Balanchivadze taught the Diaghilev dancers his *Marche Funèbre*. Ninette de Valois was one of the dancers who took part in this, and she remembers the purposeful competence with which the young man approached the task assigned him. At the end of the day, Diaghilev arrived at the rehearsal hall with his entourage and demanded to see what had been prepared. Imposing, inscrutable, his familiar monocle in place, Diaghilev sat through the performance, taking in every detail. When it was over, he swept out without a word, leaving Balanchivadze and the dancers in total ignorance of his reaction to their efforts. It must have been favorable, however, for shortly afterward, when Nijinska left the company, Diaghilev let it be known that the newcomer was to take her place. Thus it happened that at the age of twenty Georgi Melotonovitch Balanchivadze—or George Balanchine, as he would henceforth be known— found himself ballet master of the most famous and remarkable ballet company in the world.

EUROPE: BALLET MASTER TO DIAGHILEV

Serge de Diaghileffs
Ballet Russe

In a rare moment of retrospection, Balanchine once commented that his education had occurred in two stages. The first took place in Russia, where, at the ballet school and at the Maryinsky Theatre, he learned to love ballet, developed a profound respect for its history, tradition and fundamental principles and, most significant of all, acquired a mastery of all aspects of ballet technique. The second stage began when he had the good fortune to be taken into Serge Diaghilev's Ballets Russes as the company's choreographer. It was during his four and a half years with Diaghilev that Balanchine's aesthetic outlook was shaped, his canons of judgment were established, his taste was refined—that, in short, he became an artist as well as a technician.

At the time he joined the Diaghilev troupe, he was clearly a young man of extraordinary gifts, but as yet raw—talented but without taste, as Diaghilev told him not long after he had engaged him. Diaghilev remarked that the music Balanchine had been hitherto wont to use—Scriabin and such—was not really very good music, a remark which caused young Balanchine to bridle at the time but which carried weight with him. Diaghilev also pointed out that in what he had seen of his choreography false, crude or disappointing effects often marred passages of great beauty, and he added that Balanchine was like someone who carefully prepares an elegant and delicious meal and then, when his guests are waiting for just the right wine to go with it, brings them a big jug of water. Diaghilev, a noted epicure, winced with pain at his own simile.

From the very start, though, it was to be observed that Diaghilev treated Balanchine with respect, despite the difference in their ages. Since Balanchine had just come out of Russia, Diaghilev was eager to hear all that he had to say about what was going on there and what was happening to ballet. He was particularly interested in Balanchine's accounts of Goleizovsky's new productions, with their unorthodox, sculptural effects, and questioned Balanchine closely about them. "Diaghilev greatly en-

Serge Diaghilev.

joyed these conversations," writes Serge Grigoriev, who was the company's *regisseur* (or stage manager) throughout its entire existence, and whose history of those years, *The Diaghilev Ballet: 1909–1929,* is probably the most disinterested and factually accurate, and the least hysterical, of the many memoirs that have since been produced. These conversations with Balanchine reinforced Diaghilev's conviction that Balanchine was going to be a good risk as the company's choreographer. "At the same time," writes Grigoriev, "he perceived, what was less welcome to him, that Balanchine's ideas were already, so to speak, crystallized, and that he would consequently prove too independent to act as a mere instrument for the realization of Diaghilev's own conceptions." Since Fokine, none of the other choreographers—Nijinsky, Massine, Nijinska—had ever made any ballets before coming under Diaghilev's wing. As choreographers, they were entirely Diaghilev's creation. With Balanchine, Diaghilev could see, it was not going to be like that. He could teach Balanchine much, but he could not mold him as he had the others.

Still, for Balanchine, what an education it must have been merely to be associated with such a company as Diaghilev's! As Arnold Haskell has written, "For twenty years the Diaghilev Ballet was the only company that counted. Its history was the history of ballet. . . . If was, in fact, far more than a ballet company, it was a whole artistic movement." From the moment of its first Paris appearance in 1909, it made itself felt as a major influence on European culture. It is remarkable how many memoirs written by people not of the dance world contain an account of the author's discovery of the Ballets Russes as one of the major revelations of his life. The company was the darling of the smart set—Coco Chanel, Misia Sert, the Comte de Noailles, Lady Ripon, Lady Abdy and the rest—but it also spoke to the intellectuals of the day, who treasured it for being in the forefront of the avant-garde, winning spectacular victories for important new movements in other arts besides the dance. A Diaghilev première in Paris was always an event of electric excitement. There was in the air the feeling, possibly snobbish but with more justification than most snobberies are grounded on, that *everybody* who mattered was seated in that audience—the *haut monde,* the artists, the intellectuals. With tense anticipation they awaited the curtain's rise, wondering what new discoveries Diaghilev was going to reveal; what new trends in art and fashions in style were about to be set; what new reputations would be made; what scandals perpetrated.

Matisse sketch for the curtain of LE CHANT DU ROSSIGNOL.

The center of a creative ferment, the company brought to light a host of major talents. At one time or another, almost every European painter of genius, as well as a number of brilliant composers, worked for Diaghilev's Ballets Russes. The list of painters who created scenery and costumes for ballets just in the four and a half years that Balanchine was its choreographer is breath-taking. It includes Picasso, Rouault, Utrillo, Miró, Gris, de Chirico, Braque, Derain and Tchelitchev. At first, young Balanchine rather took these colleagues for granted. They were simply the painters around the place, as far as he was concerned. Not having had much experience with the pictorial arts, he did not know any better. When he was told that *Le Chant du Rossignol,* a ballet which originally had been choreographed by Massine but which Balanchine was to restage as his first major ballet assignment, had sets and costumes by none other than Henri Matisse, Balanchine replied carefully, "Oh, *really?*" and tried not to reveal that he had never heard of Matisse.

One of the things for which he is grateful to Diaghilev is that the latter took some pains to develop Balanchine's knowledge and appreciation of painting. Diaghilev believed that a choreographer should be cultivated in all the arts. For Diaghilev himself, paintings were not merely a pleasure but a passion, a necessity. When he stood before a picture, he seemed to be not just looking at it but imbibing it. During the first two summers he was with the company, Balanchine spent part of the time with Diaghilev in Italy; and when they were not engaged in planning the forthcoming season's new works, Diaghilev would take him along with him to museums and churches. The party would generally include Serge Lifar, the handsome but still awkward young dancer who had become Diaghilev's favorite after the defection of Massine, and Boris Kochno, Diaghilev's secretary, an intelligent, striking-looking young man, somewhat of a dandy, who was doing most of the librettos at this time and whose opinions Diaghilev valued highly. They went to Florence, Venice, Siena, Assisi, Ravenna and Rome. Diaghilev always carried his Baedeker with him. He was as inseparable from his Baedeker, Kochno has written, as a priest from his breviary. "He pored over it in the train and as soon as he arrived in town would set off to see the pictures he knew so well already as if late for a romantic rendezvous."

Balanchine remembers with appreciation that Diaghilev seldom lectured him about how he was supposed to react to the paintings he was showing him, but would merely usher him up to some picture and command, "Look!" Then he would leave Balanchine alone to gaze at it. Gradually some of the paintings he was being shown began to become meaningful to Balanchine and give him pleasure. He grew especially fond of Perugino. Once, Diaghilev led the group into a part of the Vatican that, he said, was adorned entirely by paintings by Raphael. They looked about. "That one," said Balanchine diffidently after a while, pointing to the central painting in the ceiling, "looks to me more like a Perugino."

Lifar scoffed at Balanchine's assertion. "Don't quarrel," said Diaghilev. "Let's look at the book." He turned to the pertinent section in his Baedeker and read it aloud. The book said that the paintings in this section were all by Raphael with the exception of one in the ceiling which was by Raphael's master, Perugino. Diaghilev congratulated Balanchine, who felt quite pleased with himself at this small, unexpected triumph.

Considering his youth when he joined Diaghilev's Ballets Russes, Balanchine might well have been forgiven if he had panicked upon being suddenly entrusted with choreographic responsibility for a company of such intimidating reputation, but he met the challenge coolly. Even at that age, he was a thorough professional, and he had perceived at first glance something that the public had not yet noticed—that the company, though it offered manifold delights in the way of scenery, new music, avant-garde librettos and over-all style of presentation, really did not dance very well. At that period in its history the Diaghilev group had only forty dancers—a handful compared to the huge ensemble Balanchine had been accustomed to at the Maryinsky. The soloists were good, but the corps de ballet was ragged. Diaghilev, who had never set up a ballet school of his own, had always counted on getting new dancers from the great Russian companies—the Maryinsky and the Bolshoi—but with the Revolution that source of supply had been cut off, except for an occasional defector. That was one of the reasons, Balanchine thinks, that Diaghilev came to focus so much attention on decor and costumes; he was trying to distract the public from the inadequacies of the dancing.

At first, Balanchine's appointment as ballet master had been greeted with grumbling and a certain amount of passive resistance on the part of some members of the company, who were suspicious of change and were not disposed to welcome a callow stranger in so authoritative a role. Before many rehearsals, though, he managed to gain their confidence and allegiance. "Easy brilliance, strong individualism, humour, and a rare intelligence"—these were the traits that Ninette de Valois, who was a soloist with the Ballets Russes at the time Balanchine joined the company, noted about him then. Others in the company recall his unfailing courtesy and spontaneous charm, his gaiety and his lack of temperament. Though he was, as he still is, sparing of praise, he was easy to get along with. In these respects he was an agreeable contrast to some of the other choreographers the company had known: the brooding, withdrawn Massine; the unhappy, severely disturbed Nijinsky; and especially Fokine, who frequently flew into rages and threw chairs about during rehearsals.

Among those who have recorded their memories of Balanchine during his early days with the Ballets Russes is Vladimir Dukelsky, a young Russian composer who never fulfilled his early promise in serious music, but who later, under the name of Vernon Duke, became a successful writer of musical comedy and film scores. Dukelsky was working on his first commission for Diaghilev, the score for a ballet to be called *Zephyr and Flora,* when Balanchine joined the company. He has written, in a volume of breezy reminiscences called *Passport to Paris,* that his very first memory of Balanchine is actually quite dim because he was so charmed by the sight of Tamara Geva, Balanchine's wife—with her pale skin, fair hair, cool blue eyes and lissome body. This was at a rehearsal of *Scheherazade.* "She startled Grigoriev, the stern disciplinarian, by wearing pink Russian boots to rehearsal; since *Scheherazade* is a character, not a classical, ballet, he let it pass. She also wore a pink ribbon in her lemon-blond hair and had seductive little wrinkles at the corner of her mouth when she smiled—I never saw a prettier girl." To George Balanchine he paid little attention at first. "Unaware of George's prodigious gifts as a choreographer I thought he was merely an inevitable nuisance in his lucky role as Tamara's husband." Dukelsky, who was just enjoying his first splash of fame as a composer and who fancied himself as a Beau Brummel, promptly began ogling Tamara and trying to start a flirtation with her. Soon, however, he began to be aware of Balanchine as well, and when he did, developed a great admiration and affection for him—which did not stop Dukelsky from continuing to try to flirt with his wife. After all, thought Dukelsky, they were men of the world, weren't they, and twenty-one (just barely, both of them)? They became good friends, a friendship that was to endure many years. Dukelsky delighted in Balanchine's sense of fantasy and his untranslatable humor; he called him "a Tiflis pixie." He enjoyed watching Balanchine making his way by mimicry in countries where he did not know the language, and usually, though not always, succeeding in communicating his meaning. He remembers one occasion when they were dining together in Florence, and Balanchine wanted a glass of milk, which was not to be found on the menu. "On all fours, he made a stupid face and uttered several heart-rendering 'moos'; the waiter smiled, snapped his fingers, nodded repeatedly and, a few minutes later, triumphantly produced a large steak."

Bedazzled as Dukelsky was in those days by the lure of money and worldly success, he was much impressed by Balanchine's casualness about such matters. He was also struck, as were most composers who knew him, by Balanchine's rare musicality; and he could not help regretting that his *Zephyr and Flora* was being choreographed by Massine, who, though now on cool terms with Diaghilev, had been engaged for this occasion as guest choreographer, rather than by Balanchine. "Massine had no musical intuition; he didn't know or feel why a certain passage was right, another wrong," he has written. "He never guided me the way Diaghilev did, by talking, or the Balanchine way, by sitting down at the piano and improvising the sort of music he needed."

Ballet dancers—even the vainest, most narcissistic and hysterical of the breed—are first and foremost professionals. Ultimately, a choreographer wins a company's allegiance not by compliments and pleasing ways but by his abilities. From a capable choreographer dancers will patiently tolerate almost any kind of treatment; the only thing they will not put up with is incompetence. The members of the Ballets Russes thought it was very nice that Balanchine was such an agreeable young man, but what most endeared him to them at the start of his tenure was the freshness and imagination, the easy inventiveness, with which he carried out the first chore Diaghilev gave him—which was to revise the opera ballets in which it was the company's task to dance during the winter season at Monte Carlo as a way of earning its bread and butter at its home base. Dancing in opera ballets had always been sheer drudgery for the company but Balanchine managed to make it a pleasure; and Ninette de Valois remembers that they were all grateful to him for this liberation. "How refreshing was his originality!" she wrote in a volume of reminiscences called *Come Dance with Me*. "I can remember taking part in many small duets and ensembles arranged by him for the various operas: he charged those dreary experiences with new life and interest, and no demands on him could curb his imaginative facility. His great musical sense never failed to make the most of the material offered to him, even when confronted with that outlet so universally dreaded by all choreographers—the opera ballet."

Diaghilev was also gratified by the results. That season it became quite the thing among the fashionable set at Monte Carlo to attend the opera just for the dancing.

During his first year Balanchine choreographed two major ballets. The first, which made its debut in Paris in June of 1925, was Balanchine's new version of *Le Chant du Rossignol,* made necessary because Massine's original version of it, five years before, had been forgotten by the dancers and had never been much liked anyway, receiving only two performances. Balanchine's choreography matched well the enchantment of the fairy-tale libretto and the mysterious lyricism of Stravinsky's score, and the ballet was never out of the Diaghilev repertory thereafter.

Among other features, *Le Chant du Rossignol* was noteworthy as the ballet in which Alicia Markova, then a mere fourteen years of age, made her debut. She danced with much success the part of the Nightingale, in a role that Balanchine, always remarkably percipient and adept when it came to devising choreography that showed off a dancer to best advan-

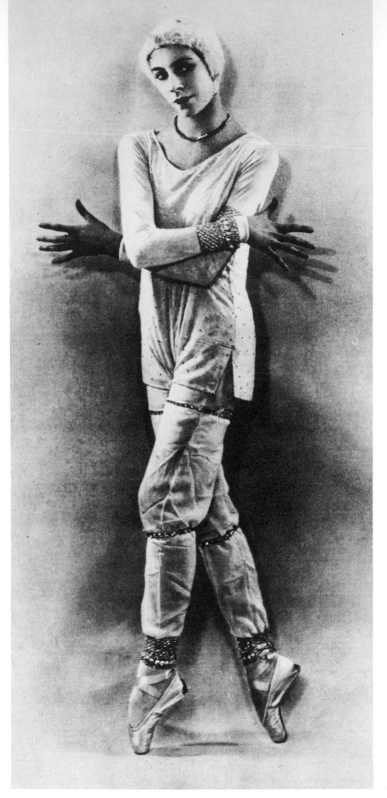

Alicia Markova as The Nightingale in LE CHANT DU ROSSIGNOL *in 192*

tage, had fashioned especially to suit the ethereal fragility of her style and appearance. "I think I could claim," she has written, "to be the first Baby Ballerina discovered by Balanchine." She recalls that Balanchine was instrumental in Diaghilev's engagement of her. She had danced several times for Diaghilev at the studio of her teacher Astafieva in London during the previous winter. Diaghilev was much taken by her, but the decision as to whether he would engage her was still pending when, one day, she received an urgent call to come to the studio again. This time Diaghilev brought Balanchine with him. "I remember dancing for them for about two-and-a-half hours on end, with Mr. Balanchine asking me to do all kinds of difficult technical and acrobatic steps, which, strange to say, however difficult, I was able to accomplish. I felt he seemed very intrigued and interested, and rather amused; and later I learned he had told Diaghilev I would be right to create the role of the Little Nightingale in Stravinsky's ballet, which was to be the first work he was to choreograph for the Diaghilev Company."

Dealing with a child ballerina created unexpected problems from time to time. One such arose in connection with her costume. A magnificent white costume had been made for her, in accord with Matisse's sketches. When little Alicia saw it, she burst into tears. She had been told that she was going to be a nightingale, and a nightingale wasn't white. It was a drab little brown bird, and she wanted a drab little brown costume. Nobody was able to pacify her, not even her governess or mother. But Balanchine had a little talk with her and somehow managed to cheer her up and reconcile her to the sumptuous white costume. She remembers that he had a nice way with children, perhaps because he was not too far from one himself then. He was, after all, only about six years older than she.

The second Balanchine ballet of the year, *Barabau,* a broad, earthy, knockabout farce, was about as different a ballet from *Le Chant du Rossignol* as could be imagined. "These two works," writes Boris Kochno in his very handsome historical survey *Le Ballet,* "the one solemn and lyrical, the other Italian buffoonery, inspired by popular song, allowed the young choreographer to show the diversity of his gifts." *Barabau* was a setting by the youthful new composer, Vittorio Rieti, of an old Italian nursery rhyme. It used a vocal chorus, had sets by Utrillo, and was danced by Woizikowsky, Lifar, Sokolova and Tamara Geva. Most of the dancers wore false noses, padded bottoms and coarse peasant garb. *Barabau* brought a fresh breath of pure garlic to the ballet stage. It was probably the first ballet that was funny enough to set an audience to laughing aloud. Sokolova remembers how surprised she and the other dancers were at first to hear such a sound coming from the other side of the footlights. *Barabau* was given its first performance at the Coliseum in London on December 11. Though it was to prove extremely popular on the Continent thereafter, the English did not take to it, particularly the English critics. "Merely vulgar and rather tedious," was Cyril Beaumont's verdict. "As a whole," he wrote, " 'Barabau' filled me with misgivings as to the wisdom of Diaghilev's choice of Balanchine as choreographer."

The English did not care to be shaken up by new things very much. They had rather a rigid code of propriety concerning what they expected ballets to be like, and they felt rather put off and wounded if Diaghilev's company offered them anything different. They tended to be sentimental about the older ballets, including those which, now properly wooled up in their thoughts by nostalgia, they had at first rejected as too experimental. They liked best to see their old favorites, danced by their favorite dancers. That was nice; that was cozy. Diaghilev had decidedly mixed feelings about the English audience. "He valued his English friends above others," wrote Arnold Haskell, one of his biographers, "and knew that he could rely upon them; he valued the fidelity of the public, and at the same time he deeply resented the conservatism that prompted it." The Paris audience was much

The comic BARABAU.

more fickle, but Diaghilev cared far more what Paris thought. In Paris the decor and costumes were the chief focus of interest, followed by the music. London tended to be more interested in the dancing, the dancers' personalities and the story. Elsewhere, on tour, there were still other reactions. Each city seemed to have its own preferences. The least predictable was Berlin. There what had been warmly greeted one year might be received with apathy the next.

It had been only two years before Balanchine's advent that the company had found its haven at Monte Carlo, under the patronage of the Princesse Héritière de Monaco. Before that the company had been very much itinerant entertainers, lugging their baggage with them, going from one crisis to another and never being sure that the whole enterprise was not on the verge of collapse. The Monte Carlo arrangement provided a substantial measure of security at last. From about November or December until about May Diaghilev's company would generally be in residence at Monte Carlo, where it would present a season of its own, dance in the opera ballets and prepare new works. In late May or early June, its all-important Paris season would take place, followed by a couple of weeks in London. After that the company might disband for its annual summer vacation period of two months. When it reassembled, there would be a tour of such cities on the Continent as Diaghilev had been able to arrange, with perhaps another week or two in London, and then once more it would settle in for the winter at Monte Carlo.

A wonderful place to work, Monte Carlo was, for the Diaghilev company: a haven, a storehouse, a laboratory, a resort. Balanchine loved the place from the first moment he saw it—the sea, the mimosa, the flowered hillsides and winding streets, the café terraces and the little shops, with whose proprietors he became friendly. He was at home there. Life for him in those days was by no means all art and high purpose. Sometimes Diaghilev told him that he worked too hastily. But then the rehearsal hall was in a windowless basement of the opera house, lit only by electricity. "Outside it was so beautiful, and I was young," Balanchine later recalled. "There were times when I would finish up a task more quickly than I should have, because I couldn't bear to linger in that dungeon another minute." During one slack period, he and Grigoriev thought they were safe in cutting the morning rehearsal sessions short and giving the company the time off, because Diaghilev never attended those rehearsals; he usually rose late, chatted in his hotel with Grigoriev for a while, and about one o'clock emerged from his hotel. But somebody betrayed them. Grigoriev arrived at Diaghilev's hotel one morning to find Diaghilev already up and dressed. He had decided to attend Balanchine's rehearsal, he said, and to make sure that Grigoriev would not dash ahead and warn Balanchine, he asked Grigoriev to wait and go with him. When they reached the rehearsal room, the porter there of course told Diaghilev that everybody had left half an hour before. No comment was made by Diaghilev, but none was necessary. Balanchine cut no rehearsals after that.

Balanchine and Tamara Geva lived at first in a pension at the Hôtel de Prince. Dimitriev, Efimov and some of the other members of the company also stayed there. The food was good, and lunch, following the morning rehearsal, was a leisurely, pleasant, often merry affair. In the evenings, after a performance or the evening rehearsal, there might be little parties at the apartment of one or another of the dancers—though often by that time most of the dancers were too exhausted from their day's work to do anything but sleep. At these parties Balanchine would often be called on to improvise at the piano or he might strum a guitar and sing, in a lugubrious voice, bawdy and nonsensical lyrics to mournful Russian tunes. Sometimes he would prepare a gala meal. He had discovered in himself, once he began to appreciate the delicate wonders of French cuisine, a talent as a chef, and became eventually quite famous for this within the company. Doubrovska remembers one occasion, some time after Balanchine had joined the company, when she invited Diaghilev to a little party that she and her husband, Vladimirov, were giving, and was only able to gain his acceptance by promising that Balanchine would be preparing the meal.

They had good times, but it was not all the high brilliant gala that romantic accounts have suggested. They worked exceedingly hard, these dancers. The standard salary for those below the top rank of stars was only fifteen hundred francs a month, or about sixty dollars. Balanchine, because of his additional duties as choreographer, was paid 2,500 francs. Each month Balanchine, Tamara Geva, Danilova and Efimov would contribute a fifth of their salaries to Dimitriev. They felt obligated and grateful to him for being the instrument that had brought them out of Russia; besides, they had signed a contract with him stipulating that they would do so. After this, not a great deal was left to live on. Most of the Diaghilev dancers lived rather like sharecroppers, begging advances from the management and always in debt to it. Meanwhile the smart set were nightly tossing away fortunes in the Casino, which incidentally was supposed to be off limits to the dancers and other entertainers, a rule which had been put into effect shortly before the war as a consequence of a gambling spree by Chaliapin, during which he lost his entire season's fee. During all his years in Monte Carlo, Balanchine only once slipped into the Casino. This was one evening just after he had been paid his monthly salary, which he found amounted, after he had given Dimitriev his share and paid back what he had borrowed from the management, to a total of twenty francs. It seemed better to Balanchine to be completely penniless than to hoard such a pittance. He walked into the Casino, tossed his twenty francs down on number 13 and, without waiting for the wheel to spin, turned and walked out again. A moment later, an acquaintance who had observed this rushed after him to give him the handful of money Balanchine had won; the wheel had turned up 13. Delighted, Balanchine took his winnings and paid his rent with it. It is typical of his nature, albeit somewhat curious, that he never felt any urge to try his luck again, not even just once.

The glittering soirees in Paris and London, around which legends have accumulated, were not attended by most of the Diaghilev company, except on the occasions when they were invited to dance for the guests. For such chores, they got no extra pay, had to put out from their own pockets for taxi fare back to their hotels late at night, and were lucky if they even got fed. Only the brightest luminaries among them were lionized guests at such parties. Balanchine was not in that category. The choreographer was all-important to the company, but he was not, in those days, a star or public personality unless he also happened to be the leading dancer or Diaghilev's special protégé. Once, during the Paris season not long after Balanchine had joined the company, one of Diaghilev's coterie of patrons, Lady Abdy, was being honored at a fête at Claridge's. Diaghilev asked Balanchine to come to the affair and stage Lady Abdy's various entrances with all due elegance and theatricality. When Balanchine attempted to pass into Claridge's that evening, the doorman barred the way. Balanchine said he had been invited to the gala for Lady Abdy. The doorman looked him over with an expert eye and sniffed disdainfully. When Balanchine persisted, the doorman called two large policemen who expertly tossed him into the rain-filled gutter. Balanchine argued no more but made his sodden way home. In later years as Balanchine became better known, he would occasionally be invited, as a guest, to such affairs; but he never enjoyed them anyway and sought to avoid them whenever he could. Unlike Nijinsky, Massine or Lifar, he would never play a dazzling part in the glamour of the Diaghilev epoch. The chic world would never fawn on him; Picasso would not sketch him; the papers would not be full of fascinating stories concerning his latest tantrum or exploit. It caused him no regrets. He could well do without all this.

With Diaghilev—*"cet homme charmant et terrible,"* in Debussy's apt characterization—his relations remained friendly but always rather formal. Their mutual respect was tinged with a certain mutual wariness. Balanchine, it was obvious from the start, was one of those men who, as Diaghilev chose to put it, "had a morbid interest in women." He was not going to be a candidate for the homosexual entourage. This left him out of some of the opportunities which Diaghilev reserved for his favorite, but it simplified life for him immensely. He was spared the hysteria that went with the favorite's role. No detectives would shadow him, at Diaghilev's behest, as they once did another of Diaghilev's ballet masters when Diaghilev began to suspect the latter of infidelity—and with a woman, at that. Balanchine's private life would be his own.

After the success of his first year, Diaghilev counted on him for two or three new ballets a year, along with such other occasional dances, divertissements and ballet revisions and refurbishments as might be required. His facility was considered extraordinary; only Fokine could be compared with him in this respect. One of the most popular of his ballets for Diaghilev, *Les Dieux Mendiants,* or *The Gods Go A-begging,* was one that Balanchine put together backstage in just a week's time during the 1928 London season, choreographing it in spare moments between rehearsals and performances of other ballets. With Handel music arranged by Sir Thomas Beecham, it had been intended by Diaghilev as no more than a complimentary gesture toward his faithful English audience; but the ballet unexpectedly turned out to be a success that delighted audiences everywhere, even Paris.

Of the other ballets he did during the first half of his tenure with Diaghilev his most applauded works were *The Triumph of Neptune* and *La Chatte. The Triumph of Neptune* was another work that was specially created to please the British audience. It had a book by Sacheverell Sitwell, music by Lord Berners, and sets and costumes designed in the style of the nineteenth-century English toy theatres. The whole long ballet, in its twelve

Lifar and Nikitina in LA CHATTE.

scenes and fantastic, sensational plot, marvelously evoked the atmosphere of the Victorian pantomime. With its jolly jack-tar and bustling London streets, its clowns and fairy queen and apotheosis of Britannia at the end, it captured an English essence—"the puerile romanticism," as the Russo-French dance critic Levinson wrote, "of a race of grown-up, laughing children."

La Chatte, the following season, was very different from this tribute to sentimentality. It was a thoroughly modern statement. The constructivist sets, of transparent talc against a background of black cloth, were by Gabo and Pevsner. The story was an Aesopian fable, though turned upside down in a way that really destroyed the fable's point if anybody had stopped to consider it, and the dancers in their gleaming cellophane costumes resembled science fiction characters. Paradoxically, despite all the novel elements, the ballet succeeded in suggesting, more powerfully than a traditional treatment might have, a quality of classic mythology, an ancient Greek ideal of physical beauty. In this ballet Serge Lifar achieved his first important triumph. As a dancer, he had come a long way in just four years from the apologetic awkward youth who, in 1923, had tagged along, uninvited, when

Lifar's entrance in LA CHATTE.

Nijinska sent to Russia for some of her promising students. "Who is this boy who has no sense of rhythm and no ear?" Diaghilev asked when he first saw him, but Lifar was allowed to stay with the company on sufferance. Driven by ambition, he worked as probably no other dancer has ever worked, for none of the other great ones had ever started so late. He practiced his parts incessantly. Long after Balanchine had begun yearning to get out of the rehearsal hall and into the sunshine, Lifar could be heard begging him, "Please, George, go over that bit just once more with me, won't you!" Maurice Tassart has described him well:

"He did not command quite as much elevation as did Nijinsky, and his batterie *was not nearly as clean. But he had the same grace and radiance, and undoubtedly much more fire and dramatic power. In addition to this, he was taller, with a much more beautiful figure: broad shoulders, narrow hips, perfectly shaped legs. His strange, unforgettable face was both childish and diabolic. Far from trying to soften his Asiatic features, he emphasized them deliberately when he had his naturally upturned nose surgically flattened in 1928."*

Though Lifar never quite succeeded in overcoming all his technical faults, Balanchine, fitting his choreography to him like a glove, was able to conceal such inadequacies as remained and provide for him the kind of movements —something of a daring synthesis between the classic dance and the suppleness of the circus and music hall performer—which were his most superb expression. "It was Balanchine who provided Lifar with the necessary outlet for his talent," wrote Pierre Michaut. "Here was the ideal dancer for Balanchine's choreographic compositions."

Originally, Balanchine himself was called on to do considerable dancing for the Diaghilev company as well as choreographing. How good a dancer he was has been the subject of some dispute. Ninette de Valois has drily dismissed his dancing as having been "less than indifferent." He resents this imputation fiercely, whereas criticism of his ballets provokes nothing more than a careless shrug from him. He says he does not see how anyone can be a choreographer without having first been a first-rate dancer, since the choreographic ideas are all communicated by demonstration. "I was, as a matter of fact, a wonderful dancer," he says forthrightly—not as a *danseur noble,* but as a character dancer. While at the Maryinsky, he had won ac-

claim for his performance of the hoop dance as the Jester in *The Nutcracker*.
Danilova and many other of his colleagues concur as to his abilities. They
say that his leaps were prodigious—that, in fact, they never saw anybody,
except Nijinsky, with better elevation. "He could jump like a flea," recalled
Danilova once, "and he could dart and whirl about the stage like a string
of firecrackers. I never saw anybody dance a better *Lezginka* than he." And
Cyril Beaumont, in his book *The Diaghilev Ballet in London*, singled out
as one of the outstanding dances of *The Triumph of Neptune* the "remarkable solo by Balanchine as the Negro, Snowball; a dance full of subtly
contrasted rhythms, strutting walks, mincing steps and surging backward
bendings of the body, borrowed from the cake-walk, the whole invested
with a delicious humour derived from the mood of the dance, a paradoxical
blend of pretended nervous apprehension and blustering confidence."

Be that as it may, the question of Balanchine's dancing ability was
rendered academic early in 1927, shortly after the season in which *The
Triumph of Neptune* was given its première, when he suffered a severe knee
injury during rehearsal. He had to have an operation, and his leg was in a
cast for a month. It was fortunate that Balanchine had choreographic talent,
or all his years of rigorous training would thus have come to nothing, for he
had difficulty with strenuous roles after this operation and for quite some
time could not even kneel with ease. "Good! Now I won't have to work so
hard," Balanchine remarked when he first learned the bad news that his
knee would never be strong again—an unexpected reaction but not an in-
explicable one. It is of a piece with Pablo Casals' exclamation when, at the
age of twenty-one, a rock smashed his left hand: "Thank God I won't have
to play the cello any more!" It was a cry of relief from the agonizing burden
of responsibility his talent meant. For a performing musician, his instrument
is his chariot to heaven, but it is also the stubborn enemy with which he has
to wrestle—"my intimate enemy," Enesco called his violin. How much more
intimate is the enemy for the dancer, whose instrument is his own body.

Of the various performances Balanchine gave as a dancer, the one
which those who saw it are least likely to forget was the time, about a year
after he had joined the company, when he danced Alicia Markova's role
of the Nightingale in *Le Chant du Rossignol*. The work had been scheduled as a command performance for the Princesse Héritière of Monaco,
whose favorite ballet it was that season. At the last moment little Markova
fell ill. None of the dancers knew her part, except the choreographer Balan-

chine. So Diaghilev waved aside Balanchine's demurrals and ordered him into the breach.

Le Chant du Rossignol is based on the fairy story which tells of the Emperor of China, dying of melancholy, whom nothing whatever can cheer, until at last he is given a nightingale in a cage, who sings for him with such exquisite, innocent joy that his heart is touched, and he revives. Markova, in the cage, looked delicate and winsome, a wisp of a thing. She may have weighed all of eighty pounds in those days. By comparison Balanchine, at about one hundred and forty, was a great hulk. Clad in an improvised

Balanchine, in costume for his part in CARNAVAL.

nightingale's costume, sewn together in haste backstage, he just barely managed to squeeze into the cage. Pressed against the bars, with his muscles rippling and bulging, he looked—one witness recalls—more like an ape in a cage than a nightingale, a white-faced ape with a beak. Tchelitchev, who was present, thought he looked like a stuffed rabbit. As soon as the maidens of the Emperor's court glimpsed this apparition, they began to titter. Grigoriev, the company's stage director and disciplinarian, was playing the dying Emperor. "Shut up, girls!" he threatened under his breath, as he languished feebly on his couch. "I'm going to fine you all a week's pay." But then, opening his eyes, he caught sight of the caged Balanchine and choked with laughter himself. It was hard on his melancholy. Once the cage has been brought on, the Nightingale is supposed to hop out lightly and dance for the Emperor. Balanchine wormed his way out and began his solo. He danced it beautifully. Being a superb mimic, he even managed somehow to look fourteen years old, and ethereal—suggesting many of Markova's mannerisms. Diaghilev all the while was rolling about in his box with mirth at the sight. Had it been Paris, instead of Monte Carlo, Diaghilev would have cancelled the performance rather than substitute a man for Markova; but he did not care much what the Monte Carlo audience thought. The Princess, it is said, witnessed the whole performance gravely. Afterward she is supposed to have remarked judiciously that Mr. Balanchine was very good but that she still preferred the little Markova girl.

In the summer of 1927 Balanchine's marriage to Tamara Geva, which had been growing increasingly shaky for some time, came to an end. She was restless and bored with the narrow world of ballet. She was not, as most of the others were, a graduate of the Russian ballet academies, and she had other interests than the dance. She was eager to get about more, to see more of the world, to live. To her mind, Monte Carlo was a dull place. It annoyed her that Balanchine was so satisfied with things. "What are we going to do tonight?" she would ask. "Why do we need to do anything?" he would reply. Then they would quarrel. Once Dukelsky came along in the midst of such a quarrel, just as she was walking out in a huff. He promptly proposed that they elope to Nice. She said it was a splendid idea. He hired a horse carriage and off they went. After about ten minutes, though, she decided that perhaps it wasn't such a good idea after all. Dukelsky sheepishly agreed and, feeling like an ass, had the carriage driver turn around and deliver her back to her husband. But the time eventually came when she could no longer contain her restlessness. She let Balanchine know that she was leaving him, and the company as well. She joined the Balieff Chauve-Souris and traveled with it to America, where she later made a theatrical career.

Balanchine was wounded by her leaving him, but not mortally. Their marriage had been impetuous. He was young; he had by now come to accept change and rootlessness as part of his life, and he did not, as a matter of principle, show his feelings. They healed before long anyway, his wounded feelings. The balm for this healing process, if it was needed, was supplied by the charming Alexandra Danilova, in whom he had long taken delight, as a fascinating dancer as well as person, and for whom, as she says, he had been an object of adoration since their school days. For Danilova, Balanchine had just made perhaps the finest role she had danced so far—the Fairy Queen in the *Triumph of Neptune*. Other brilliant roles would follow. What better love tokens could a choreographer offer a ballerina!

CHAPTER SIX

"Before the war, Diaghilev created a vogue for Russian ballet, but after the war he merely created a vogue for vogue."

Constant Lambert's cutting summation has its truth, though, like most aphorisms, it leaves out much. Certainly, the history of the Diaghilev Ballet in the postwar years for the most part reflects a restless search for novelty, for modernism at any cost. The watchword of the epoch was the fiat that Diaghilev had issued when Cocteau, having undertaken to prepare a scenario for a new ballet, asked what his employer would like him to do. *"Étonne-moi!"* Diaghilev replied. And Cocteau tried his very best to astonish him, as later on did Boris Kochno and nearly everybody else in Diaghilev's service.

It was a period in which the artists around Diaghilev deliberately cultivated the banal and the trivial for shock effect. Thereby they caught the spirit of the postwar age, antiheroic and contemptuous of bourgeois morality as it was, and distrustful of all causes—the era of "So what?" The clever person cultivated assiduously his disbelief; he did not commit himself, his emotions or his faith to anything, if he could help it.

Lambert's witticism leaves all that out—the psychological effect of the war—and it imputes to Diaghilev more power than he actually wielded, powerful as he was. When Diaghilev in 1921 sought to go against the times with a revival of a full-length classical ballet, *The Sleeping Beauty,* he suffered a financial disaster that almost destroyed the company.

Joining the Ballets Russes at the end of 1924, Balanchine naturally participated in the making of the clever modernistic works that were the vogue. Sometimes he did them very well indeed, as with *La Chatte.* At other times, as with *La Pastorale*—a complicated ballet in twelve scenes concerning the romance between a Telegraph Boy and Movie Star who meet while she is in the midst of making a film—the results were less notable. The *pas de deux* in this one was more of a triangle, the third element being the Telegraph Boy's bicycle. As entertaining as anything that happened on stage in *La Pastorale* was the sight of Lifar, who played the Telegraph Boy, in the wings before the curtain went up. While the other dancers were rehearsing their *pirouettes* and *arabesques,* Lifar was to be seen earnestly pumping up his bicycle tires.

It is a question how congenial all this kind of thing was to Balanchine's nature as a steady diet. He was adaptable and bright, and he was a child of this era; but it is likely that he was not wholly at ease in the atmosphere of smart cynicism and delicious triviality. Presently he found his own way out of the confusion of the times. This artistic salvation came with the creation of *Apollo* (originally *Apollon Musagète*) in 1928. "I consider *Apollo* the turning point of my life," he has said. Here, for the first time, he struck the unmistakable Balanchine note. At the height of the jazz age, he returned to classicism—or, rather, he evolved a new classicism, which serenely embodied the classical virtues of clarity and grandeur and yet in spirit and in style of movement was more up to date and adventurous than the run of ultramodern ballets. With *Apollo*—"a work of capital importance in the arts of the twentieth century," it has been called—Balanchine started out on what was to be the central, though not the only, line of development in his career.

The ballet had its première in Paris on June 12, 1928. As usual, there were last-minute improvisations—such as the lovely *pas de deux* for Apollo and Terpsichore which, according to Nikitina, Balanchine choreographed in half an hour at the Studio Wacker in Paris—but most of this ballet was prepared with special care at Monte Carlo during the preceding spring, and with a clear sense on the part of all concerned that something new and significant was being made. Nicholas Nabokov, a young composer whose *Ode,* choreographed by Massine, was one of the other new works of that season, has given a vivid account in his autobiography *Old Friends and New Music* of a glimpse he had of *Apollo* in preparation. The occasion was his first sight of Balanchine, with whom he was shortly to become close friends. Nabokov had just arrived in Monte Carlo, having come to work on *Ode.* At the rehearsal hall, when he entered it, looking for Diaghilev, he saw the massive figure of André Derain, whom he already knew, leaning against the upright piano. Diaghilev was seated to the left, and next to him was a funny-looking little man with thick glasses and a crooked goatee, who was dressed in a disheveled manner and who giggled in a bleating voice. This odd figure, as Nabokov later learned, was André Bauchant, a primitive painter whom

Bauchant's curtain for APOLLON MUSAGÈTE.

Diaghilev had commissioned to do the sets in order to avoid, he said, a false Hellenism. Bauchant, whom the Paris art dealers were pushing as a successor to Rousseau, always had his pockets bulging with photographs of his work. If someone said anything in Bauchant's presence about a cucumber, according to Derain, Bauchant would immediately pull out a photograph and say, "Here's a still life of mine with a cucumber. Won't you buy it?" If someone mentioned that he was going to America on the *Lafayette*, Bauchant would pull out of his pocket a "Lafayette Meets Washington." On that particular day Diaghilev was in bad temper with Bauchant because on walking into Bauchant's studio he had found him painting a still life instead of working on the *Apollo* sets. But at the moment of Nabokov's arrival, Diaghilev was completely absorbed in what was going on in the center of the floor—so absorbed that he did not even look up to greet Nabokov.

> *There, in the center of it* [writes Nabokov], *a group of three ballerinas were clustered around and over a male dancer. The ballerinas were Tchernicheva, Doubrovska, and Nikitina. . . . The male dancer was Serge Lifar. That group's pose has since become famous in the annals of choreographic*

classicism: Lifar knelt between the three ballerinas, who dipped forward and their necks stretched upward so that they looked like three drinking swans whose precarious balance was maintained by a trembling hand firmly clutching Lifar's shoulder. In front of the group stood its inventor, the slight and incredibly young-looking George Balanchine, Diaghilev's recent discovery, his new choreographic genius.

After a moment Diaghilev turned around and greeted Nabokov curtly. Without waiting for an answer, he pointed at Balanchine; and Nabokov heard him saying to Derain, "What he is doing is magnificent. It is pure classicism, such as we have not seen since Petipa's."

The events with which *Apollo* deals are simple, compressed, evocative: Apollo is born, discovers and displays his creative powers, instructs three of the Muses in their arts, and then ascends with them to Parnassus. The theme is creativity itself—Apollonian creativity, vigorous but lucid, untortured,

Lifar and Danilova in APOLLON MUSAGÈTE.

civilizing. Edwin Denby, a poet and former dancer who has written some of the most perceptive dance criticism of our time, has said of this ballet:

Extraordinary is the richness with which he can, with only four dancers, create a sustained and more and more satisfying impression of the grandness of man's creative genius, depicting it concretely in its grace, its sweet wit, its force and boldness, and with the constant warmth of its sensuous complicity with physical beauty. "Apollo" is an homage to the academic ballet tradition—and the first work in the contemporary classic style, but it is an homage to classicism's sensuous loveliness as well as to its brilliant exactitude and its science of dance effect. . . . And it leaves at the end, despite its innumerable incidental inventions, a sense of bold, open, effortless and limpid grandeur.

It was Stravinsky's music for this ballet that showed Balanchine the way to the technical and aesthetic discoveries he made in *Apollo,* and to Stravinsky he gratefully admits his indebtedness. Balanchine recalls that in his previous ballets it had been his wont to heap all styles of movement together, as in a sort of goulash. The score that Stravinsky provided for *Apollo* —restrained, disciplined, yet uncommonly lyrical—taught Balanchine the most useful lesson of his career: that he, too, could clarify his art by reducing all the multitudinous possibilities to the one possibility that was inevitable, that he could, as he has since put it, "dare to not use all my ideas." As he studied the score, which left with him the strong impression as of a white-on-white canvas, Balanchine for the first time realized that, like tones in music and shades in painting, gestures have certain family relations which, as groups, impose their own laws. All the choreography he has done since then, Balanchine says, has been affected by this realization.

It is characteristic of Balanchine and of his work that his greatest choreographic discoveries should come by way of a musical experience. He would seldom, in the course of his life, be able to do first-rate choreography to second-rate music. Many choreographers are just the opposite; they find it intimidating and inhibiting to have to cope with a musical masterwork. It is also typical of Balanchine that he should frankly give pride of place to the composer. "A choreographer can't invent rhythms," he has said, "he only reflects them in movement. The body is his medium and, unaided, the body will improvise for a short breath. But the organizing of rhythm on a

grand scale is a sustained process. It is a function of the musical mind."
Already, at the time he began work on *Apollo,* he admired Stravinsky's
music to the point of veneration. When he heard it, he felt moved to try to
make it visible. If he himself could write music, Balanchine felt, that was
the way he would want it to sound.

As a youth in Russia, Balanchine had been intrigued enough by the
score of *The Rite of Spring* to ask the Maryinsky's director for permission
to stage it, and as soon as he had heard *Pulcinella,* he had begun trying to
make dances for it. Appropriately, his first major assignment for Diaghilev
had been the restaging of Stravinsky's *Le Chant du Rossignol.* But *Apollo*
was the first ballet in which he and Stravinsky worked together. Stravinsky,
who had in the past not been easily pleased by what choreographers had
done to his music, was this time altogether satisfied. The choreography for
Apollo, he wrote, with its "groups, movements and lines of great dignity and
plastic elegance as inspired by the beauty of classical forms," was exactly
what he had wished for when he had composed its music. Thus, with
Apollo, began what was to become perhaps the most exquisitely matched
and most notable collaboration in the history of ballet.

The première of *Apollo* at the Théâtre Sarah Bernhardt, with Stravinsky conducting, was a gala event, and for many in the audience, a profound
experience. Gordon Craig wrote that he found the ballet so beautiful that he
left the theatre during the intermission that followed it, without seeing the
rest of the program, because he wanted to retain its loveliness in his memory
as long as possible. As Apollo, Lifar was superb. Backstage, after the performance, Diaghilev kneeled down and kissed his leg in homage. "Remember it, Seriozha, for the rest of your days," Diaghilev said to him. "I am
kissing a dancer's leg for the second time in my life. The last was Nijinsky's,
after *Le Spectre de la Rose.*"

Nobody offered to kiss the choreographer's leg. He would have laughed
if anybody had tried. There was no need for extravagant gestures. Balanchine knew well what he had achieved and what had happened to him in
the course of making this ballet; and he was content.

For all its success, *Apollo,* surprisingly, proved to be the cause of the
one serious disagreement which Balanchine had with Diaghilev. At the next
performance after the première, Diaghilev peremptorily ordered Terpsichore's variation cut out. He said it was boring. Balanchine protested in-
dignantly. Of the three Muses' variations, Terpsichore's was not only the

APOLLO *danced by Lew Christensen.*

APOLLO

A series of moments from APOLLO. *In most of these photographs the Apollo is Jacques d'Amboise.*

APOLLO *danced by André Eglevsky.*

loveliest but the most personally meaningful to Balanchine—his testament to the goddess of the dance. Balanchine told Diaghilev that it was not the variation that was boring but the dancer whom Diaghilev had insisted on casting for the part, Nikitina.

Balanchine had from the start very much wanted the part to go to Danilova, but Lord Rothermere, the newspaper magnate who had provided the financial assurance for the London appearances of the Ballets Russes during the previous two seasons, had urged Diaghilev to give Nikitina the part. Nikitina was Lord Rothermere's favorite. He made her one of his "adopted daughters" (he had two), as she relates with filial piety in her memoirs; and he gave her one of his Rolls-Royces (he had eight). He was very good to her and, on her account, to the Ballets Russes. But unexpectedly, just before the 1928 season opened, Lord Rothermere had withdrawn his patronage. Diaghilev, who could be petty on a grand scale, now could no longer stand the sight of Nikitina and addressed rude and cutting remarks to her in front of the whole company.

Balanchine felt that Diaghilev, not wishing to admit that he had been wrong and venally motivated in the first place, was now taking his revenge on the role. He threatened to quit. Angry words were exchanged. Diaghilev refused to alter his stand. The second performance proceeded without Terpsichore's variation, but when it came to the place where the variation should have been, some members of the audience who were aware of what had happened began to shout their disapproval. Ultimately, the variation was restored, with Danilova alternating with Nikitina in the Terpsichore role.

It was not long after this quarrel that there occurred the episode in regard to Balanchine's contract which Grigoriev mentions in his book. One day shortly after the summer holidays Grigoriev, aware that Balanchine's contract was about to expire, asked Diaghilev if he had remembered to renew it. At this question, Diaghilev began fiercely heaping abuse on Balanchine. He was very much of a mind, Diaghilev said, not to renew his contract at all.

Grigoriev was shocked and astonished but discreetly forbore to ask questions. He said merely that he wished to know if Diaghilev intended to retain Balanchine. If so, then he would go ahead and make the contract arrangements himself. After a pause, Diaghilev said, "Do as you like."

To Grigoriev, these words came as a great relief, and he hastened to get Balanchine safely under contract as soon as possible. There had been a

Some of the Diaghilev Ballet in Edinburgh in 1929.
L to R: Business agent (in bowler), Woizikowski, Soumarskova, Lifar, Doubrovska,
Danilova, Balanchine, Tchernicheva, Markova, Markova's mother.
In back, Roger Désormière.

time, some sixteen years before, when on being warned by Benois that the company was in danger of losing Fokine, Diaghilev had been able haughtily to reply, "That's not so great a calamity. What is a ballet master? I could make a ballet master out of this inkwell if I wanted to." But those times were past. There had been too many painful crises in the intervening years resulting from the departure of a choreographer for Diaghilev to repeat so haughty an assertion now. Nor would he again be so glib about how easy it was to make a ballet master. By now he, and all concerned, were well aware that a good choreographer was rarer than diamonds, and that for the company to lose its ballet master was calamity indeed.

By the following season, which, though no one could have guessed it then, was to be the last season of the Diaghilev Ballet, it is Grigoriev's impression that the breach between Diaghilev and Balanchine had been healed and that they had resumed the correct and formally friendly relationship they had always maintained. Grigoriev feels certain that Balanchine would have gone on working for Diaghilev after that if Diaghilev had lived. Balanchine himself thinks so. There were others, however, who, noting a growing sense of independence in Balanchine, were sure that it would have been merely a question of time before an irrevocable rupture developed between him and Diaghilev. By 1929, Kochno writes in *Le Ballet,* Balanchine seemed already to have "emancipated himself," so that it was necessary to be think-ing about his eventual replacement if the company was not again to find itself in the disastrous situation caused by Massine's departure in 1921.

Some memories of Balanchine which are, of course, vivid and perti-nent ones, are those which Danilova has supplied. They thought of each other as man and wife in those days, though, because Balanchine did not have a divorce from Tamara Geva at the time, they had been unable to marry. They lived in a pension at Monte Carlo, and they had also taken an apartment in Paris, which they were keeping as a year-round base. Recalling their four years together, Danilova, long afterward, touched on many of Balanchine's traits, some of which had two sides for her—his spontaneous generosity which, to someone who was sharing his life, could also be ranked as frightful improvidence; his honesty, which could sometimes be painful, and which on occasion turned into stubbornness and pride; his evenness of temper, which made him easy to be with but difficult to engage deeply. She remembers with appreciation his simple but helpful wisdom about things that mattered. "I used to worry about how much money other dancers were being paid and what parts they were getting. He told me to just sit down and

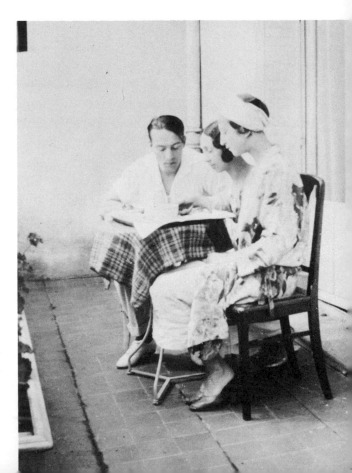

Breakfast on the hotel terrace at Vichy in 1929, with Danilova (in flowered gown) and Doubrovska.

think about what I wanted to do, never mind worrying about others." Envy was not one of Balanchine's characteristics. Herself of an effervescent nature, she naturally enjoyed Balanchine's gaiety and fantasy. He liked to clown. At one period it amused him to wear a billboard around the apartment instead of a dressing gown. He would often, when doing one of the mime roles he generally performed after his knee was impaired, put on fantastic makeup which would look conventional enough when seen from the audience's distance but had a hilarious effect on the others on stage with him. In one ballet, in which he had a solemn part, his face, when seen from close up, looked exactly like a Christmas tree. And he had a special fondness for puns, particularly multilingual ones, and other verbal nonsense.

Despite his generosity to strangers—to anyone, as she pungently put it, "who would cry in his pocket"—he could be forgetful about those nearest to him. Once, she felt hurt because she got no flowers from Balanchine on a night when she was dancing one of his parts for the first time. It had not occurred to him that she might expect them. When their friend the conductor Roger Désormière reproved him the next day for his negligence, Balanchine clapped his hand to his head and, rushing off, spent all his money on a bouquet of a hundred roses for her for the second night's performance.

"I think, perhaps," she said speculatively, "he had not learned in those days how to love another human being. Perhaps if he had not been separated so much from his family, he might have learned that—and learned not to bury his feelings. And there was all the upheaval of the Revolution we lived through, affecting him and all of us. In a way we were like little wild animals. We were forced to bring ourselves up, to improvise our lives—and that left its mark."

Of the ten ballets which Balanchine made for the Diaghilev Ballet only two have survived and may be still seen today. One is *Apollo*. The other is *Prodigal Son,* which had its first performance on May 21, 1929, in Paris, just three months before Diaghilev's death, and was the last new ballet to be presented to the public by him. It was one of two new works which Balanchine choreographed in 1929; the other one, *Le Bal,* with music by Rieti and extremely interesting but perhaps overwhelming sets and costumes by Chirico, was given its première in Monte Carlo a few weeks before.

Balanchine and Doubrovska in LE BAL — *one of the rare photos to be found showing Balanchine as a dancer.*

For *Prodigal Son* Diaghilev commissioned Georges Rouault, the greatest of modern religious painters, to design the decor and the costumes. It
was Rouault's first theatrical commission. He stayed at the Hôtel de Paris
in Monte Carlo for many weeks while this ballet was in preparation and,
Balanchine remembers, often attended rehearsals. A small, rather shabby,
gray-faced man, he would sit and watch with interest but would say very
little. Once, during an intermission in the rehearsal, he showed Balanchine
and some of the other members of the company how to balance a chair on
his nose, and did it very skillfully. When Diaghilev would ask him how the
designs were coming along, he would reply, "I'm thinking." As time went
by, Diaghilev began to grow increasingly anxious about the designs. He kept
asking Rouault to show him some of the sketches he had been doing, but
Rouault always put him off. Rouault, as Diaghilev must have been aware
when he engaged him, was extremely loath to show a work until it was
finished, and it was always a great struggle for him to concede at last that a
painting might be finished; he liked to keep a painting by him for years,
pondering it, and every now and then adding a brush stroke. Finally, Diaghilev could wait no longer. From the hotel's concierge, he obtained a key
to Rouault's room, into which he stole one day while Rouault was out.
There Diaghilev found hundreds of sketches lying about. He snatched up a
handful. From this loot, used as a rough guide, the company's scenic artist,
the extremely capable Prince Shervashidze, was able to execute the ballet's
two magnificent sets, so unmistakably Rouault in their profundity of spirit
and their somber, glowing palette of color; and from these sketches also
Vera Soudeikine (who later became the wife of Igor Stravinsky) was able
to derive the basic conceptions for the costumes.

Prodigal Son was yet another new kind of work for Balanchine to
attempt. Indeed, in many respects, it was a novel experience for the whole
company. It seemed a surprising return, though utterly different from them
in approach, to the emotionality and passion of the early Diaghilev ballets
of twenty years before. How strange the members of the company found it
during rehearsals, after years during which Diaghilev had firmly suppressed
any signs of histrionics or emoting he detected in their performances, to be
now urged, even implored, by him to let themselves go, to give free play to
their feelings. In this ballet Diaghilev took a greater personal interest than
any he had prepared in years. It was a return to the kind of close supervision of the early years, for which he had been famous. Perhaps it was that

the subject was closer to Diaghilev's heart than the chic, clever ballets he had been conjuring up to keep ahead of the vogue. *"Assez de musiquette!"* he had been heard to say of late—"Enough of this music-hall triviality!" Perhaps, as Grigoriev suggests, he felt his supervision required because he had doubts as to whether Balanchine, whose previous ballets "had been almost entirely devoid of drama and feeling," could cope with what was required in this one. "Gifted though Balanchine undoubtedly was," Grigoriev wrote, "his approach was almost exclusively intellectual, and any manifestation of emotion was foreign to him."

New also, for a Diaghilev ballet, was the Biblical theme and the religious spirit. The Soviet musicologist Nestyev, in his biography of Prokofiev, who composed the score for *Prodigal Son,* finds Diaghilev's choice of a Biblical theme symptomatic. "In seeking 'eternal themes,' in turning to artistic devices of the remote past, the artists of the West sought to save themselves from the complete intellectual and artistic degeneration toward which their rootless experimentation was inevitably leading." Though Nestyev's tone is slighting, his point has some validity. *Prodigal Son* anticipates the trend toward religion and orthodoxy which characterized much of the art in the thirties and forties. It was Diaghilev's fate to be in the forefront of the vogue, even when he thought he was turning his back on vogue. It may be remarked, incidentally, that religious feelings came more naturally to those who collaborated in the production and performance of *Prodigal Son* than to many European, American or Anglo-American artists who later adopted theology. Balanchine's faith was certainly not spurious.

Prodigal Son derives in theme and action from the parable in St. Luke. For clarity, some unessential elements, such as the good elder brother who remains at home while the sinful prodigal wanders, were omitted. The libretto was, as usual, by Kochno. Balanchine and Kochno often argued over the librettos. Even in those days Balanchine was an advocate of making the story for a ballet as simple and clear as possible. Kochno was wont to indulge in witty complications which were a delight to read but impossible to dance. "Paper will withstand anything," Balanchine would say to him, "but a stage is different. Not every idea is suitable for dance." Or sometimes Kochno, at a loss for an action, would simply write *"Promenade"*—leaving Balanchine with numerous measures of music to fill up, somehow or other. "It's all very well for you to write *'Promenade,'* " Balanchine would say in exasperation, "but meanwhile *I've* got to figure out something interesting for the people up there on the stage to be doing all that time." On this occasion, however, the libretto Kochno prepared was an unusually straightforward and uncomplicated one, though it did contain one or two *"Promenades"* with which Balanchine had to cope. For some of the action, such as the Prodigal's return, Kochno drew on a Pushkin story, "The Stationmaster," in which are described in detail several engravings, depicting scenes from the Biblical story, which hang on the walls of the little post station, somewhere in the middle of Russia.

Thus *Prodigal Son* had a Biblical theme, but as seen through Russian eyes and filtered through Russian souls, and, as Balanchine choreographed it, one that was expressed in a thoroughly twentieth-century manner. His choreography was symbolic and expressionistic. It conveyed the central significance of each action and situation poetically—though the poetry was often the poetry of the grotesque—but with never a literal or naturalistic gesture. For this ballet Balanchine turned away from the classical vocabulary he had employed so gracefully in *Apollo,* but he remembered the lesson he had learned in that ballet about unity of tone. This time his palette of movement contained borrowings from gymnasts, circus performers and acrobats, enriched by Balanchine's fertile powers of invention. In an interesting article, "Acrobatics and the New Choreography," published in *Theatre Guild Magazine* shortly after *Prodigal Son*'s première, Agnes de Mille discussed some of these devices and the uses to which Balanchine had put them: the circus trick employed in the duet between the Siren (Doubrovska) and the Prodigal Son (Lifar)—"one of the most important seductions to be found on any modern stage," she wrote—in which Doubrovska wraps herself around Lifar's waist like a belt and then slides slowly down his body to the floor where, as he sinks down beside her, their limbs intertwine in an inextricable tangle; or the tumbling stunt used to hurl her up to the shoulders of her depraved attendant revelers, where, from a height of ten feet, she stands looking down at her subdued lover, towering over her prey; or the horror of depravity conveyed by the back-to-back scuttlings of these inhuman revelers among whom the Prodigal Son has fallen; or, utterly different in mood, the tenderness achieved at the end by the father's lifting up of his returned son from the dirt and folding him in his cloak. Such steps and movements had never been seen on a ballet stage before, but they had been introduced by Balanchine not for show but to communicate inexorably the heart of the matter. There are very few modern works, in any art form,

that can match the horror and conviction of this ballet's sense of degradation and sin or the tenderness and wonder of the sense of redemption and forgiveness that the ending achieves.

As usual there were last-minute inspirations at rehearsal. It was only at the last rehearsal that Balanchine got the idea of having the revelers be hairless, with bald pates—a most effective gargoyle touch. And it was just a few hours before performance time that he improvised the boat scene near the end when, finding himself at this point with music but no movement choreographed for it, he had the revelers turn over the fencelike structure and use it as if they were sailing away in it, with the Siren, her body bowed backward and her long magenta cloak stretched out behind her like a sail, in the pose of a figurehead. Balanchine planned to change that part the next night when he had time, but it looked so good that he has kept it ever since.

There were also last-minute altercations and emotional crises. Prokofiev, when he arrived in Paris for the final rehearsals and to conduct the pre-

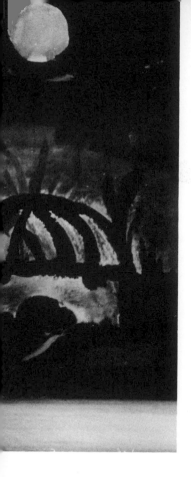

The boat scene from PRODIGAL SON, *as performed by Yvonne Mounsey in the 1952 production.*

mière, was appalled at what he saw. He hated Balanchine's stylized choreography. It was not at all what he had had in mind. He had envisioned the whole thing being done naturalistically. He wanted it to be "real"— with real wine to drink and real cushions to lounge on in the orgy, as in the orgy in the ballet *Scheherazade* twenty years before. He complained strenuously to Diaghilev, but Diaghilev sided with Balanchine.

Throughout the rehearsals of this ballet the company had been unusually wrought up, and tension grew as the first night approached. Doubrovska, whom Balanchine affectionately used to call his guinea pig because he liked to try out his most unusual new steps on her, was feeling uneasy because her poses and movements were so suggestive. She had never danced anything like that before. Lifar was suffering in his soul even more than usually, first because his beloved Serge Pavlovitch Diaghilev had turned against him of late and second because he simply couldn't fathom what the role was supposed to mean, he couldn't *feel* the part. In one of his many memoirs—this one a book purporting to be a biography of Serge Diaghilev—Lifar has

related how at long last, in the course of several agonized minutes on his
bed in his hotel room just before the curtain went up, he "created" the
"Prodigal Son." It is worth quoting at length.

In it, he tells first how, an hour before curtain time, Diaghilev's cousin
and factotum, Korebut-Kubetovitch, called at his hotel to fetch him, and
how, racked by doubts and torments as he was, he refused to go. He wasn't
going to dance tonight, he told the poor cousin, he simply couldn't. Seven-
thirty arrived. Then eight, then ten after eight. Korebut-Kubetovitch's face
was white with anxiety. Lifar lay on his bed, suffering:

*A terrific struggle was going on inside me. Somberly, sadly, I thought
of Serge Pavlovitch, he who was my spiritual father, and of our relations
together. I thought of the past, that life I had offered up as a sacrifice to
him, uselessly and so unnecessarily. Why? To what end? Then visions out
of the remote past came thronging around me. I saw myself in Kiev, on
my father's threshold, returning from my first unsuccessful effort, to fly
abroad. . . . I, a prodigal son, waiting for dawn to dare to enter my
home. . . . The love, tenderness and care Serge Pavlovitch had lavished
on me, the manner in which, through him, I had become an artist; all, all
rose before me again, and a feeling of intolerable poignancy, of pity for the
ailing, weary, aged old man—for suddenly he had begun to seem much
older—sent a wave of endless commiseration pulsing through my being.
Was it possible I could betray him? . . .*

*The memory of things past, my sudden vision of the old man, merged
into one vision of . . . The Prodigal Son. I am that prodigal son of his.
. . . In my ears there sounded Prokofiev's music. Suddenly I saw light. I
began to understand. From out of the depths of chaos and turmoil emerged
the creative instant of clear and calm perception.*

I leaped out of bed.

*"Let's be off to the theatre. I have created my Prodigal Son. . . . It is
myself."*

His performance that night did, in fact, move the audience to tears.
Balanchine says that Lifar was, without doubt, the most exciting Prodigal
Son of all those who have ever danced the role, as he was also the most
impressive Apollo; but Balanchine laughs at Lifar's account of his creation
of the part. He commented, when it was first drawn to his attention, "His

Lifar in PRODIGAL SON.

PRODIGAL SON — *Dolin and Woizikowski as the two friends*

performance would have been just as good, whether he had ever discovered or not that the Prodigal Son was really him in disguise, because he had been given interesting steps to perform and had been rehearsed very carefully." One may question this, as one may also question whether Balanchine, in working out the choreography of this ballet, was really as unmoved, as preoccupied with purely technical considerations as he likes to say he was. When one sees a performance of *Prodigal Son* one finds this hard to believe.

On the night of July 26, 1929, when the company concluded its London season, Balanchine saw Serge Diaghilev for the last time in his life. At

The seduction scene from PRODIGAL SON — *in a performance
by Yvonne Mounsey and Francisco Moncion.*

Diaghilev's request, the entire company had assembled backstage so that
Diaghilev could bid them farewell for the summer. He was going to Paris
and then, by stages, to his beloved Venice, while the company was scheduled
to leave the next morning for a performance at Ostend. When all were
gathered, Diaghilev came onto the stage and made them a little speech,
courteous and charming as only he could be. "You are leaving tomorrow,"
he said, "and I shall not see you again until the autumn. I wish you all to have
a good rest and return to work refreshed and invigorated. We have a busy
year before us. All my contracts are signed, and for the first time in our
whole career we have an uninterrupted series of engagements already fixed.

I thank you for the excellent work you have done, which has been largely responsible for any success we may have had. Good-bye—and good luck."

With that he passed among them and shook hands with each member of the company. Among Balanchine's memories of that night there persists an olfactory one that, in some way, suggests the complex quality of the whole ballet enterprise—the fragrance of the almond blossom pomade that the fastidious Diaghilev always used, mingled with the dusty smell of the backstage props and scenery and the acrid odor of the dancers' sweat. Diaghilev looked ghastly that night. His cheeks were as pale and lifeless as dough; his eyes, under which were dark circles, glittered feverishly. His massive head drooped and he moved with painful effort, as if his body were a burden too great for him to carry. When he spoke it was in a voice so low that one had to strain to hear him.

Yet his appearance, though awful, did not alarm Balanchine or the other members of the company that night as much as perhaps it ought to have, for they, and Diaghilev's other acquaintances, had by now become accustomed to Diaghilev's continued ill-health. He was terrified of death, which no one might safely mention in his presence, and he took all the elaborate precautions of a superstitious hypochondriac. He would wipe his

Larionov's drawing of Diaghilev near the end of his life
He is studying the score of PRODIGAL SON

hands with a handkerchief to get rid of the germs after opening a door; rather than cross a black cat's path he would turn about and walk all the way around the block; when he rode in a carriage he worried about the possibility of catching glanders from the carriage horse; he was in constant anxiety whenever he had to cross the Channel, for a fortuneteller had once told him he would meet death by sea; he wrapped himself up with the greatest care against drafts, which he could discern in rooms where no one else might be aware of even the slightest breath of air stirring. Yet he willfully neglected the simpler safeguards his physician had prescribed to cope with the actual ailment from which he suffered: diabetes. On an impulse he would stuff himself with chocolates or drink a bottle of champagne, even though he had been ordered to avoid sweets and alcohol; and, despite his obvious exhaustion, would stay up till the early morning hours at a party with his latest young protégé rather than admit that his sick, aging body required rest. To this, too, all who knew him had by then become accustomed. They assumed his extraordinary will would always revive his flagging flesh when need be, just as for twenty years, through all vicissitudes, it had animated his Ballets Russes. They were used to seeing startling changes in his appearance within a few hours, brought about by the sheer force of his spirit. "He could look the oldest man in the town when you met him at noon," wrote Gordon Craig, "and at eight, when the curtain was about to go up, he would look the youngest." They imagined he would somehow go on this way indefinitely.

The morning after that leavetaking scene backstage the company proceeded to Ostend, and from thence to Vichy, where it performed for a week before an audience of fashionables and notables, a number of whom had been following the company with adoration since its inception: it was a quintessential Ballets Russes audience. August 4 was the last night there, after which the company was scheduled to disband for the summer vacation. No novelties were performed that evening, but cherished favorites—an all-Massine program: *Cimarosiana, Le Tricorne* and, for the closing ballet, *La Boutique Fantasque,* with Danilova, Tchernicheva, Balanchine, Woizikowsky and Lifar as the principal dancers. Balanchine danced a mazurka in this ballet. At its close there were clamorous ovations, fortified by resounding basso "bravos" from Chaliapin, who had attended every evening of the week, and repeated curtain calls. Amid that applause of its devotees the curtain was rung down for what was to be the last time on the Ballets

Russes de Serge Diaghilev—one of the most exciting and influential theatrical manifestations since the Renaissance.

From Vichy Balanchine went back to England, where he was to choreograph a dance sequence for a film called *Dark Red Roses,* produced by
Sinclair Hill, which, as it so happened, was to be the first talking picture
made in England. A romantic melodrama, the film concerned a sculptor
who suspected his wife of infidelity with a musician; the dance sequence in
it was used as is the mousetrap play in Hamlet—as a kind of fantasy re-
enactment of the crime to be played out before the eyes of the guilty ones
at a party. The dance Balanchine made for this was a quasi-Oriental affair,
to music from Moussorgsky's *Khovanchina,* and the dancers were Balanchine,
Lydia Lopokova and Anton Dolin. During part of the time he was in
England in connection with this film, Balanchine was a guest of Lopokova
and her husband, the economist John Maynard Keynes, at their country
home in Sussex. Balanchine was extremely fond of Lopokova, as indeed it
was difficult to resist being. A doll-like figure—tiny but with a perfection of
grace, and possessed of an effervescent vitality—she had been, when she
was a member of Diaghilev's company, before her marriage, Diaghilev's
most enchanting and delightful comedienne. She could be very witty and
even wise, in a piquant, spontaneous way; Balanchine thought of her as a
kind of small, merry wizard. Keynes, too, for all his erudition, was of a gay
and high-spirited temperament—enough so as to move him to dance the
can-can with his wife at Bloomsbury parties on occasion—and Balanchine
remembers his visit there with great pleasure. With Keynes he got along
beautifully, for Keynes loved to talk about ballet and Balanchine loved to
talk about economics, on which subject he held decided, if rather whimsical
and untutored, opinions. One afternoon, when he happened to find himself
in Keynes' study, Balanchine caught a chastening glimpse of a paper dealing with economic theory that Keynes was working on. It was covered with
formulae and calculations of which Balanchine could not make head or
tail; he resolved promptly to make no more pronouncements on economics
to Keynes.

The dance sequence for *Dark Red Roses* was to be filmed on August
19. Dolin, Lopokova and Balanchine went out to the film studio at Isleworth in the late afternoon, got into costume and waited for the director to
give them their call. In French, Russian and tags of English they sat chatting
as they waited. Lopokova had a few lines to say in the film before the dance

Lydia Lopokova, by Picasso.

began—a conventional compliment addressed to the sculptor, to the effect of, "I wish I could do as well with my feet as you with your hands." She was conscientiously reciting it over and over, for she was afraid she was going to get it backward when the scene was shot. Balanchine was doing his best to mix her up by inventing absurd variations on her lines: "I wish I could do with my toes as well as you can do with your nose," and such like. With that sort of help, the more she rehearsed, the more mixed up she got, to the hilarity of Balanchine and Dolin.

In the midst of this a news vendor came around with the afternoon papers and Dolin walked over to him to get one. On the front page, as he glanced casually at it, Dolin saw a small picture of Diaghilev such as might accompany an announcement of some surprising new spectacle which that prince of surprises and splendors was planning. But there were to be no more such announcements. Crying *"Serge Pavlovitch est mort!"* Dolin ran back to where Balanchine and Lopokova sat and showed them the paper,

A scene from the movie DARK RED ROSES — *with Balanchine (with sword),*
Lopokova, and Dolin.

with its brief item carrying the information that Diaghilev had succumbed
to death in Venice from diabetes in the early hours of the morning. "Big
Serge, poor, poor Big Serge," murmured Lopokova, her eyes full of tears,
"he was so tired, so very tired." Not talking much, the three of them, sad
figures dressed up in the costumes of exotic mummery, sat on in the gloom
and damp chill of the studio until two-thirty in the morning, when, at long
last, the call came for them to do their dance before the cameras.

Soon those who had been Diaghilev's associates would begin to vie as
to who could claim to be his true and sanctified spiritual heir. In Venice, at
the funeral, Lifar would throw himself into the grave, like Hamlet, and he
and Kochno would compete in their lamentations. Such was never Balanchine's style. He recoiled instinctively from hysteria. He would make no
contribution to the various cults of Diaghilev that would arise. Then, and
always, Balanchine distrusted cults—even cults celebrating undeniably
exceptional persons, including, when that time would come, cults about
himself. All such expressions, he felt, inevitably generated enough spurious-

ness to contaminate whatever was being thus celebrated. On the other hand, he would certainly not go to the other extreme, as some of Diaghilev's collaborators—such as Fokine and Benois—would do and assert that Diaghilev had made no creative contribution to ballet at all but had merely been a skillful, parasitical exploiter of the artists he had been fortunate enough to garner. A score of years later, at the request of *Dance News*, Balanchine contributed an appreciation of Diaghilev and an evaluation of the role he had played. It is worth quoting here.

Perhaps it is only today, almost twenty years after his death, that all contemporary choreographers begin to realize the true proportions of the enormous artistic debt we all owe to Serge Diaghilev. If we analyze the work we have done since his death in 1929, we see that we are still following in his footsteps, still adhering to the principles laid down by him during the twenty years he guided the fortunes of his unique Ballets Russes. Were he alive today, Diaghilev would probably find a new direction in his beloved art form, a new approach to the creation and presentation of ballet. He was always twenty-five years ahead of his time.

Diaghilev had the capacity to see not only the potentialities inherent in an artist, be he choreographer, composer, designer or dancer, he also knew what work, what style, what period suited that artist best. Great though it was, his genius for discovery would not have been so overwhelming had he not had that innate and cultivated taste which alone distinguishes true artistic quality from a sense for novelty and craftsmanship.

If I were to describe Diaghilev simply, I should say that he was a man of high culture. It so happened that he was a great ballet impresario, a patron of the arts, but he could just as easily have been a statesman, an ambassador: he could have held any post that required knowledge, intelligence, culture, taste. He was at home in world literature, music, painting and sculpture. He spoke three languages with the fluency and in the idiom of the native. Never a professional musician, he could read a musical score as one reads a book.

Stravinsky has described Diaghilev's intimate musical knowledge in his Autobiography *and Nicholas Nabokov, who also composed his first ballet for the Ballets Russes, has written of Diaghilev's great understanding of music in his book* Old Friends and New Music. *Never a choreographer or a dancer, Diaghilev knew what was exactly right and what was wrong about a particular ballet or in any portion of it. Never a painter, he possessed an unerring and intimate knowledge of art.*

These qualities made Diaghilev a creator, a real producer. He was not just the director or manager of a ballet company who guessed what the public would accept and what it would reject. He did not follow the public; the public followed him. He did not really care very much whether people agreed with him or not. What mattered to him was the work done by the best and most suitable choreographer, musician, designer and dancers. If they succeeded, their work was a success. Diaghilev so inspired the artists who worked under his direction that it is not too much to say that any ballet created for his company bore his personal stamp as well as that of the composer, painter and choreographer. . . .

During his five years with Diaghilev, Balanchine, as has been said, had remained on rather formal terms with him as far as their personal relationship was concerned. Still, that night at the Isleworth film studios, as he sat sadly waiting for the camera call, with the newspaper on the floor at his feet, he mourned Diaghilev with a keen sense of personal loss. How could he not? This man had been his great benefactor. He had reposed confidence in him at a time when Balanchine was a mere untried youth, had recognized the promise of his inherent talents and had provided him the conditions and opportunities for realizing them; he had taken pains to educate him and cultivate his sensibilities; he had, in short, as Balanchine has never hesitated to acknowledge, helped transform him from a craftsman of ballet to an artist. For all this Balanchine was grateful then and remains so to this day. "It is because of Diaghilev that I am whatever I am today," he says.

CHAPTER SEVEN

How important Diaghilev was to his Ballets Russes became unmistakably apparent at his death. Without him the ballet company collapsed immediately. Diaghilev himself had never been wealthy. He had been, in Cocteau's phrase, "a sublime pauper," dependent on the favors of his rich patrons for the realization of his luxurious fantasies. For years the duns had followed him about, waiting to pounce. At his death they instantly seized what they could lay their hands on of the heavily mortgaged sets and costumes. A deluge of unpaid bills washed away Diaghilev's dance empire; his dancers were left stranded—jobless and bereft.

For Balanchine, however, a notable opportunity appeared almost immediately. A few weeks after Diaghilev's death, Balanchine was approached by Jacques Rouché, the director of the Paris Opéra, and invited to stage a new version of Beethoven's two-act ballet, *Les Créatures de Prométhée* as part of the centenary commemoration (two years late) of Beethoven's death, which France was then observing. The Prometheus ballet was to be the Opéra's major event of the year; more than that, it was to be, Rouché hoped, a decisive effort toward the achievement of his ambition to resurrect the glory of French ballet at its ancient home. In centuries past the ballet of the Paris Opéra had been the most admired in the world; it had served as the very model of what ballet should be; but it had been in sad decline since the latter half of the nineteenth century. No one took the Opéra ballet seriously any more. People attended the performances not to look at the ballet but to be seen themselves in the Opéra's elegant and distinguished surroundings. The house lights were not even turned off during the performance. The spectators could sit in their boxes and chat and wave at their friends; during lulls in the conversation they could divert themselves by ogling the girls onstage. Season ticket holders were permitted to wander about backstage, where they might pinch from behind what they had ogled from in front. Rouché—a wealthy, dapper, bearded little man who looked himself like a *boulevardier,* like one of the *vieux abonnés* he despised, but was actually a man of considerable discrimination and artistic integrity—had long wished to change all this; but first, he rightly felt, he had to produce ballets that were actually worth looking at and taking seriously: that was what he hoped Balanchine would do for him. He told Balanchine that he would very much like him to become permanent *maître de ballet* and assured Balanchine that the position could be his if he wished to take it.

Balanchine was not at all sure at the moment that he wanted to become the Opéra's ballet master. He relished the prospect of having a big stage to work on, like that of the Maryinsky, where ingenious scenic effects were possible, and of having at his disposal a large company, basically well trained in the fundamentals of the classic dance despite the faults they had fallen into, with a constant supply of new talent from the Opéra's ballet academy. But he did not much look forward to the rest of what went with the position—the politics; the intrigue; the social calculations as to whom it would be expedient to charm, whom appease and who could be safely scorned; the herculean efforts involved in effecting any changes and innovations in a state institution so bureaucratically and hierarchically organized. For these aspects he had little talent or inclination. He lacked the kind of ferocious, obsessive ambition for "success" it took.

And he was young. When he was not in the studio, engrossed in making his ballets, he wanted to be free to enjoy the rest of what life had to offer. Still, there was that tempting big stage and huge company of dancers, and the fine orchestra that went with it all. . . .

But no decision was required as yet. The immediate question was *Les Créatures de Prométhée,* and Balanchine had no hesitation about accepting the engagement to stage that work, even though one of his friends, Eric Wolheim, who had been the British agent for the Diaghilev company, urged him fervently to have nothing to do with it. *Les Créatures de Prométhée* had been a bad-luck ballet from the moment that Salvatore Vigano had commissioned it from Beethoven, he told Balanchine, and recited a long list of disasters associated with it throughout its history.

Balanchine began choreographing the ballet in late October. Within two weeks he fell desperately ill with pneumonia. At one point it was doubted he would live. French physicians in those days still treated pneumonia by cupping, an ancient form of bloodletting; thick glass cups, inside which burned tapers, were clapped to the patient's flesh, which turned bruise-colored when they were removed. It was supposed to draw out the inflammation. Balanchine managed to survive both the pneumonia and the treatment, only to learn, as he convalesced, still feeble, that he had developed pleurisy, the consequence, possibly, of the malnutrition and other hardships endured during the postrevolutionary years in Russia.

As soon as he was able to receive visitors, Balanchine was called on by an aide of Rouché's, wanting to know if he was going to be able to continue with the Prometheus ballet: time was growing short. Balanchine told him there was no chance of that. He urged that Lifar, who had the leading role in the ballet, be given the opportunity to finish choreographing it. Up till then, Lifar had choreographed only one ballet in his life, a rather grotesque version of Stravinsky's *Renard,* with acrobats and dancers doubling in the roles, which the Ballets Russes had presented, with only moderate success, the previous May. The Opéra management had qualms about entrusting a major work to such a tyro but accepted Balanchine's recommendation, having no alternative except to cancel the ballet. Surprisingly, Lifar proved diffident. "Do you think I can do it, George?" he kept asking anxiously, as he paced, with all the pantherlike vitality of his superbly conditioned body, about the small bedroom where the ailing Balanchine lay.

"Certainly you can," Balanchine assured him. Weak as he was, barely able to keep his head propped up on the pillow, he could not help wishing that Lifar would just sit still for a bit.

"I mean, George, do you *really* think I can?"

"Of course. Don't worry about it. I'll help you in any way I'm able."

Recovered from his brief siege of humility, Lifar agreed to try. The two settled between them that Lifar could enjoy sole credit on the program as choreographer and that Balanchine, who was going to need all the money he could lay his hands on for his medical expenses, could keep for himself the ten-thousand-franc fee for which he had contracted with Rouché. (Lifar, of course, was to receive a substantial fee from the Opéra for his dancing.) In the two weeks before he had fallen ill, Balanchine had sketched the basic plan of the ballet and made a start on the choreography. Now, as work on the ballet resumed, under pressure to make up for lost time, Balanchine's bedroom became a workshop. Designers, musicians, personnel from the Opéra—all came and went, each with some urgent problem requiring attention. Daily, Lifar would appear at Balanchine's bedside so show him how the choreography was progressing. Propped up by pillows, Balanchine would make comments and suggestions, interlarded with words of encouragement and reassurance.

This went on for some days until Balanchine's doctor, who had been grumbling about the strain to which his patient was being subjected, put a stop to it. The pleurisy, it was discovered now, had turned into tuberculosis. Balanchine would have to go to a hospital right away. By this time the ballet was taking shape. Lifar was growing in confidence. He no longer needed Balanchine.

The tuberculosis sanitarium which the doctor recommended was in the Haute-Savoie, amid pine woods and within sight of Mont Blanc. There, in that Magic Mountain environment—a self-contained world, introspective and remote, with its own values and concerns—the next three months of Balanchine's life were passed. He was supposed to lie as still as possible, this young master of the art of movement; to eat as much food as he could, even though he had little appetite; to avoid the direct rays of the sun—these were the main prescriptions of his treatment. Swaddled in blankets against the biting winter cold, he spent his days on the veranda outside his room, his gaze absently taking in the prospect before him—the snow-covered fields, the dark green pine masses, and the austere and formidable mountainside, over whose ice fields the blue cloud shadows wandered. He was feverish most of the time, and in a vague state. Time flowed by in dreamlike fashion. These months were an interval of suspended animation for him. He had no visitors. He did very little reading, or even thinking. No ideas for ballets occurred to him. He had never been able to do much away from a studio. For his imagination to be stimulated he had always needed, besides music, to have the dancers he was going to create for right before his eyes—assembled in the mirrored studio, waiting, idle but expectant, for the choreographer to make use of them. Up there in the mountains the world of ballet seemed as far away as the moon.

Still, all of his expectations were centered upon returning to ballet as soon as he was able. No other life could be imagined now. When the sanitarium's doctor wished to perform a pneumothorax operation on him, Balanchine flatly refused to allow it, for fear his career would be jeopardized. The unsuccessful knee operation had left him suspicious of surgery, anyway. If he were left now with only one lung, as well as a damaged knee, how could he ever expect to carry on the strenuous physical activity that choreographing required? The doctor was less concerned about that question. His interest was to preserve Balanchine's life, which was more threatened than

Balanchine was aware of at the time; but seeing that Balanchine was adamant, he gave up trying to persuade him.

Shortly after this, as it happened, Balanchine's fever abated. He grew stronger. By the middle of December he was well enough to be taking walks about the sanitarium grounds and into the woods, and early in January he was considered sufficiently improved to be permitted to leave the sanitarium. Portions of both lungs had been permanently impaired, but the progress of the illness had now been arrested—at least for the time being. For many years afterward he was to be harassed by symptoms indicating that the infection had not been completely suppressed. He would start out a day feeling healthy and vigorous, but then in the afternoon he might find himself suddenly feverish and weak and liable to break out into a clammy perspiration at the least exertion. This condition he accepted as something he would have to live with; he did not let it interfere with his work, or with his pleasures either, for that matter. It has been a source of amazement, to those who have known him, that he has been able to pursue so taxing a career under such a handicap.

The next few years were to be rootless ones for him—years in which he would wander from one place to another, putting his hand to whatever he could. They were years in which he was without security, yet also, characteristically, quite without care on the whole. If he worried, he seldom showed it. On leaving the sanitarium, he went directly to Paris. Unacclimated as yet to the real world of the flatland, after his sojourn on the Magic Mountain, he found himself at first affected by a rather eerie sense of unfamiliarity amid the familiar sights, as if Paris or he, or both, had altered in some subtle way during his absence.

The next day he sought out Lifar. They greeted each other convivially. With great enthusiasm Lifar told Balanchine about the success he had scored with Prometheus at the ballet's première at the end of December. There had been a dozen curtain calls. What a triumph! Balanchine was pleased to hear of Lifar's success. After a while Lifar asked Balanchine what his plans were for the immediate future. Balanchine replied that he was in need of work and was thinking of talking to Rouché about the ballet master job that Rouché had spoken of to him before he fell ill.

Lifar did not seem to think that was a very good idea. "They don't like foreigners here, you know," he said.

"What about you—and Efimov? Aren't you foreigners?"

"Well, we're here already. But I don't think they want any more."

Balanchine got the impression from that conversation that even if he could manage to overcome the Opéra's antipathy to foreigners and become engaged as ballet master, he would not find the atmosphere congenial. With a shrug, he said he guessed he would forget about it and would look for something else—he was sure something would turn up somehow. Lifar heartily wished him the very best of luck. They shook hands and parted. Not long afterward, the Opéra announced the appointment of its new ballet master: Serge Lifar.

Why Balanchine never pursued the position further if he had wanted it, at least to the extent of discussing it with Rouché, is difficult to explain —except that it is in keeping with his character that in some situations he is diffident about pushing himself forward, while in others he assumes a dominating role without question. Once he had turned his back on the Opéra prospect, he suffered no regrets over it. He was a fatalist by nature— a lighthearted fatalist. He believed that, since human beings were incapable of foreseeing all the circumstances and surprises which destiny had in store for them, it was a waste of time to try to plot out one's future. To calculate too finely is to presume on God's role, and he who does so can expect to meet with frustration, disappointment and humiliation. The revolution he had experienced combined with the mystical religious training of his child- hood to reinforce this philosophy in him. All that a person ought to do was make the best of whatever turned up. "As a human being, you cannot know in advance what will be best for you," he has always said. All his life such would be his attitude. Like ballet itself, which, in Auden's phrase, inhabits a continuous present Eden, he would live intensely in the present, with no laments for the past and little regard for the future. He would never carry insurance. When insurance men would call on him, he would tell them, with an air of grave plausibility, that he would be happy to do business with them if their company would reverse its usual procedure, paying him a lump sum right off, to enjoy while he was young and able to enjoy it, and letting him repay it bit by bit in his old age. They would depart, perplexed, and never call on him again.

As for the Paris Opéra, hindsight suggests that Balanchine would probably not have been content with the conditions he found there, and may well not have been able to function effectively. Whereas Lifar, as is now history, turned out to be just what the institution needed, a triumph of personnel placement, in effect. In him the Opéra obtained not only an interesting enough choreographer and the most compelling male dancer of his epoch, but also just the kind of flamboyant and strenuous public personality the situation required. His love of the limelight, his flair and appetite for publicity, his copious memoirs and treatises on ballet, his feuds and well-advertised but happily bloodless duels, all enabled him to become himself something of a French institution, like Brigitte Bardot. Indeed, so well known was he to become that in France his name would eventually pass into the language as a lower-case noun. When a French paratrooper would put on his long underwear under his uniform, it would be his sergelifars he was getting into. Such is fame.

Meanwhile, to return to January of 1930 and Balanchine, he had said confidently that something would turn up, and within a few days something did in the shape of an offer from the English showman, Sir Charles B. Cochran, who was just about to begin putting together his *Cochran Revue* of 1930. After quickly choreographing for Nemchinova's little company in Paris a ballet to music by Poulenc called *Aubade,* Balanchine crossed the Channel for England. There, in a period of about eight weeks, he prepared three ballets, a finale and a couple of lesser dance numbers for the revue. Balanchine experienced no distress at finding himself working for a showman now, for Cochran was a unique figure—one of the great showmen of the century. In his time he staged a wide range of spectacles—revues, Shakespeare, contemporary comedies, Ibsen, prizefights, rodeos, religious pageants—all with zest and with exactly the appropriate quality of taste each required. "Cochran was the center of elegance and excitement in the theatre, with just that touch of toughness that brought in the crowds—and the money," recalls Beverley Nichols, who was the author of the book and some of the songs for the 1930 revue.

Cochran's revues had a flavor all their own. International, lavish, chic, they had the esteem of the intellectuals as well as the white-tie-and-tails set. His revues, Cochran said, "are not for the tired businessman." His aim, he declared, was to be "intelligently amusing." He commissioned sets from such artists as Derain and Bérard and he engaged some of the finest Diaghilev dancers, including Nikitina, Lifar (who also choreographed one ballet for the 1930 revue) and Efimov. He had the taste to hire superlative talent, and the sense and modesty not to interfere with his employees.

The ballets in these revues could only be miniatures, in size as well as time, because the Pavillion Theatre—a charming theatre, with a personality all its own—possessed a tiny stage, not much larger than a dining table. The backstage area was equally cramped. It had only one narrow entrance to the stage; if a scene called for hoop skirts, the costumes had to be hung from the flies and lowered onto the performers before the curtain went up.

Lifar in a moment from LUNA PARK *in the Cochran Revue of 1930.*

IN A VENETIAN BOX — *another little ballet from the Cochran Revue.*

In these circumstances Balanchine yet managed to make works of art out of the little ballets he created and to achieve quite magical effects. They were ballet quintessences. Cecil Beaton, the designer and photographer, has written in his book, *Ballet,* about the impression these numbers made on him at the time. He recalls attending the *Cochran Revue* several times to see them, thankful to find ballet being kept alive in some form or other after the demise of the Ballets Russes. One of the ballets that particularly caught his fancy, he remembers, was a carnival ballet called *Luna Park,* with music by Lord Berners, in which the dancers were sideshow freaks. The ballerina, Nikitina, was reduced to one shapely leg; Serge Lifar had been given two extra pairs of arms; and there was a two-headed man and other such attractions. Balanchine had obviously had a fine time working out the choreographic possibilities of those odd appendages and parts. "It was all very strange, and, in its peculiar way, beautiful," Beaton wrote.

Making a virtue out of necessity has always been one of Balanchine's fortes—in ballet, as in his life as a whole. So, in one of his ballets for the *Cochran Revue* Balanchine triumphed over the confined area of the Pavillion stage by devising a work in which the dancers did not move about at all. *In a Venetian Box,* it was called, and was to the music of the pizzicato movement of Tchaikovsky's Sixth Symphony. In this little work an ensemble of female spectators are seen as they sit watching a play; they weep, laugh, applaud, gossip, look about them. The choreography featured only the movements of their arms and upper bodies, yet succeeded in maintaining variety and interest. The young dance critic of the *New York Times,* John Martin, then in Europe for a summer visit, wrote an appreciative review of the ballets in the Cochran show, singling out *In a Venetian Box* as a particularly delightful and subtly realized conception.

There was some talk in those days of Balanchine going to America to work. In an interview John Martin had with him, Balanchine was quoted as saying that he was sure he would be in the United States by the autumn somehow, though he had no specific offers or projects in mind. A few months before this, the *American Dancer* had carried the report that Balanchine was slated to join Anna Pavlova's troupe on its American tour in the forthcoming season. In fact, Pavlova and her husband, Victor Dandré, had met with Balanchine in Paris just before he fell ill and had asked him if he would create some of his "modern" ballets for her, but when he showed her some of his conceptions, she found them, predictably, not at all to her taste. What she was looking for really was a modern *Dying Swan;* neither Balanchine nor any other choreographer could provide her with such a fowl.

America seemed to beckon to the expatriate Russian; he thought of it as the country of the future; but all talk of his going there was premature then. Instead, Balanchine made his way next to Copenhagen, to take up for a season the duties of guest ballet master for the Royal Danish Ballet. He stayed in Copenhagen from August, 1930, until the following January. It proved to be not a very stimulating sojourn for him, or very satisfying for the Danes either. His assignment was to stage six works from the Diaghilev repertory: Fokine's *Scheherazade* and *The Legend of Joseph;* Massine's *The Three-Cornered Hat* and *La Boutique Fantasque;* and his own *Apollon Musagète* and *Barabau*. He would have much preferred making new ballets to restaging old ones, even his own old ones; he has always tended to lose interest in a ballet quickly once he has completed it. For their part, the Danes, whose company is to this day a kind of wonderful living museum of the dance—the only one in the world that tries to present a whole repertory of ballet almost exactly as it may have been danced a hundred years ago—did not take to Balanchine's approach, which is always vitally contemporary even when he is paying homage to tradition. He freely altered all of the ballets he staged in Denmark, and for *The Legend of Joseph* did completely new choreography from start to finish. Summing up Balanchine's tenure in Copenhagen, Kragh-Jacobsen has commented in his historical work, *The Royal Danish Ballet,* "He did not make the impression his ability had promised."

From Denmark Balanchine wended his way back to England. There he did a stint for Sir Oswald Stoll, the impresario of the Coliseum. In Sir Oswald's variety show, the little troupe of dancers that Balanchine had gathered ("16 Delightful Balanchine Girls 16," the billing ran) performed various "popular" ballets, which were supposed to furnish relief of a sort between the clowns and trained-dog acts. Some of the relief was unintentionally comic, the comedy being supplied by the efforts of the Coliseum orchestra, a notably inept group, to cope with Balanchine's notion of popular music—Auric, Stravinsky and the like.

Working for Stoll was naturally not so satisfactory as working for Cochran had been. Still it paid handsomely. Best of all, it permitted Balanchine to live in England. England pleased him very much at that time. "It is very dignified life here," he was heard to say approvingly. Cravatted and bowler-hatted, he used to go riding in Hyde Park of a Sunday. He had his suits made at Anderson and Sheppard and he learned to roll an umbrella. With umbrella impeccably rolled and trousers impeccably baggy, he fancied himself the very model of an English gentleman. Elegant he no doubt was, in his own exotic way, but nobody could possibly have mistaken him for an English gentleman any more than, now that he lives in America and has taken to wearing bright, pearl-buttoned Western shirts, a black string tie and frontier pants, anyone seeing him hurrying along New York's upper Broadway to his rehearsal studios would mistake him for a cowboy.

If he could have had his way, he would have been happy to go on living in England for a goodly while. Unfortunately for him, the depression had begun to make itself felt in the theatre world and he found himself out of work. Without a job he could not get his residence permit extended, even though John Maynard Keynes interceded for him with the authorities; and so, with regret, he had to take leave of England and return to Paris.

With the money he had earned from his engagement at the Royal Danish Ballet, Balanchine had bought his first car, a sporty, green Willys roadster, which he had had imported to Copenhagen from the United States. When he had moved on to England, he had had it shipped after him. Now that he had to depart from England, he tried to take it along with him to France; but when he debarked at Calais, he found himself in a dilemma. He could not bring the car into France because, impoverished as he now was, he could not pay the import duties. He couldn't leave it at the dock, because he couldn't pay the storage fees. From this dilemma Balanchine neatly freed himself by making a present of the car to the nearest bystander. That's the way the money went. He lived, during those odd-job years following Diaghilev's death, sometimes like a prince, sometimes like a pauper. Saving or budgeting was not in his nature. When he worked and had money, he indulged his fancies without stint, gave presents to friends and casual acquaintances, entertained with parties and banquets in the grand manner. Between jobs he seldom knew where his next meal was coming from.

Alexandra Danilova was waiting for Balanchine's return in their Paris apartment. When he arrived, she was particularly distressed to learn what he had done with the car, because she had just bought herself a complete outfit to go with it—green hat, green shoes, green dress, green bag. All that Balanchine had to offer her as a present was a bottle of toilet water he had bought in London. She regarded it with astonishment. Her blue eyes sparkled with icy incredulity, her proud neck arched regally. She looked magnificent. "Toilet water? To Paris! How very kind of you—I can see you've been thinking of me night and day." And she took the bottle and threw it at his head.

On that *opéra bouffe* note the curtain was rung down on their romance. It had in any case been fading away. Both had enjoyed other companionship during the frequent periods of separation from each other. Since his illness, Balanchine had been feeling that he was not so interesting to Danilova as he had once been. For her part, she had been chafing increasingly at the insecurity of their lives. The following year she married an Italian engineer, Giuseppe Massera, hoping to find a source of stability outside the world of the theatre, but the marriage did not long endure.

During the autumn of 1931, not long after Balanchine's return to the Continent from England, still another major opportunity materialized for him. He was asked by René Blum, the director of the theatre at Monte Carlo, to become the *maître de ballet* of a new company which Blum was organizing. Periodically, since Diaghilev's death, there had been rumors and announcements of new ballet troupes being formed to fill the gap left by the disappearance of Diaghilev's Ballets Russes; Blum's company—the Ballets Russes de Monte Carlo, as it was to be eventually called—would be the first such to actually come to fruition. In addition to Balanchine, Blum early solicited as collaborative talents Boris Kochno, Christian Bérard and André Derain. For his *regisseur* he engaged Serge Grigoriev. And as a managerial colleague he took on, to his ultimate regret, Wassili Grigorievitch Voskresensky, a one-time military police and Cossack captain better known to the world by his assumed name and title of Colonel W. de Basil.

A tall, gaunt man with thick-lensed glasses behind which gleamed cold, shrewd eyes, de Basil was a strange but powerful personality—a man of great energy and resourcefulness, with a reservoir of charm he could turn on at will and a natural propensity for the devious and the Machiavellian. He had little cultivation in the arts and next to no knowledge of ballet, but he did possess an instinctive theatrical flair. In recent years he had been associated with Prince Zeretelli in bringing performances of a Russian opera company to Paris, and in 1931 had arranged for the appearance in Monte Carlo of a small troupe of dancers who had taken part in the Zeretelli opera. As soon as he got word of Blum's venture he hurried to Blum to offer his services. By that time Blum had already succeeded in establishing the basis of the organization. All that de Basil brought to Blum, as Blum later wistfully noted, was "vague promises of backing and contracts," yet so compellingly did he work on Blum that, almost before Blum knew what he was doing, he found himself taking de Basil into partnership and bestowing on him the title of co-director.

Balanchine had little to do with de Basil at first. His early dealings were with Blum, for whom he had great respect and with whom he was in excellent rapport. Blum, who was a brother of the French Socialist leader Léon Blum, was a gentle amateur of the arts—sensitive and cultivated. If de Basil was a character who would have been at home in the pages of a Dostoevski novel, Blum could better have been imagined gracing the world of Proust. Indeed, he had been one of the earliest admirers of Proust's work at a time when that author was unknown and had helped make possible the publication of the first volume of *À la Recherche du Temps Perdu.*

It was Balanchine's conviction that the new ballet company should be *new* in almost every way. He did not wish it to rely on the Diaghilev repertoire or to present itself to the public as the true inheritor of Diaghilev's beaver-trimmed mantle. As he saw it, if Diaghilev had left any heritage, it was the message that one should dare to be oneself. Diaghilev was noted for his lifelong, almost phobic reluctance to repeat or even imitate himself. Sharing this feeling, Balanchine wanted to see the new company demonstrate its independence boldly from the start. He was even averse to using the word "Russe" in the company's name, since it suggested a speciously glamorous link with the past. He would have preferred that the company forthrightly call itself Ballets de Monte Carlo.

Full of enthusiasm and ideas, Balanchine went out looking for dancing talent to recruit. The general expectation was that he would be signing on as many of the former luminaries of the Diaghilev company as he could round up, but Balanchine had different ideas. By chance, one day when he was in Paris, he met Danilova. She had heard the news of the new company being formed and was all agog. Naturally she assumed that she would figure prominently in it. "When will we be starting, George? You'll be needing me, won't you?"

"No, Shoura," Balanchine replied. "I don't think so."

"But why not?"

"Because, frankly, you're too old."

"Too *old?*" Danilova cried, momentarily more astonished than outraged.

"That's right," Balanchine said. "For the kind of ballet company I have in mind, much too old."

At that time Danilova was twenty-seven years of age. She was just reaching her peak. Ahead of her were to be more than twenty years of glory and adulation, during which time she would reign as the prima ballerina of the era, at least outside of Russia. So it is understandable that Balanchine's words left her fuming. The fact was, however, that compared to the ballerinas Balanchine planned to employ, the twenty-seven-year-old Danilova did, indeed, seem venerable. While in Paris on this occasion Balanchine had discovered three prodigies, children of Russian émigrés, whom he had engaged. These were the trio upon whom American publicity agents were before long to pin the label of "the baby ballerinas"—Irina Baronova, who was twelve; Tamara Toumanova, who was thirteen; and Tatiana Riabouchinska, who was all of fifteen. The first two were pupils of Preobrajenska and the latter a student of Kchessinska. They could perform feats of amazing virtuosity with innocent ease. Apparently nobody had told them that *fouettés* were supposed to be difficult. Though by St. Petersburg standards they were much too young for leading roles, Balanchine intended to feature them prominently in the new works he planned to create for the company.

Toumanova and Riabouchinska were to join the company in Monte Carlo when it began rehearsals after the start of the year. Baronova meanwhile was to have a part in the Offenbach operetta, *Orpheus in the Underworld,* which Balanchine staged in the fall of 1931 at the Mogador Theatre in Paris. "The sensation of the evening," as André Levinson wrote after that work's highly successful première, "was the tiny child Baronova, who went through the final galop like a whirlwind."

Baronova herself, in an article she wrote some years later, gave an amusing and rather touching account of what being a "baby ballerina" was like. "At the age of twelve I found myself in the magical and hardworking world of ballet. In the years to come I found out that the hard work was always there but the magic was not always present. Of my debut at the Mogador Theatre I shall always have the happiest of memories. It was a delightful operetta; working with Mr. Balanchine was sheer joy, and all of us were madly in love with him. To show my admiration, I used to buy little bags of sweets (he loved sweets) and shyly offer him some; and to my delight he not only took a sweet but invariably grabbed the whole thing, which by then usually was rather a sticky little bag."

She remembers Grigoriev's perplexity when she arrived at Monte Carlo and was introduced to him as the newest member of the cast for whom he, as *regisseur,* would be responsible. "You are such a child, my angel!" he exclaimed. "Oh, dear, what am I going to do with you?" And she also recalls that in Monte Carlo a favorite off-duty diversion for the baby ballerinas, when they were away from the rehearsal hall where they had each been striving their utmost to appear as sophisticated and mysteriously glamorous as a Russian ballerina is supposed to look, was to go to Pasquier, the famous teashop, and have a competition to see who could eat the most pastries. "Sometimes I would win by eating twelve pastries or more in no time at all, and I must confess without much effort."

It was, of course, most incongruous. Sometimes they seemed mere children, no different from other schoolgirls; at other times, as one watched them practicing, with intense concentration and extraordinary skill, some traditional ballerina role, one wondered if they had ever had a childhood at all. In the ballets he created for them Balanchine succeeded in making a remarkable synthesis—a new artistic essence—out of these incongruities. He achieved this most tellingly in *Cotillon,* a ballet to music by Chabrier, with sets by Bérard, and which featured Toumanova, pale and mysterious, with her long black hair hanging down her back. Here dazzling choreography, which showed off the technical precocity of Toumanova and the others in the ballet, was combined with a wistful, bittersweet atmosphere, shy yet sophisticated, and somehow terribly poignant even in the midst of exuberance. *Cotillon* was a heartbreak ball which seemed to express, for all its tenderness, the insecurity and desperate gaiety of one moment of time, over which hovered a sense of fatality and doom. A. V. Coton, in *A Prejudice for Ballet,* has written: "As a creation of atmosphere—in the absolute sense, not an atmosphere of a time and place—nothing else in ballet compares with 'Cotillon.'" Many who saw it still regard it as Balanchine's masterpiece.

In addition to *Cotillon,* Balanchine fashioned two other new works for that first season: *Bourgeois Gentilhomme,* with music by Richard Strauss and scenery by Benois, which proved an agreeable but not memorable ballet; and *La Concurrence,* with music by Auric, and gay decor by Derain, who was also responsible for the conception of the ballet. A madcap ballet depicting the rivalry of two tailors, who go to shameless extremes to lure customers from each other, *La Concurrence* won favor from the start; it provided Baronova with an opportunity to show her talents and featured an extraordinary burlesque variation for Woizikowsky, in the role of a ragged tramp. There was one other new work, it being *Jeux d'Enfants,* which Massine prepared, as guest choreographer. With these as the showpieces of its repertory, the Ballets Russes de Monte Carlo made its debut on April 12, 1932, in the elegant, small theatre in Monte Carlo.

Out front the fashionable audience was delighted by what it saw. Behind the scenes, however, the picture was somewhat less delightful. Ballet

Tamara Toumanova in COTILLON

companies have, of course, always been famous for the amount of intrigue that goes on in them, but those with which de Basil got involved were to be notorious in this regard. He thrived on intrigue. It was as salubrious an atmosphere for de Basil as a dank cellar is for a fungus culture. From the moment of his arrival at Monte Carlo he had begun his own intricate backstage ballet of maneuvering and finagling—fostering rumors, setting factions of the company against each other, elaborating schemes whose aims were never quite what they appeared. Steadily he managed to gain increasing control over the company's affairs; soon he seemed to have his hands in everything. Years later Balanchine was asked, on one occasion, to characterize de Basil. "De Basil was an octopus," Balanchine replied. Then he added, after a moment's thought, "A crooked octopus, and with bad taste."

René Blum had a fine automobile. Before long, de Basil could be seen riding about in it. He had persuaded Blum that the car should be considered part of the enterprise. Not long after that he got Blum to give him a bill of sale for it. Balanchine remembers talking with Blum one day when Blum was trying to puzzle out what had happened. "You know what?" Blum said wistfully to him. "De Basil has just bought my car from me with my own money." In that way, during the next few years, the entire enterprise was to pass from Blum's ownership to de Basil's. In a power struggle the gentle amateur of the arts was no match for the former Cossack officer.

Frequently, during the company's formative months, Balanchine recalls that de Basil would come to him with a receipt for ten thousand francs (or some such sum), which he would ask Balanchine to sign. Balanchine would ask why he should sign a receipt for money he had not received. De Basil would then give a complicated explanation, not exactly plausible yet somehow very nearly persuasive, to the effect that this would in some manner or other facilitate de Basil's raising funds for the company's use and thus enable it to put on more splendid and costly ballets. Balanchine always demurred. He is sure, however, that others of his colleagues—particularly Bérard, who would amiably sign anything put before him—did sign such fictitious receipts for de Basil; and he suspects that de Basil used them as a way of obtaining money from Blum.

On one occasion Balanchine had strong words with de Basil when he learned that de Basil had solicited fifty thousand francs from a young American would-be ballerina, giving her to understand that by making this contribution she could hope to get ahead in the company and get good parts from Balanchine. Balanchine was offended at the suggestion that roles in his ballets were for sale and, beyond that, outraged that de Basil had apparently left the impression with the girl that some of her contribution was to end up in Balanchine's pocket. De Basil seemed surprised and rather amused that Balanchine should get worked up over such a trifle. He shrugged, adopting his suavest man-of-the-world tone. "She's a rich girl, with nothing better to do with her money. Why get yourself all upset? You are an artist—you have your beautiful ballets to create. Leave these onerous money problems to me. That's what I'm here for. Ah, my dear Balanchine, you have no idea what an expensive luxury a ballet company is."

Balanchine also had words with de Basil about the latter's encroachment on the artistic policies of the company. Increasingly, he sought to alter the fundamental image of the company on which Balanchine and Blum had agreed. De Basil wanted to risk no commercial failures. He was eager to exploit to the hilt all the company's Russianisms. He aimed to peddle nostalgia, dressed up in what Balanchine regarded as phony glamour. The core of de Basil's clientele and patrons was to be all the White Russian exiles, weeping in their champagne for a Mother Russia such as never was. And additionally he sought, of course, to clutch Diaghilev to his bosom as a sacred relic, and to present the Ballets Russes de Monte Carlo to the world as nothing other than a kind of miraculous resurrection of Diaghilev's troupe.

All this was most uncongenial to Balanchine. Under such conditions he might have been expected to assert his principles and quit. He debated it; and while he was debating, de Basil quietly fired him and replaced him as *maître de ballet* with Leonide Massine. This took place in June, during the company's Paris season. The first that Balanchine heard of this transaction was when Danilova telephoned him one day to say that she was perplexed, for she had just been asked by Massine to join the Ballets Russes de Monte Carlo with top billing and she wondered why Balanchine was giving up his position. Danilova professed great indignation on Balanchine's behalf when she heard what he had to say about how he had been treated by de Basil, but she would have had to be less than human if she had not also experienced a certain delicious satisfaction at one aspect of the turn of events: the company she was now being courted to join was, after all, the same one her former lover had told her she was too old for the year before.

Objectively speaking, it must be said that even if Balanchine and de Basil had not been at odds, there were a number of respects in which it was more advantageous to the Ballets Russes de Monte Carlo to have Massine as *maître de ballet* than Balanchine at that time. Of the two choreographers, Massine was then the bigger name. His ballets had wider appeal than Balanchine's. He appeared to have yet unlimited potential ahead of him as a choreographer and was a magnetic presence as dancer. In addition, he brought with him, in his negotiations with de Basil, the rights to a number of the old Diaghilev sets and costumes, which he and an American theatrical agent named E. Raymond Goetz had acquired.

For one brief season, after his break with de Basil, Balanchine had the chance to try to put into practice something much closer to his conception of what he thought a ballet company should be—experimental and creative, international in its cultural orientation, making use of the dance techniques which the Russians had brought so near to perfection, but not trading on the Russian atmosphere. And with no "Russe" in its name. Les Ballets 1933 it would be called.

It started out in January of that year amid an atmosphere of dedicated poverty, with a pittance of 25,000 francs to work on. The chief collaborators with Balanchine at first were Kochno, who had withdrawn from the Ballets Russes de Monte Carlo after Balanchine's dismissal, and Derain. There were also a handful of dancers from the Monte Carlo company, of whom the most prominent were Toumanova, Rostova and Jasinsky. No one was being paid more than bare subsistence, but they met daily to prepare Balanchine's new ballets and their enthusiasm was so great that they refused to worry about whether money could be raised to present the works to the public. They would put them on somehow, they vowed. Derain suggested that they buy a wagon which he would decorate, just as Toulouse-Lautrec had done for La Goulue, and that the troupe would travel around in it to fair grounds and public squares, giving performances wherever they alighted.

Around this time the wealthy young British socialite Edward James came along. James was looking for some token of affection to give to his estranged wife, the Viennese dancer and mime Tilly Losch—for whom Balanchine had once choreographed a dance number in one of the Cochran revues—and he decided to make her a present of a ballet company, in which

Roman Jasinski and Toumanova in MOZARTIANA.

she could display her talents. A ballet company as a present for one's loved one is a more princely gift than a diamond necklace from Cartier's. The one season Les Ballets 1933 existed—in which not more than a score of performances were given, in all—was to cost James over a million francs. It is to be hoped that James enjoyed the ballets which resulted from his largesse, for he gained little in the way of domestic or other bliss. He found himself harried and maligned by various disappointed composers and artists, who thought they should have been commissioned to contribute their precious efforts to the venture, some of whom he had to buy off to obtain respite; he had his face slapped on the stage of the Savoy Theatre in London after the curtain fell one evening by Lifar, who called him "an amateur," an incident which precipitated one of the celebrated bloodless duels and near-duels of Lifar's history; and within a short while his marriage to Tilly Losch broke up for the last time, culminating in one of the more sensational divorce suits of the era.

With the arrival of the bountiful James on the scene, Balanchine's little Cinderella troupe found itself suddenly able to have almost everything it could wish for. A number of other dancers were engaged, including, besides Tilly Losch, Diana Gould (who later married Yehudi Menuhin) and the beautiful British dancer Pearl Argyle, of whom Balanchine was briefly, and rather shyly, enamoured. A brilliant group of designers, librettists and composers were assembled, among whom, in addition to Derain, were Tchelitchev, Caspar Neher, Bérard, Berthold Brecht, Kurt Weill, Darius Milhaud and Henri Sauguet. In collaboration with such stimulating figures, Balanchine, applying himself to the task at hand with his typical calm but intense concentration, regardless of whatever hysteria or emotional turbu-

Two scenes from THE SEVEN DEADLY SINS, *a 1958 production of the ballet* LES SEPT PÉCHÉS CAPITAUX. *At right Lotte Lenya, who appeared in both the original and later production, with Allegra Kent. At left, Allegra Kent.*

lence may be in the air, produced in a remarkably short while six new ballets
—*Errante, Songes, Fastes, Mozartiana, Les Sept Péchés Capitaux,* and *Les
Valses de Beethoven.* These, together with a brief oratorio, *Job,* by Nicholas
Nabokov, made up the entire repertory.

By the night of the company's première, which took place in Paris on
June 7, the atmosphere of dedicated poverty in which the troupe had begun
its work had been long forgotten. The fashionable and avant-garde intellectual elements of Paris had adopted the much discussed, though as yet
unseen, new company as their pet of the hour. The season was held in the
glittering Théâtre des Champs-Élysées—a far cry from the painted wagon
Derain had romantically suggested a few months before—and the opening
night turned out to be one of the poshest social events in years. *The New
Yorker's* correspondent, Genêt, wrote in her Paris letter shortly afterward:

*The French are still fond of dancing. As proof, the opening of the
newly organized "Les Ballets 1933" at the Champs-Élysées was the most
brilliant first night of* tout Paris *since the* ouverture *of Comte Étienne de*

Beaumont's "Soirées de Paris" in '24, which was probably the most brilliant première since Diaghileff's "Sacre" in the spring of '13. Which was probably the most brilliant debut since Fanny Elssler's at the Opéra in 1834, which was probably the most brilliant first night since the court ladies of Louis XIV applauded themselves as ballet girls in Lulli's "Triumph of Love," by special request. For four hundred years Parisians have been regally addicted to ballet, and if the 1933 group lacked Bourbon appreciation, it enjoyed Ritz royalty, much more tastily dressed.

Yet, for all that, Les Ballets 1933 fell flat. There was a moderately appreciative response for the lighter, more conventional works, but the public, with only a few notable exceptions, did not take to the three more experimental and more consequential ballets—*Errante, Mozartiana,* and *Les Sept Péchés Capitaux.* The first they found scandalous, the second dull and the third disagreeable. Paris' most distinguished and thoughtful ballet critic, André Levinson, wrote a lament in the newspaper *Candide,* grieving over the course that Balanchine's career seemed to be taking. "By a phenomenon as regrettable as it is curious," Levinson wrote, "this artist, having proved himself last year by guiding his world in the direction of a choreographic classicism rejuvenated by fortunate audacities, abdicates his role of leader and resigns himself to the auxiliary role of a kind of illustrator who comments, by vague dance steps, on the musical concepts of composers or the pictorial concepts of designers." In trying to satisfy so many contrary and uncongenial demands on his talents, Levinson wrote, Balanchine seemed plunged in perplexity, "totally disoriented, riddled and shaken up by contradictory esthetics. . . . It is for us to hope that this almost total eclipse of a choreographer in whom we had founded the most justified hopes, is only temporary; moreover it is necessary that he be taken in hand again by a patron capable of orienting his vacillating will."

During the same time as Les Ballets 1933 was appearing at the Champs-Élysées, de Basil's Ballets Russes de Monte Carlo, in direct competition with the new company, was presenting its Paris season at the Théâtre du Chatelet. To add to Balanchine's mortification, his former company was heralded as sheer delight and far better in nearly every way than it had been the previous year, when he had been its *maître de ballet.* In London the ballet war continued, with Balanchine's company opening at the Savoy on June 28 (with the addition to the repertory of a Lifar ballet, danced by Lifar and

ERRANTE, *as seen here in a 1934 production wi* *William Dollar and Tamara Gev*

Nikitina) and de Basil's company opening at the Alhambra on July 4. The results were the same there as in Paris. Les Ballets 1933 could sustain only a few performances and then had to capitulate, leaving the Ballets Russes de Monte Carlo triumphantly in charge of the field. The latter company had scheduled a three weeks' engagement at the Alhambra, but as its triumphs mounted and the laurels heaped up, it kept on having to extend its engagement week after week to satisfy the adoring public. It did not close until it had played twelve weeks; its reception at the box office had surpassed even that which had been accorded to the Diaghilev company at its peak.

In London Balanchine's company was to disband in mid-July. Balanchine was at loose ends once again. The four years since Diaghilev's death had been restless ones for him; the future seemed to hold no promise of any greater stability. There were job possibilities on the horizon, but nothing that he craved. He was now twenty-nine years old. In the nine years since he had left Russia he had choreographed twenty ballets along with numerous lesser dances. Most of these works had already vanished, never to be seen again, and as far as Balanchine could judge, the few still in repertory were shortly doomed to follow the others. Balanchine did not mourn them. By its nature, ballet is the most ephemeral of the arts. It is like ice sculpture or sand painting, threatened with dissolution from the moment of its creation. The awareness of its mortality contributes to the poignancy of the spectator's experience. Balanchine always accepted this, without distress, as a fundamental condition of his art. "Ballets are like butterflies," he would say. "Who wants to see last season's butterfly?"

But not to be able to engross himself in new creation, not to have a company for whom he could fashion the next season's butterflies—that would be the great frustration for him. He sat backstage at the Savoy one night after a performance, despondently weighing his possibilities. He had just danced the taxing male role in *Errante* that night, substituting for the injured Jasinsky, and he was exhausted as well as in a state of uncertainty.

It was at that point that the American, Lincoln Kirstein, entered his life.

AMERICA: A SCHOOL, A STYLE, A COMPANY, A REPERTORY

Les Ballets 1933 existed only long enough to present a very few evenings of ballet in Paris and London, yet it had at least one outcome of permanent significance: it brought Balanchine an invitation to establish himself in America, and this invitation initiated the events that led, in the ripeness and vicissitudes of time, to the founding of the New York City Ballet. It was after watching Les Ballets 1933 that Lincoln Kirstein, the ballet-struck scion of a wealthy Boston merchant family, sought out Balanchine and suggested that he come to the United States. Thus was begun the close but informal working relationship that has persisted to this day, and in which Balanchine has the role of artist and Kirstein has the unusual multiple role of patron, impresario, polemicist, adviser, advocate and friend. Balanchine creates dances and dancers to the top of his bent while Kirstein devotes himself to the top of *his* bent to providing the conditions that make it possible for Balanchine to do this. It is doubtful if any other choreographer in history has had so devoted a patron and ally.

Since childhood, Kirstein had been enamoured of ballet. At the age of nine, when his parents refused to take him to see a performance of Diaghilev's company in Boston, during the one American tour it made, he harbored vengeful fantasies of running away and becoming a famous dancer. (At just about the same age, it will be recalled, Balanchine was being granted what would have been Kirstein's dearest wish by being enrolled, despite all his protestations, in the Imperial Ballet School at St. Petersburg.) As a young man, Kirstein essayed various arts, showing some talent in all of them. He won a prize at Harvard for freehand drawing, he had a book of poems published, he wrote and published a novel, he played the piano better than competently, he collected art works and wrote articles on painting and photography, he was one of the co-founders of the Harvard Society for Contemporary Art, which is generally credited with being the germinal source out of which grew New York's Museum of Modern Art, and, while still in college, he helped establish the highly regarded literary quarterly

Lincoln Kirstein, about 1934.

Hound and Horn, which he later edited.

But it was ballet that gripped him most. He first saw the Diaghilev company in London in 1924, when he was seventeen years old. "The first blaze of its great adventure was over. A small theatre housed the company, and it was by no means a good season. But I never knew that," he has written. "It was exactly as if I had come home to that splendid country for which I knew I had been destined, but which up to that time I could not seem to find." Every season thereafter he traveled to Europe to see the ballet, and soon he began noting appreciatively the works that Balanchine (just three years older than Kirstein) was creating. "Ballet became an obsession with me," he has said. "Far more than the ordinary influence or attractions of Harvard, the ballet seemed my real education. As time passed, I was increasingly magnetized toward some direct participation in it."

This growing conviction that ballet was to be his special destiny was reinforced by an episode which occurred when he was twenty-two. It was August of 1929, and he was a tourist in Venice. He was searching through the back alleys one hot morning for a church in which El Greco might have worshiped. As he approached it, he found a barge of black and gold moored to the church steps. Entering the church, he perceived in the gloom a bier, blanketed with heaped-up flowers, below a great Byzantine iconostasis of burnished bronze. "Suddenly he became aware of mourners, and the fact that this was, indeed, a funeral," he wrote in *Hound and Horn,* portraying himself in third-person form. "Faces, somehow familiar, ignored him as he passed out into the sunlight, and leaving, heard the first words of the Greek Orthodox service for the dead. Not until three days later, reading the London *Times,* did he learn that he had unwittingly attended, in San Giorgio dei Greci, the obsequies of a great Russian."

It was the funeral of Serge Diaghilev. The episode affected him strongly; he dwelt on it in detail in the novel, *Flesh Is Heir,* which he wrote two years later. That he should have been led to that scene at just that moment seemed to him, if one were susceptible to portents, no mere chance but a sign that Fate was making to him, perhaps even a revelation of a role he might someday assume.

Preparing himself, he plunged into extensive research in the history of the dance, the fruits of which appeared in his book *The Dance* a few years later, which was described at the time of its publication as the most comprehensive history of the dance to date. He also helped Romola Nijinsky with her biography of her ill-fated husband. And at the age of twenty-five Kirstein—six feet three inches tall, ungainly, self-conscious and cerebral—began taking elementary ballet lessons from Michel Fokine in New York, exposing himself to the derision of that great but by then embittered ballet master.

"How can Kirstein be a director of a ballet company?" Fokine some years afterward commented scoffingly to Anatole Chujoy, the editor of *Dance News.* "He took some ballet lessons from me, and he can't get his feet off the floor." To this, Chujoy replied that, after all, Diaghilev had never taken a ballet lesson in his life—an apt reply but one not likely to impress Fokine, who nursed the aggrieved conviction that, as a ballet company director, Diaghilev had been a baleful influence. For Kirstein, taking these lessons was the act of an intellectual deciding intellectually that he ought to be less intellectual in his relationship with so physical and immediate an art as ballet—a groping attempt to share to some small extent the experience of the working ballet practitioners. It has been one of Kirstein's sadnesses all his life to feel himself a mere cultivated amateur in the midst of professionals whose professionalism he admires beyond words.

When Kirstein set sail for Europe in the summer of 1933, he was ready to make his decisive commitment to ballet. To implement his aspirations he carried with him tangible assurance of financial assistance from friends and relatives, particularly Edward M. M. Warburg, of the banking family, the classmate with whom he had collaborated in founding the Harvard Society for Contemporary Art. "I felt that I was about to put all the pieces together in my puzzle—pieces I had been unconsciously collecting for the previous ten years," he has written. The pieces fitted together into a vision, and one that, in the perspective of history, was of an almost imperial grandeur. He wanted to bring ballet to America. He was not content to have some Russian or Russianesque company come here on tour but, rather, it was his idea to have ballet take root and prosper as a vital, indigenous art in the United States—to establish a ballet academy, a ballet company, a ballet repertoire and a ballet audience. Such a transplanting had succeeded only three or four times in the three hundred years since the first ballet company was chartered by Louis XIV, and each time it had taken a monarch with ample coffers to achieve it. Each time, too, it had been effected by the importation into the new country of a great ballet master from the old, who brought the art with him, like Prometheus bringing fire.

Even before Kirstein saw what Balanchine had wrought in Les Ballets 1933, he knew that it was Balanchine he wanted as the instrument of his ambition, and what he saw that year reinforced his conviction, despite the audience's lukewarm response. "Why did I choose Balanchine?" he asked in a retrospective article he wrote for *Theatre Arts* in 1958. "Because I was in love with dancing and had seen 'La Chatte' in 1927 and 'Apollon Musagète' the year following. No one else could do dances like these. There was no question of choice, even if Fokine, Massine, or Lifar had been accessible to me, which they were not (although subsequently they might have been); I knew that what Balanchine made meant ballet to me, because ballet was about dancing to music, not about painting to pantomime."

The initial meeting of the two men was arranged by Romola Nijinsky, who took Kirstein backstage after a performance of Les Ballets 1933 at the Savoy Theatre in London. That was the night when Balanchine, at short notice and despite his bad knee, had been required to step in and dance Jasinsky's role in *Errante*. Seeing how weary Balanchine looked, Kirstein made no attempt to discuss his plans then. A few afternoons later, at Kirstein's invitation, Balanchine called on him at his hotel, and there, in the parlor of the small hotel—"dusty with propriety and full of provincial beauties who had come up to London to be presented at court," as Kirstein remembers the scene—the two of them talked, conversing in French. Two more dissimilar young men it would be hard to imagine—the one wealthy and dilettante, earnest and torrentially articulate, and the other gay by nature, distrustful of solemnity about his craft, and without a penny to his name. That afternoon in the parlor, Kirstein poured out his admiration for Balanchine's creations, his grand dreams for ballet in America, his lofty ideals for the future of the art, his fervent hope that Balanchine would join him in the endeavor. Balanchine said that he would like to try it. As far as he was concerned, Europe had become a museum; in America he sensed the promise of new possibilities. He added that, furthermore, he would dearly love to go to a country that produced girls as wonderful as the movie star Ginger Rogers. It can only be guessed what Kirstein thought of that remark or what Balanchine was up to when he made it—whether he actually meant it (as he well might have) or was pulling Kirstein's leg (as he also well might have been doing), or both.

After Balanchine left, Kirstein sat on in the parlor, his imagination soaring even higher than before. At the next table, having tea, were three girls in white court dress, with plumes in their hair—just returned, most likely, from the court photographers. "I could not discover whether they were the three Muses of Apollo or the three Fates," Kirstein writes, in his characteristic style of scholarly hyperbole. "My mind jumped forward in time and I saw the completed school achieved and functioning, and even more, a great stage swarming with dancers the school had trained, situated somewhere in America. It was exasperating to think concretely of ways and means to make the mirage a miraculous reality."

Balanchine arrived in New York aboard the *Olympic* on October 18, 1933. With him was Vladimir Dimitriev, for Balanchine had insisted, as a condition of his own acceptance, that Dimitriev should be in charge of the school's administration. Balanchine still felt a debt of gratitude to Dimitriev for the enterprise he had shown in organizing, nine years before, the little ballet exodus from the Soviet Union; and, though he was no longer the inexperienced youth he had been then, he still looked to the older man for guidance on practical matters.

The times could scarcely have been less propitious for an attempt to introduce into the United States so exotic, costly, aristocratic and useless an amusement as ballet. The arts were expected—according to the dominant critical and intellectual attitude of the depression period—to be somehow committed in the social struggle, to portray reality in all its harshness, or at least to be earthy and "of the people." Classical ballet certainly did not meet any of those conditions. Modern dance seemed closer to the earnest temper of the time than classical ballet. Actually, there were comparatively few people in the United States, even among the sophisticates, who had ever seen any ballet. Famous ballet stars and their troupes—Pavlova, Mordkin, Bolm, Fokine and others, including, one year, Nijinsky and the Diaghilev Ballets Russes—had made American tours or given performances in this or that large American city, with varying degrees of acclaim, during the past twenty years; but there was no settled tradition of ballet in the United States, no significant standard of reference. People who had never seen ballet naturally did not feel that they were missing anything, while among those who had seen it an ultrasnobbish conception prevailed that Americans could never master ballet techniques and simply did not have the "soul" (a word Balanchine cannot abide) for ballet.

Initially, the plans drawn up by Kirstein, in consultation with his

wealthy young colleague, Warburg, had called for the new institution—
the School of American Ballet, as it would be known—to be established
at Hartford, Connecticut, under the auspices of the Morgan Memorial
Museum there. The theory was that the school should be conducted in a
sheltered, tranquil atmosphere, like that of a university, sufficiently remote
from New York to be unaffected by that city's pressures and demands, by
the ambitions and crises under which the performing arts labor there. The
museum, in addition to offering the ballet school the dignity of its sponsorship, would be able to make available to it a completely equipped auditorium and excellent classroom facilities. It seemed, in theory, a most advantageous arrangement. Kirstein, who had worked very intensively and
persuasively to effect it, was entitled to feel satisfied with himself at having
these details all worked out in time for Balanchine's arrival. There was,
however, one major human factor that he had neglected to take sufficiently
into account: Balanchine.

After having received his training in the capital city of Russia and
gone on from there to show his wares in Paris and London and other
great cities of Europe, Balanchine did not fancy the idea of now settling
down in a provincial American town, whose name he had never even heard
before. This was not what he had come to America for. He and Dimitriev
announced to the flabbergasted and crestfallen Kirstein that they would
rather return to Europe than go to this Hartford place. They might well
have done so if Balanchine had not fallen seriously ill at that point, with a
recurrence of tuberculosis. He had to spend several weeks in bed. During this
time Kirstein and Warburg frenziedly revised their plans. They had begun
to get an inkling of the crisis-ridden existence they had let themselves in for
in getting mixed up with ballet, in aspiring, as they put it in one of the
many grandiose public announcements they issued, "to further the tradition
of classical theatrical dancing in order to provide adequate material for
the growth of a new art in America." Reluctantly they gave up their
carefully secured Hartford connection. After some search, they found a classroom on the fourth floor of an old building on Madison Avenue at Fifty-
ninth Street. The classroom was in a studio which Isadora Duncan had once
occupied.

The official opening date for the School of American Ballet was
January 1, 1934, and classes began the next day, with some twenty-five
students in attendance. Dimitriev had the title of director of the school.

Balanchine was chairman of the faculty—a very small faculty, consisting of just two other members. One was Dorothy Littlefield, a young dancer from Philadelphia, who was to teach the junior grade. The other was Pierre Vladimirov, a former partner of Pavlova's and once Nijinsky's successor as *premier danseur* at the Maryinsky. It was just by chance that this distinguished dancer became available to the school. At the time the school was being formed, he happened to be in New York, as a member of a small troupe which Lifar had brought to America, and became dissatisfied with it. Balanchine had always admired Vladimirov greatly and thought it very lucky that the school had been able to obtain his services. Ballet is an art of example. No textbooks can supplant the living presence of a teacher, who embodies a link with tradition. For the inexperienced American students who would be joining the school henceforth, merely to see the way Vladimirov comported himself was an essential lesson in the fundamental tradition of the classic dance.

An interesting relic of those early days of the School of American Ballet is a snapshot which is the first photograph taken, so far as is known, of Balanchine rehearsing American dancers. Dated June, 1934, it shows him out in the open air, on a small, tree-rimmed stage, preparing a group from the school for its first performance. Looking at the snapshot, one can readily see why it was felt that ballet dancing was no activity for Americans. It just does not seem possible that anything remotely like a ballet troupe could ever emerge from this hodgepodge of chubby, self-conscious girls in homely, one-piece bathing suits. A couple of them have their arms upraised in an ethereal attitude, and appear to feel pretty foolish about it. Another has a hand clapped to her head, as if she were asking herself, "Now what was I supposed to do on Count Three?" Still another suggests a shopper in a department store; her feet hurt, but she won't give up. A hefty creature with a bandanna on her head, standing at one side of the group, half-crouched, with her legs apart and solidly planted, looks more like a prospective line-backer for the New York Giants than a future ballerina. Balanchine is to be seen in the midst of this forlorn, chaotic scene, tugging at one of the girls in an effort to haul her approximately into position. He is the only person in the picture who does not seem to be aware of the manifest hopelessness of the whole enterprise.

If it is strange to reflect that the brilliant New York City Ballet developed out of so unpromising a beginning, it is almost as astonishing to

The first known photograph which
shows Balanchine working with American dancers —
June, 1934, at White Plains.

SERENADE, *as danced by the New York City Ballet.*

realize, as one looks at this funny picture, that the ballet Balanchine was working on with the girls must have been *Serenade*—a work of enduring loveliness, which is today to be found in the repertory of many companies throughout the world. *Serenade* was the first ballet that Balanchine created in the United States, and the first of any consequence ever created for American dancers. It is a choreographic tour de force. Balanchine devised it as a lesson for the students in his school's advanced class. He wanted to show them how the fundamental steps they were painfully trying to master can become transformed, when shaped by a choreographer, into something more than routine exercises, and he also wanted to bring home to these novices that ballet, for all its ancient heritage, is a living, contemporary art, not to be worshipfully thought of, as most people thought of it then, merely in terms of *Giselle* and *Swan Lake*. So, with a string serenade by Tchaikovsky for his music, he improvised choreography around his students. The first evening he worked on it, seventeen girls were present, so he choreographed the opening scene for seventeen, demonstrating how that awkward number of dancers could be arranged on the stage in an interesting manner. The next evening, only nine girls were present, and the third evening six; at each session he simply choreographed to the music with whatever students he had. Male students began attending the classes, and he worked them in. At one point, where the girls were supposed to rush out, one fell down and began to cry. He choreographed the incident right into the ballet. Another evening, a girl showed up late. That went in, too. It must have been not only an illuminating but a delightful series of lessons. Subsequently, when Balanchine decided to make a stage work of *Serenade,* he elaborated some parts, dropped others, and made the whole thing more theatrical and dramatic, embodying in it an elusive suggestion of a story about ill-fated lovers. What *Serenade* is really about, though, is not that hint of a story; it is about the classical ballet itself—how the young, inexperienced, unsophisticated dancers we see on the stage achieve mastery of the art, and how they are refined and transfigured in the process. So it opens with the dancers standing in diagonal rows, as if in a classroom, with one arm upraised, feet together and toes pointed forward. Then, on a chord, they open their feet to the first position. This is the most elementary movement in ballet, yet Martha Graham, whose own career in the dance has been a long revolt against formal ballet, recalls that at that moment, the first time she saw the work, tears sprang to her eyes. "It was simplicity itself," she has said, "but the simplicity of a very great master—one who, we know, will later on be just as intricate as he pleases."

In this first American ballet of his, Edwin Denby has written, Balanchine was devising, intentionally or unintentionally, an approach to ballet that would be natural for American dancers. The problem was that Americans were as yet too self-conscious to dance in the grand classical manner, and Balanchine tackled it by making the company as a whole more important than any individual stars. Denby writes:

He had to find a way for Americans to look grand and noble, yet not be embarrassed about it. The Russian way is for each dancer to feel what he is expressing. The Americans weren't ready to do that. By concentrating on form and the whole ensemble, Balanchine was able to bypass the uncertainties of the individual dancer. The thrill of "Serenade" depends on the sweetness of the bond between all the young dancers. The dancing and the behavior are as exact as in a strict ballet class. The bond is made by the music, by the hereditary classic steps, and by a collective look the dancers in action have unconsciously—their American young look. That local look had never before been used as a dramatic effect in classic ballet.

Recently, when Balanchine was asked what he thought of Denby's exegis of *Serenade,* he replied, "Too fancy!" And he added, "I was just trying to teach my students some little lessons and make a ballet that wouldn't show how badly they danced"—the kind of ingenuous, deadpan statement that he often makes and that he may or may not entirely mean.

At any rate, one does know that *Serenade* has been a work which has been of some importance to Balanchine throughout the years since he made it, and he has retained a special fondness for it. It is not likely to be allowed casually to slip into oblivion, as has happened to many other lovely Balanchine ballets, and is kept up with rather more care than most of the other ballets in the repertory. From time to time over the years he has turned to *Serenade* and worked it over in one way or another—adding some elements, omitting others, consolidating or expanding individual roles. The ballet seems to serve him as a certain archetype, or perhaps a kind of journal or copybook, in which some of the maxims he cares about may be set down. A present friend of Balanchine's has a recollection of standing with Balan-

On the following pages, another moment from
SERENADE, *in a New York City Ballet performance.*

chine, at the latter's usual vantage point at the rear of the center aisle, watching a performance of this ballet with him one evening in 1959. When the curtain came down and the friend praised the work, Balanchine replied, with evident pleasure, "Yes, it stands up not too badly—considering it's twenty-five years old. For a ballet, that's a long time to last."

The two men went across the street to a café during the intermission. Over their drinks Balanchine began talking about some of the dramatic themes in *Serenade*. "It's like fate," he said, in regard to one motif. "Each man going through the world with his destiny on his back. He meets a woman—he cares for her—but his destiny has other plans."

The friend listened with some amazement as Balanchine went on in this vein, since in all the years he had known Balanchine he had never heard him discussing the literary content of any of his plotless works, or even admitting that they had any. "That's fascinating," he commented. "Did you tell any of that to your dancers when you were choreographing the ballet?"

Balanchine drew back in horror. "God forbid!" he said.

The original performance for which this ballet was being rehearsed when the all-too-candid snapshot was taken was an "invitation only" affair, given on an outdoor platform on the estate of Felix Warburg—Edward Warburg's father—near White Plains on June 10, 1934. A few months later Balanchine and Kirstein decided that the school's students were now ready to perform before the general public. A separate corporation was established for the performing group, which took the name of the American Ballet. Whereas the ballet school was subsidized chiefly by Kirstein and his family at this point, with assistance from Nelson Rockefeller, a friend of Kirstein's, the funds to support the performing company now came mainly from Edward Warburg, supplemented by donations from Mrs. W. K. Vanderbilt and some other benefactors. Warburg took the title of director of the American Ballet; Balanchine, naturally, became ballet master; Kirstein, who is made uncomfortable by the trappings and titles of rank, had himself put down as secretary. After a couple of out-of-town tryout engagements, the American Ballet played its first season in New York—two weeks at the Adelphi Theatre, on Fifty-fourth Street, beginning March 1, 1935—with a small repertory of Balanchine ballets: *Serenade, Dreams, Transcendence, Alma Mater, Errante,* and *Reminiscence.* For these performances, the company numbered twenty-six dancers from the school, plus two guest artists: Tamara Geva, with whom Balanchine worked in the easy rapport which

ALMA MATER, *with William Dollar as the janitor, Heidi Vosseler as the coed and Charles Laskey as the football hero.*

he would always seem to maintain with his ex-wives, and Paul Haakon, a protégé of Fokine's.

The new company and Balanchine's new ballets aroused no great enthusiasm among either the public or the critics. In 1952, in his book *Modern Ballet,* John Martin, the *New York Times* dance critic and for many years the only dance critic of consequence in the United States, was to write: "The bringing of Balanchine to America in 1933 was an event of considerably greater moment than anybody realized at the time except perhaps Lincoln Kirstein, who brought it about." But in those earlier years, when Balanchine and the American Ballet were first trying to get established in the United States, Martin was not merely lukewarm on the subject of Balanchine but actively antipathetic. His reaction to the ballets presented during that first appearance in New York was that *Errante* was "cosmic nonsense"; *Dreams* was "scarcely worth the labor that has been spent on it"; *Transcendence,* though of greater interest than *Dreams,* was "largely incomprehensible" and manifested a "straining for choreographic novelty." Best he liked *Reminiscence,* a frankly derivative collection of divertissements in the old Russian ballet manner, which Balanchine had put together purely

Gisella Caccialanza in DREAMS.

as an entertainment. Of *Serenade,* Martin wrote: "It is a serviceable rather than an inspired piece of work. No doubt Mr. Balanchine had his problems in devising choreography for an inexperienced company, but whatever the reasons, *Serenade* lacks spontaneity to a great extent." In his initial reviews and subsequent estimates, Martin repeatedly attacked Balanchine's approach as precious and decadent, an example of the kind of "Riviera esthetics" that America should be spared. "While every region is entitled to whatever decadences it pleases, there is nothing to be gained by our importing them." At this point, he wrote, the very best thing that the American Ballet could do would be to get rid of Balanchine, with his international notions, and hire a good American dance man.

The criticism that Balanchine was not American enough to be entrusted with nurturing a truly American school and style of ballet was one that was frequently heard in those days. Even Balanchine's admirers kept urging him to do more ballets with American subjects—such as, say, *Uncle Tom's Cabin,* or *The Winning of the West.* Kirstein, himself, felt the attraction of folk-lore themes, as did many city intellectuals then. The ones who did not were the American folk, who were, on the whole, leaving the farm as fast as they could or mechanizing it to resemble an agricultural factory. Balanchine had no interest in such themes. He had taken to America from the moment of his arrival and felt at home in it. He liked the way it all looked and smelled and sounded. He felt in tune with its tempo, its vigor, its directness. His intuitions as to what being a twentieth-century American meant would prove much truer and more persuasive eventually than the notions of his folklore-loving critics. Most of all, he liked the way the people moved—their athleticism and unself-conscious freedom of gesture, which showed in their games and daily activities, even if not yet in their dance. The long-limbed girls he found a pleasure to behold, and compared their configuration favorably with the Boucher cherub kind of body which had been the standard model of the dancers at the Maryinsky when he was young. "The land of lovely bodies," he called America.

Friends of Balanchine from that period remember that, unlike most expatriate Russians, he was seldom nostalgic for the old country, nor could he be heard, as was something of a practice among the intellectual Russians, continually praising Paris at the expense of New York. His closest friends and cronies tended to be Russians, as would always be true for him—among them, in those days, Tchelitchev, Nicholas Nabokov, Dukelsky, Nicholas Kopeikine, the company's rehearsal pianist, and George Volodine, a dancer. In addition to these, he soon came to know a great number and quite extraordinary variety of people around New York. People were attracted to him—"perhaps," as one who has known him for a long time has said, "because he doesn't misunderstand what they say or do but always watches attentively for the truth." Or, perhaps, simply because he was gay and easy to be with. Despite being continually surrounded by people who considered themselves his friends, or who simply enjoyed being with him, he struck some who knew him as essentially a lonely person—with the loneliness of those who think they do not need others and who avoid deep involvements. He could be spontaneously kind, but without ever giving up an abiding aloofness or detachment. "If one of Balanchine's friends got into trouble," one of his associates once said, "Balanchine would always be ready to help, with all the money he had or with whatever he could do for him, but he wouldn't weep over him." There was in his makeup what one friend has called "a gentle ruthlessness," which has enabled him to pursue his course through life with less detours than most people experience. Kirstein liked to describe him admiringly as "sinister." To reporters and others who inquired as to what Balanchine was like, Kirstein would often say, "He's Georgian, you know—just like Stalin." A characteristic of Balanchine's that impressed others was his decisiveness. When something had to be done, he simply made up his mind and did it—and never fretted about it afterward. This applied to just about everything except letter writing. He had, his whole life long, an almost physical aversion to writing, so that he would telephone long distance almost anywhere rather than write a letter and, when pressed to write, would invent improbable and ingenious reasons for avoiding it. He did not even care to read letters if he could help it. Rieti, who had moved to America a few years after Balanchine and resumed a friendship with him which had originated during their collaboration for Diaghilev, remembers that Balanchine's mailbox would always be full of unopened mail. Inquisitive by nature, himself, Rieti could hardly bear Balanchine's indifference. "George!" he would exclaim, "Aren't you going to read your mail?" "I will—I will," Balanchine would reply with a wave of his hand. "Not now—later."

His living quarters were not pretentious. During his early years in New York, he seemed restless in this regard—as if looking for a place to settle, but not finding it. He lived in a series of small apartments on the East Side of New York, not far from the school. He would furnish one and fix it up, and then, after a few months, begin looking for another place. Early he acquired a car, which, characteristically, he bought on sheer impulse one day, without making any detailed inquiries or doing any comparison shopping. The friend who was with Balanchine on that occasion commented, "I spend more time buying a tie than you just did buying a car." In this automobile, Balanchine and friends, and often one or another of the girls from the school, enjoyed driving out to Connecticut or Long Island of a Saturday or Sunday. Their favorite objective was to try to find, out in the American countryside, some restaurant where they could get a nice Russian glass of tea.

Though Kirstein's advance announcements, at the time the school had been established, had stressed that no attempt would be made to rush into the production of ballet programs until some considerable maturation period had elapsed, neither he nor Balanchine had had the patience to abide by this. In the fall of 1935, they set out with their small, inexperienced company and their modest repertory of ballets on what was planned to be a fourteen-week tour of America. The tour got as far as Scranton, Pennsylvania, and then collapsed, when the company's theatrical manager suffered a nervous breakdown and suddenly it was discovered that there were no funds to meet any of the expenses. It was a disillusioning experience, but those involved with the company did not despair. They were brimming with optimism for the future. That summer, just before the tour began, there had occurred what seemed at the time the greatest piece of good fortune imaginable: the Metropolitan Opera had invited the American Ballet to become the Opera's resident ballet company, with Balanchine as ballet master. Kirstein afterward wrote: "The invitation was so unexpected, the opportunity seemingly so wonderful, there was scarcely any thought of refusal." It appeared to offer the company, at one stroke, almost everything it could desire: a home, and a distinguished home, at that; steady employment; an audience; and the chance—so Balanchine and Kirstein assumed —to present evenings of their own repertoire as well as dances and ballets for the operas.

At that time, in 1935, the Metropolitan had just undergone an administrative shake-up. Giulio Gatti-Casazza's long reign as director had been ended, and Edward Johnson was to take his place. Johnson was himself a former opera singer and reportedly intended to give more consideration to the artists' viewpoint than the opera's management hitherto had done. Johnson told the members of the ballet company that he hoped they would bring "freshness, youth and novelty" to the Metropolitan. Nobody listening to him seems to have greeted this skeptically, or stopped to consider the incongruity of such qualities as freshness, youth and novelty at the Met as it was then constituted. As Kirstein was later to recall, in a caustic, near-libelous pamphlet entitled *Blast at Ballet:* "I was so enchanted to work in the dusty labyrinth of that palatial mortuary under the cracked gilt plaster, powdery scenery and bundles of rotting costumes, that my *zeal* exceeded a crusader's. I had not yet learned the first rule of diplomacy: *Surtout point de zèle.*"

Balanchine, being less demonstrative and voluble, did not show his feelings so openly, but he was, if anything, even more enchanted than Kirstein. To work in such a setting was what he had trained for as a boy. Opera houses would always arouse memories of the Maryinsky in him; when he entered one, he always felt as if he were returning home and assuming his natural heritage. He might have tempered his optimism and delight by recalling the frustrations he had experienced at the Maryinsky when he first began to choreograph and to assert the originality of his bent; he might also have reflected that few of his achievements for Diaghilev would have been tolerated by the staid management of an opera house: but for the moment he was not able to do so. When wishful thinking has nostalgia to reinforce it, the combination is apt to overpower the sober voice of experience. Stimulated by the splendid prospect he envisaged for his company in these grand new circumstances, he found himself brimming with creative ballet ideas which he was eager to demonstrate as soon as possible. He could scarcely wait for the season to begin. In Kirstein's words, "Everything proceeded on our part with a fatal and precipitate enthusiasm."

It did not take long to discover that the ballet company's relationship with the Met was not going to be the happy and fruitful one they anticipated. As soon as Balanchine saw the dressing area assigned to his dancers— a dingy, cheerless, cramped portion of the basement—he was reminded in what low esteem the Met held its ballet troupe. Everywhere he turned, during the season, he encountered other reminders. The Met begrudged every penny the ballet company cost it. It kept nagging at the dancers not to wear out so many pairs of ballet shoes, and it fussed over the cleaning bills for the costumes. To economize, the Met's management never let the dancers rehearse with the orchestra; all they had was a pianist. That was the way things had always been done. For *The Bartered Bride* the conductor had made cuts in the orchestra score, but nobody bothered to tell Balanchine. The result at the opera's performance was, of course, sheer chaos. The critics wrote that the dancers couldn't keep step.

From the outset the Met's management and Balanchine quarreled over his conceptions of the dance. The management complained that the divertissements and ballets Balanchine devised for its operas showed no respect for tradition. To this Balanchine coolly replied, "Of course not. The tradition of the ballet at the Met is bad ballet." The Met, he went on, had always used ballet in the opera the way a diner uses a napkin—to wipe his mouth before resuming his meal—whereas he wanted to provide dances that would be tasty dishes in their own right.

As things worked out, though, the only dishes of his concocting that satisfied the management and the critics were the dances he did for *Carmen* and the kermis ballet in *Faust*. ("I think Balanchine must have composed it in a deep sleep," Kirstein said of the latter effort.) The *Carmen* divertissement, as even the management admitted, saved the opera after the Met's favorite Carmen had lost her voice. The reason for Balanchine's success in this instance, according to Irving Kolodin in his history of the Metropolitan Opera Company, was that the surroundings in *Carmen* were neutral in quality so that there was no clash between the style of the dancing and that of the staging. In other, more stylized operas a violent clash was felt.

The essence of the more knowledgeable criticism of Balanchine's work at the opera house was that his dances were not properly subordinated to the over-all intention of the operas, were too assertive, and seemed to strive unduly for effect. He may have been trying too hard to make his mark in this country, or simply taking too literally Edward Johnson's request for something fresh and new from the ballet. Some years later, in summarizing Balanchine's tenure at the Met, Kolodin wrote: "Balanchine could have made a fresh and vital thing of the danced portions of a Metropolitan production; but the production itself would have to be fresh and vital before such a departure could be regarded as adjunct rather than intrusion." As became apparent quite soon, the Met's repertory was not going to be overhauled significantly, even though major reforms had been promised at the time Johnson took over from Gatti-Casazza; and it became equally apparent that when he had asked for "freshness, youth and novelty" in the ballet what he had really meant was the same old thing but done with just a little more verve, perhaps.

Even if the Met had been willing to attempt new productions at that time, it is possible that there would still have been manifest a basic incompatibility between the style of movement Balanchine used and that of the singers. This is a point that the perceptive critic and composer Virgil Thomson made in his later analysis of what had gone wrong with the marriage between Balanchine and the Metropolitan. "Balanchine's ballet style employs a dynamic, explosive, sharply precise kind of movement, full of enormous tension and vigor. That was the style that the Russians had been developing since they imported classical ballet from France, and the style that Balanchine brought to America with him. But the style of movement employed by the singers and other stage figures in the opera houses of the West comes directly from the Franco-Italian manner and uses slow, broad, much softer gestures. I don't think Balanchine himself was aware of what a contrast the two styles made."

The difficulties encountered with the management over the opera ballets were disconcerting enough, but the greatest blow to Balanchine and Kirstein was the discovery that the Met had no intention of scheduling regular evenings of ballet, as other great opera houses of the world did. Balanchine was flabbergasted, for he thought there had been a clear understanding on this matter. The fact that his company had a repertory of ballets suitable for performance had seemed one of the main reasons why the company had been invited to enter the Metropolitan in the first place; certainly that had been the decisive reason for the company's acceptance of the invitation. But when Balanchine and Kirstein broached this subject after joining the establishment, they were informed that the Met regarded evenings devoted to ballet as a luxury that could not be afforded. "There is simply no budget for the extra orchestra rehearsals that would be required," they were told repeatedly in the course of the elementary lessons on the economics of running a great opera house they were given whenever they sought to advance their proposals.

To salvage something under these conditions, Balanchine contrived to have his company create some works to music the orchestra already knew, and thus could play without extra rehearsals. He arranged *The Bat* to the music of Johann Strauss' *Die Fledermaus*. The public found it delightful, and it was presented many times. Another work, created to meet these exigent circumstances, was *Concerto,* which represented the dancer William Dollar's first venture into choreography. It was to the music of Chopin's Piano Concerto in F Minor, another piece that the orchestra had in its repertory. John Martin was invited to attend a piano rehearsal of this work (no "dress" rehearsal could be afforded, of course), but he was turned away when he presented himself at the stage door. The custodian at the door knew his Metropolitan Opera House, and he could not believe that a critic of the *New York Times* could really be interested in seeing dancing there.

A frustrating, disagreeable relationship it was from the start, and harrowing for all concerned—for the Met as well as for Balanchine and his company. Balanchine must have been a great trial to the Metropolitan. Theretofore, it had always employed humbler dancing masters who modestly accepted their place in the Met's scheme of things. Balanchine, for all his quietness and elegant breeding, was never afflicted with an ounce of humility, and he had never hesitated to speak his mind. The Met can hardly have enjoyed learning that its ballet master, in a statement to the press, had said that New York's music critics knew nothing about dance and not much more about music, nor can it have been much amused by Balanchine's reply to a reporter's question about how he had prepared his dancers for performing with an opera company: "Generally, I instructed my dancers to dance all over the place. The dancers must pay no attention to the singing chorus. I advised them to kick the chorus if they got in the way." Such flights of brash humor were not calculated to endear Balanchine to the officials who ran the joyless, unprofitable business known as the Metropolitan Opera. To them, the very enthusiasm with which Balanchine and Kirstein approached their work seemed an appalling and vaguely menacing breach of the standards of decorum customarily observed in the gloomy, gilt sanctuary on Thirty-ninth Street. The personification of the Metropolitan Opera House atmosphere, for Balanchine and Kirstein, was embodied in Edward Ziegler, the associate general manager, in whose hands was the responsibility for the actual functioning of the administration, in all its ritualized, anachronistic complexity. A steely realist, capable of freezing with an icy, ironic smile the naïve suggestions of those who were not versed, as he was, in every detail of the house's budget, he was a formidable figure. When Kirstein would encounter Ziegler backstage, Kirstein would often recall Heinrich Heine's description of Henri Duponchel, director of the Paris Opéra in 1835: "To judge from his outward appearance one would take him for the overseer of the Père Lachaise cemetery rather than the director of the Grand Opéra."

As early as the first *Aïda,* the insiders were saying that Balanchine and company were done for, as far as the Met was concerned. The general expectation, shared by Balanchine, was that at the end of the season the Met, with a sigh of relief, would bid them farewell. No such announcement appeared. Instead, there came the surprising announcement that during the experimental, popular-priced spring season (an innovation of Edward Johnson's), which was to take place right after the close of the regular season, there would be featured a new production of Gluck's *Orpheus and Eurydice,* staged and choreographed by George Balanchine, danced by members of his company and with decor by Pavel Tchelitchev.

What led the Metropolitan suddenly to offer so fair a chance to one toward whom it had hitherto been so grudging? It is hard to say. At the time there was much intramural conjecture about the Met's motives. Some of the speculation imputed a devious malice to Ziegler and other Met officials which would have done credit to the Borgias: they had decided, it was said, to let Balanchine commit suicide in public and were going to relish seeing him measure out and administer his own poison. But it may not have been at all like that. The Met's management may have been sincerely seeking to give Balanchine's talents a fuller trial, under more ample and flexible conditions than the regular season afforded. They were skeptical, but still . . . And it would not cost the Met much, for Edward Warburg had agreed to share the production costs.

At any rate, here was a great opportunity at last for Balanchine and his young company. He and his colleagues decided to put into this work all their long-nourished conceptions as to the ideal form of presentation for lyric theatre. It was to be a revolutionary treatment of an opera: all beauty. No fat, ungainly singers would clutter up the stage. The actions and passions of the timeless legend, to Gluck's sublime music, would be conveyed visually through the "nebulous precision," in Cocteau's fine phrase, of the ballet. The singers—soloists as well as chorus—would be in the pit, out of sight, along with the orchestra.

As for the conception, Kirstein writes that they sought to present what was most living for the present epoch in the Orphic myth. They visualized it, he said, as "the eternal domestic tragedy of an artist and his wife. . . . We saw Hell as a concentration camp with flying military slavedrivers lashing forced labor; the Elysian Fields as an ether drama, a desiccated bone-dry limbo of suspended animation, and Paradise as the eternity we know from a Planetarium arrayed on the astronomical patterns of contemporary celestial science."

The leading spirit in the formulation of these ideas was Pavel Tchelitchev, who evolved set designs and costumes for the opera which recalled in

Pavel Tchelitchev.

their quality and atmosphere Piero della Francesca's paintings and at the same time suggested surrealistically something of the present workaday world. Febrile, intense, exceedingly articulate, Tchelitchev was a visionary with an intense compulsion to systematize his visions. On top of a surrealist's perceptions of the world, he erected a medieval structure of logic. He could hold forth hypnotically, if not always comprehensibly, for hours on subjects that obsessed him. Balanchine would listen to him as spellbound as a child being told a fairy tale. He had a lasting influence on Kirstein, who collected his paintings and organized exhibitions of them and wrote monographs on him. "It was Pavel Tchelitchev," Kirstein later recalled, "who showed me that theater was an amazing amusement of measurable importance, neither more nor less. His standards of taste, ingenuity and genius were icily professional; he was only interested in virtuosity; as he said: the coloratura style." On Balanchine also, Tchelitchev's personality was a powerful stimulant during the preparation of *Orpheus and Eurydice,* as it had been when they worked together on *Errante* for Les Ballets 1933; but on the whole Tchelitchev's influence on him was not so marked or lasting as it was on Kirstein, for Balanchine was less susceptible by nature than Kirstein to abstract ideas and systematizations—or, indeed, to words of any sort. Also, Balanchine had a suspicion that despite all the ardor of his fine language about ballet and the lyric theatre, Tchelitchev did not really care much for dancing—at least, not anywhere near so much as Balanchine. No painters ever did, it seemed. Many painters, Balanchine sometimes thought, would really have preferred it if the dancers would only dance behind the set instead of in front of it; that way they would not distract from the exhibition. Still, Balanchine thought Tchelitchev's designs for *Orpheus and Eurydice* very beautiful—as beautiful, in fact, as any set designs he had ever seen.

On this occasion, as always, the chief stimulant and deepest fount of inspiration for Balanchine was the music. He listened, during the intense, excited conferences that would sometimes go on far into the night, to the ideas propounded by Tchelitchev and Kirstein, but the voice to which he gave most heed when it came time to choreograph was that of Christoph Willibald Gluck—poignant, passionate, grave and noble. *Orpheus and Eurydice* had long been perhaps his favorite of all operas. For Gluck's music Balanchine created, in Kirstein's words, some of his "most accomplished erotic patterns, touching and electric encounters, and noble plastic groups."

A scene from ORPHEUS AND EURYDICE. *Left to right:*
Holly Howard, Joseph Lane, Lew Christensen and Helen Leitch.

In the principal roles were cast Lew Christensen, Daphne Vane and William Dollar. There were only three weeks to create, prepare and rehearse the opera, but all concerned, down to the members of the corps de ballet, gave themselves over completely to the work. For those three weeks they lived and breathed it. At last came the day—May 19, 1936—and the company was ready. The music began, the curtain went up, the dancers performed, in Balanchine's opinion, to near perfection.

Nothing like this had ever been done at the Metropolitan Opera before —and the official consensus of opinion was that it was awful, a most devastating failure. The critics called it silly, arty, bogus, irrelevant and ugly, and the most inept performance they had ever seen at the Met. They acted as offended as if they had been personally insulted. If New York had been Paris, there might well have been boos and catcalls from the audience, and all the rest of the furor of a *Sacre du Printemps* scandal; as it was, there were merely titters, yawns, scowls of frigid disapproval and polite applause.

Some few among the audience were deeply impressed. One was Glenway Wescott, who wrote a letter to *Time,* taking issue with that magazine's sarcastic and flippant review. Wescott called it "the only original undertaking of the opera association this season," and said: "By virtue of the strange new scenes and 20th-Century dances, I was more deeply moved by the old myth and music than ever before. . . . Balanchine is a very great man, I think. If I were to make a list of the dozen most exciting and inspiring things

A cutthroat poker game as publicity for CARD GAME —
*Warburg, Stravinsky, Balanchine and Dollar
(back to camera), with the four Queens of the ballet
as kibitzers: Hortense Kahrklin, Leda Anchutina,
Ariel Lang and Annabelle Lyon.*

I have seen in the theatre, three of his choreographic works would be on it: Apollon Musagète and The Prodigal Son and Errante."

But those of Wescott's mind were in the minority. The management of the Met permitted *Orpheus and Eurydice* a total of two performances, and then dismissed it forever.

If the Met had been seeking Balanchine's destruction as diabolically as Kirstein was certain it was, it had his head on the block now. Yet the ax was withheld for the time being. The American Ballet was permitted

CARD GAME, *as performed at the Met, with William Dollar as the Joker.*

to return for the 1937–38 season, but was manifestly there on sufferance only. Clearly the company's days were numbered. The atmosphere of the dusty caverns backstage at the Met could not have been grimmer for Balanchine and his dancers that year.

Despite all, during what remained of his tenure at the opera house, Balanchine managed to wangle one more opportunity to show his work in gala style on the Metropolitan stage—an opportunity once more made possible by the generosity of Edward Warburg, though this time with no cooperation at all from the Met's management. The occasion was a Stravinsky-Balanchine festival, presented in the spring of 1937—featuring *Apollo* and two new ballets: *Le Baiser de la Fée* and *Card Game: A Ballet in Three Deals*. The latter work had been specially commissioned from Stravinsky for the occasion. These three ballets differed strikingly from each other, both musically and balletically; yet they all bore the authentic stamp of a Stravinsky-Balanchine collaboration. Stravinsky himself conducted a seventy-

piece orchestra, hired from the Philharmonic, not from the Met's pit, and, as publicity, had himself photographed playing poker with Balanchine and Warburg. This time, to everybody's surprise, the presentation came within a hairsbreadth of breaking even at the box office. The public was delighted, and critics called it the most brilliant evening of ballet ever seen in New York.

This success, however, did not alter the fundamental incompatibility between Balanchine and the Metropolitan Opera, and early in 1938 they parted company. "The Met is a heap of ruins," Balanchine angrily told the press as he left, "and every night the stagehands put it together and make it look a little like opera." As a parting shot, he added, "The Met is always saying it wants something new. Why don't they put together all the first acts that the box-seat patrons who always come in late never see, and make a new opera from them?" He was in a rage—a rare thing in his life. The crassest of the Broadway producers for whom he later worked never shook his famous aplomb as the Met did. He could adjust himself amicably to the quirks and demands of commercial entrepreneurs, since he knew in advance how little their business had to do with making art as compared with making money. From the Met he had expected something very different. Indeed, he had been sure when he first signed his contract with the Met that this was the beginning of a lasting association and a magnificent, creative era in opera and ballet.

If it was artistically impossible for the American Ballet to function in collaboration with the Met, it was financially impossible for it to function alone. Shortly after the Stravinsky-Balanchine festival, Warburg ceased to be a patron of ballet. The art had never been his primary interest, as it was Kirstein's, and had cost him around a hundred thousand dollars in something less than three years, which is fairly steep for a side interest. He had caught ballet as one might catch the measles—and now he had got over it.

So, in the middle of 1938, the American Ballet went out of existence.

CHAPTER NINE

For the better part of the next decade, Balanchine spent much of his time being a Broadway and Hollywood dance man. He may have been too arty for the Metropolitan Opera, but he was a hit with Sam Goldwyn and George Abbott. He quickly established himself as the best in the business, and had more offers of shows than he could handle. On Broadway, he was thought of as a real pro—quick, adaptable, easy to work with, and possessed of an inexhaustible supply of clever and original dance ideas. *Variety* bestowed its succinct accolades on him: "George Balanchine has done an ace job on the terp angle." A lot of the shows he choreographed made big money, among them *On Your Toes, I Married an Angel, Babes in Arms, The Boys from Syracuse, The Merry Widow, Rosalinda, Louisiana Purchase, Song of Norway* and *Where's Charley?* His movies included the *Goldwyn Follies, I Was an Adventuress, Star-Spangled Rhythm* and the filmed version of *On Your Toes*. Along the way, during this tinsel era in Balanchine's life, he and Stravinsky—that well-known team—joined forces to do a project for Ringling Brothers Circus. The circus first engaged Balanchine, and then he made a long-distance call to Stravinsky, who was at his home in Los Angeles, to enlist his collaboration. Their dialogue is worth preserving:

"I wonder if you'd like to do a little ballet with me," Balanchine said, after Stravinsky answered the phone, "a polka, perhaps."

"For whom?"

"For some elephants," Balanchine said.

"How old?" asked Stravinsky cautiously.

"Very young," Balanchine assured him.

There was a pause. Then Stravinsky said gravely, "All right. If they are very young elephants, I will do it."

The score which Stravinsky subsequently delivered—*Circus Polka,* it is called—bears the dedication: "For a Young Elephant."

The *jeux d'esprit* that resulted from this Stravinsky-Balanchine col-

*Balanchine at Sarasota,
with some members of the cast
of his* CIRCUS POLKA.

laboration would have amused their old colleague Diaghilev. Everybody thought this ballet, as performed by a troupe of fifty elephant in tutus and fifty circus starlets, with costumes by Norman Bel Geddes, a very chic and clever thing—everybody, that is, except the elephants, they being essentially middle-class creatures, suspicious of novelty. Balanchine gaily told a reporter when he started on the project, "Elephants are no harder to teach than ballerinas," but he knew better. No elephant, perhaps no creature in the world, will work as hard or as patiently as a ballerina—particularly a ballerina in a Balanchine company. The elephants trumpeted their annoyance at the choreography Balanchine gave them, even though he tried to keep it as elementary as possible, and they flapped their ears in pain at the Stravinsky music. Their trainer was much relieved when the circus, after cashing in for a season on the publicity the number had received, dropped it from the show; he had been muttering from the start that if they kept on making his beasts do things like this, he would end up with a herd of neurotics on his hands.

The first musical comedy to feature Balanchine choreography was *On Your Toes,* which had its première on April 11, 1936. A few months before that Balanchine had made his initial contact with Broadway by way of a couple of dance numbers he did for the Shuberts' *Follies,* a show starring Fannie Brice and featuring a young comedian named Bob Hope. At considerable expense the Shuberts had brought Josephine Baker from Paris, and it was Balanchine's assignment to fashion some dances which would display to advantage her dusky elegance and her talented, world-famous *derrière.* As much as anybody else, Balanchine admired this *derrière* of hers, but there was little original he could do for it. It was already, so to speak, institutionalized and not to be tampered with. Balanchine's contribution was not of much consequence to the *Follies,* which scored no great hit as a show.

On Your Toes, though—a show that has come to be regarded as something of a milestone in the history of musical comedy—was a different story. Here Balanchine could give freer rein to his abilities; his participation was an integral ingredient to the work as a whole. Produced by Dwight Deere Wiman, *On Your Toes* had music by Richard Rodgers and lyrics by Lorenz Hart. The dancing stars were Tamara Geva and Ray Bolger, in a role so strenuous that it would nightly exhaust him to the point of collapse, but which, by way of compensation, was the role that would first bring him into prominence. The story dealt with backstage life in the ballet world, a new theme for Broadway, with a gangster fable woven through it.

At the time Balanchine worked on this production, he was still ballet master at the Metropolitan Opera. Richard Rodgers has recalled how intimidated he was at first at the prospect of collaborating with Balanchine. "I expected fiery temperament," Rodgers has said. "He had bushy black hair, gleaming eyes and an aquiline profile. He was Russian, artistic, a genius. I was scared stiff of him. I asked him how he worked. Did he make the steps first and have music written to fit them, or what? He answered, in the thick Russian accent he had then, 'You write. I put on.' For me, that was marvelous. I went ahead and wrote the score, and I never had to change or cut a note of it as far as he was concerned."

Rodgers had some uneasy moments, though, when he first sought

Balanchine's reaction to the music he had written for the big *Slaughter on Tenth Avenue* ballet, which was to be the show's climax. It was his most ambitious piece of show music, and he desperately wanted Balanchine to be impressed by it. Rodgers and the show's rehearsal pianist played a two-piano arrangement of it for Balanchine at the pianist's apartment one day. Throughout their performance Rodgers kept eying Balanchine anxiously to see how it was going over. Balanchine listened with an expressionless countenance. When they finished, he stood up and started out of the apartment. Rodgers trailed after him, thinking wretchedly that at least Balanchine might have commented, "Better luck next time." As they waited for the elevator, Rodgers could stand the uncertainty no longer. In the primitive English he, and many of Balanchine's acquaintances, employed with him in those years, when Balanchine's command of the language was limited, Rodgers asked, "You don't like?"

"What you mean—I don't like?" said Balanchine.

"You don't say anything," pointed out Rodgers.

"Am too busy staging," said Balanchine, touching his forehead. "I love."

Far from being difficult, Balanchine turned out to be, as Rodgers recalled, "a pleasure to work with—untemperamental, logical, objective. In all the shows I worked on with him, I never once heard him speak above a normal conversational tone—not even when everybody else was succumbing to hysteria. With most other choreographers I've known, it was like asking them to give up some of their living flesh if they were told that, for one reason or another, one of their dance numbers wouldn't work. But Balanchine would just take it in stride and cheerfully produce on the spot any number of perfectly brilliant ideas to take the place of what came out."

Before *On Your Toes,* the playbill credit line for the dances in musicals had always read, "Dances by ————." Balanchine asked the producer, Wiman, whether his billing might read, "Choreography by George Balanchine." This was an unfamiliar word in the United States in 1936. Wiman said he feared the public would not know what it meant. Balanchine replied that maybe it would intrigue the public to see a new word, and Wiman agreed to make the experiment. It is an index of how popular ballet has since become that this once strange word is now so common that the advertisers of a house-cleaning service in New York City recently felt free to make a pun on it. "Let Taylor Maid Do Your Chore-ography," the ad suggested.

Tamara Geva and Ray Bolger in the SLAUGHTER ON TENTH AVENU
number in ON YOUR TOE

Balanchine was much pleased when he saw this ad. "That's progress for you," he said.

The change in the credit line was the least of Balanchine's musical comedy innovations. Balanchine was able to rid musical comedy of the notion that a dance number was a couple of showy soloists backed by a line of high-kicking showgirls; this dreary nonsense he replaced by genuine choreography. To musical comedy Balanchine brought, it was generally agreed, an elegance, sophistication and range of reference—all conveyed subtly and with a light touch—such as Broadway had not previously known. In addition, his dances in *On Your Toes*—particularly the memorable *Slaughter on Tenth Avenue*—were the first ever seen in a Broadway musical that were not just interludes but functioned as an essential, active aspect of the plot. This paved the way for what was done by Agnes de Mille a few years later in *Oklahoma*. Thus Balanchine began a trend in American musical comedy that has helped make it one of the brightest of this country's current theatrical forms.

This is not to suggest that Balanchine at the time thought of himself as engaged in a historic mission labeled "The Reform of American Musical Comedy." He would have been the last person in the world to take such an approach. If his conception of the very finest achievements of classical ballet was that they are by nature ephemeral, iridescent bubbles in the air, if he wasted no energies mourning over the fact that such masterworks of his as *La Chatte* or *Cotillon* had lived for only a few performances and then had disappeared forever, how much less likely was he to be engrossed with delusions of immortality in regard to the entertainments he was now designing for the commercial theatre. Still, in all that he did for Broadway he did not stint himself and used all the skills required. He took the job seriously and himself lightly.

To the show-going public Balanchine's approach was a refreshing change; to the dancers in his shows it was an absolute liberation. "If the rules of Equity permitted," Brooks Atkinson wrote in 1940 in his *New York Times* review of *Cabin in the Sky,* "probably the dancers would be glad to pay Mr. Balanchine something for the privilege of appearing under his direction, for he has released them from the bondage of hack dancing and ugliness." Many of the dancers considered their association with Balanchine something of an educational experience. Ray Bolger, who performed in three shows that Balanchine choreographed, once commented that working with

In the country, near Westport, Connecticut, about 1939.

Balanchine was like spinning from Juilliard to the Louvre to the Royal Academy of Dramatic Arts to Stillman's Gymnasium.

Among Balanchine's personal traits, perhaps none made such an impression on those who worked with him as his gentle, mannerly demeanor and his even temper—a deportment so different from the general run of behavior in the frenzied world of show business as to inspire some beholders with awe. This effect was registered most markedly, perhaps, on the occasion, in 1942, when Balanchine did his stint for the circus. Connie Clausen, who was one of the circus' fifty starlets that year, has described, in a charming book of reminiscence of her circus experiences entitled *I Love You Honey, But the Season's Over,* the impression which Balanchine made from the moment he appeared at the circus' headquarters at Sarasota, Florida, to begin work on his elephant polka. "Balanchine's romantic good looks and soft-spoken courtesy were such a contrast to the cigar-filled faces of the circus men and the sarcasm of Mr. Anderson [the musical director] we'd have walked into a cage full of hungry lions for him," she wrote. Backstage life at the circus, Miss Clausen had found, had little glamour, but was crude, callous and rather menacing; she was terrified of the elephants, and just about as scared of the elephant trainers, with their steel hooks, led by the fearsome Walter McClain. "In Balanchine's presence," she noted, "Walter McClain's manner changed. To our astonishment he broke into a wide smile and held out his hand. If Balanchine was abashed by the elephants, by McClain or his crew of tattered assistants, he gave no sign. He maintained then (and always) an almost formal politeness. At first it bewildered, then delighted the men, and, I sometimes suspected, the elephants as well."

A starlet was to perform with each elephant. The girls had to learn how to mount onto the elephant's trunk and balance gracefully there. Over and over Connie Clausen worked at it, during that first rehearsal, with the elephant Ginny, with which she had been paired, and its trainer, Dooley. Before long she was bruised, scratched, weary and frustrated. Balanced high in the air, after she had fallen some twenty-two times, she was just beginning to think she had finally mastered the task when suddenly her foot slipped and she crashed to the ground once more. "Dooley winced. Walter McClain spat. Ginny looked bored. And Balanchine, who suddenly appeared on the ring curb, said in his gentlest voice, 'You must try to land on the balls of your feet, my dear.' "

Another trait of Balanchine's much appreciated by his colleagues and an asset to the shows he worked on was his sense of humor. Some of his best musical comedy numbers were spoofs, like the trio for two tap dancers and a ballerina on her points, in *The Boys from Syracuse,* and the riotous burlesque of the old classic war horse of a ballet *Scheherazade,* in *On Your Toes.* A feature writer for one of the New York afternoon newspapers wrote wonderingly about the *Scheherazade* parody at the time. He seemed perplexed, even a bit shocked, by the willingness of this noted ballet master to poke fun at one of the accepted classics of his art. The newspaperman's attitude was indicative of the prevalent attitude in those days. Americans did not like ballet, but they were solemn about it. Balanchine loved ballet, so he did not need to be solemn. Moreover, as a serious artist, with a career in ballet still ahead of him, he had a real stake in parodying *Scheherazade;*

such great hunks of well-preserved wreckage blocked the channel through which his new ships would someday have to pass. The real connoisseurs of ballet enjoyed his *Scheherazade* parody, as they did nearly all of his musical comedy work. As Denby wrote, apropos of *Song of Norway* in 1945, "Balanchine's Broadway choreography does not falsify ballet as most musicals do on the grounds that adulteration is the first principle of showmanship. Balanchine's numbers are simplified ballet, but of the purest water."

It was the success of *On Your Toes* which aroused Samuel Goldwyn's interest in Balanchine and brought Balanchine to Hollywood for his first American film. Here, it seemed, was just the dance director Goldwyn was seeking for his new picture—a choreographer of international repute who could also do smash-hit dancing. Goldwyn had aspirations for this picture—*The Goldwyn Follies*. It was to be not just a colossal; it was to be an *artistic* colossal. He offered Balanchine twelve hundred dollars a week to stage the dances, a sum which Balanchine thought both artistic and colossal. It was the most money he had ever made. One of Balanchine's terms was that the dancers should be selected from his American Ballet Company, then still in existence. Goldwyn agreed to hire twenty-five members of the company for the five months or so it would take to make the film, and to provide adequate facilities for them—which meant fitting out a ballet school on the set, complete with mirrored walls, hardwood floors, dressing rooms, showers and all the other necessary appurtenances. On that kind of thing, there was no problem from Goldwyn, who, unlike the Metropolitan Opera, was not niggling about money. When the time came, he turned his studio's workmen loose on the project and they built a complete ballet school in one day. In the grandeur of such gestures Goldwyn reminded Balanchine of a Russian nobleman of the days before the serfs were emancipated.

As the film's ballerina, Goldwyn engaged Vera Zorina, who was then starring in the London production of *On Your Toes,* and who was a soloist with the Ballet Russe de Monte Carlo, where she had been a protégée of Massine's. Goldwyn hired Zorina for the *Follies* on the strength of the rave reviews she received for *On Your Toes,* without requiring the customary screen test. Then he grew nervous and cabled to London for "shots of what I have bought." When these rushes arrived, Goldwyn was so delighted with what he saw that he expanded Zorina's role in the film beyond merely a dancing part. She was then twenty years old and one of the most beautiful women in the world. Born in Berlin, of Norwegian extraction (her real name was Eva Brigitta Hartwig), she had long blond hair, an oval face with high cheekbones, gray eyes and a generous, expressive mouth. She was slim and long-limbed. She dressed with flair and taste—a rare trait in a ballerina—and she was witty and intelligent. It would not take long, once Balanchine began to work with her, before he would become entranced by her.

In the weeks before his departure for Hollywood, Balanchine was as busy as he had ever been in his life. It was then that he was preparing the Stravinsky festival at the Met. At the same time he was choreographing *Babes in Arms* for Wiman, a Rodgers and Hart show, with a cast of talented youngsters headed by Mitzi Green. He would work part of the time at the Metropolitan Opera House, fashioning intricate choreography to match the most advanced Stravinsky music; then he would rush over to the Shubert Theatre and turn out a clever dance number to Richard Rodgers' popular strains. It was a remarkable display of versatility, as well as sheer energy. One can wonder what he might have done if he had not been plagued by ill-health, as he was constantly during that period of his life. The Stravinsky project was his great challenge and delight; but even so, as a professional, he did not slight his musical comedy assignment, or speak patronizingly of it. Both at the Met and at the Shubert, during those hectic weeks, he was as creative as was appropriate to each situation. Among the dances he did for *Babes in Arms* was a charming fantasy called *Peter's Dream,* which was the first dream ballet to be seen on Broadway. It set off a vogue; for some years thereafter the dream ballet became virtually an obligatory feature of American musical comedy. *Babes in Arms* opened, to much acclaim, on April 14, 1937 (it was to have a run of 380 performances—the first Rodgers and Hart show to play more than a year). The Stravinsky festival took place two weeks later. Balanchine knocked off for a few days rest and then set out for Hollywood.

He made the journey by train, accompanied by Kopeikine. On his arrival at the railroad station in Los Angeles, he was met by a bevy of press photographers and studio publicists. His appearance and deportment perplexed them. Soft-spoken, smooth-skinned, with a grave countenance in which dark eyes gleamed impishly under haughty eyebrows, he appeared younger than his thirty-three years. Somehow he did not look quite like their notion of a fiery Russian ballet master. As usual, the press set about enthusiastically to rectify reality. They tried to get him to pose in various melodramatic attitudes, more in accord with their notion of a Russian genius of ballet, whatever that might be. Balanchine courteously refused. He had discovered by now, as he at one time commented to a friend, that if you were a Russian in America it was automatically taken for granted you were a genius. That would not be so bad, he had added, if Americans didn't also assume that all geniuses were crazy or dumb.

Frustrated, the photographers suggested to Balanchine that he should at least smile for them. He replied that it was too early in the morning; he did not feel like smiling.

"But everyone smiles!" the photographers said.

"I am not everyone," he retorted. "I am myself. Only one person."

He and Kopeikine had rented a house on North Fairfax Avenue, not far from Hollywood Boulevard. It was a white, two-story house—not palatial by any means, but ample. Its best feature was a pleasant garden. Balanchine took great delight in being able to have slices of lemon from his own trees in his Russian tea. Goldwyn, if he had been disposed to quibble over money, could probably have persuaded Balanchine to come to Hollywood for a lesser salary simply by promising him fresh lemon slices in his tea. Such gratifications always meant more to Balanchine than mere money. The heaped stalls of fresh fruit and vegetables at the markets also pleased him exceedingly. On one of his first shopping trips he bought a wheelbarrow load of fruits and vegetables which he wheeled home himself, refusing to let the store deliver it because he wanted to be able to feast his eyes on it all the way home. He was also charmed, as might be expected, by the profusion of pretty, lightly clad girls to be seen wherever his eyes chanced. He liked the place. The warm dry climate was good for his health. The balmy air, the vivid flowers and foliage, the broad vistas, with the mountains nearby and the sea not far away, and the leisurely tempo at which life went on were, at that time, a welcome contrast to New York City. It all made Balanchine feel, he used to say, somewhat as if he had been transported to the ancestral Georgia he had never known.

Shortly after his arrival in Hollywood he was summoned to his first conference with Samuel Goldwyn. It is a shame that the conference was not filmed, for it was sheer farce. Goldwyn had heard that Balanchine did not understand English very well, so he had asked George Gershwin, who was under contract to write the music for the *Follies,* to act as an interpreter. Goldwyn, of course, spoke pure Goldwyn. When Goldwyn had delivered one of his utterances, Gershwin would turn to Balanchine and convert this into pidgin English, along with the facial gestures one might use when talking to a very bright two-year-old. Ira Gershwin, who was present, could not bear it. "George!" he exclaimed to his brother. "What kind of language are you using? Even Balanchine can't understand you!" Balanchine demanded to have an interpreter of his own, to deal with Goldwyn's interpreter.

Gershwin had looked healthy and vigorous at that conference. His face, shaped rather like a ram's, with large, forceful features, had a good tan. His intense black eyes were keen and alert. He had been taking pains to keep himself in condition—playing golf, taking long walks with his wire-haired terrier and getting in a weekly tennis match with his Beverly Hills neighbor, Arnold Schönberg. His chief physical worry till recently had seemed to be his thinning hair, for which he spent half an hour a day having has scalp massaged in a contraption he had purchased, the size of a refrigerator. Of late, though, he had begun to suffer from headaches. The *Follies* was to be his last motion picture job for a while; he was planning to move back to New York and devote himself to some serious composing—another opera, a symphony, perhaps a string quartet.

Shortly after the meeting with Balanchine and Goldwyn, the headaches grew so painful that he began to find it difficult to concentrate. He laid off work, but the headaches did not abate. Once he reported a strange and disagreeable smell, like that of burning rubber. He felt increasingly tired and vague, though the doctors could find nothing organically wrong with him. Balanchine called at his house one day, near the end of June, to see how he was coming along and to discuss with him plans for the ballet they were supposed to create together for the film. He found Gershwin in bed, in a darkened room. Gershwin talked with him feebly for a few minutes in a strange, faraway voice. Balanchine came away distressed and full of foreboding. Within a few weeks after this George Gershwin, aged thirty-eight, was dead—of a brain tumor.

Before his headaches became acute, Gershwin had written five songs for the *Follies,* including "Love Walked In," one of his most attractive tunes; but he had not done any of the ballet music. It had occurred to Balanchine even before Gershwin's death that Gershwin's *American in Paris* suite might be suitable for ballet, and now together with Ira Gershwin he worked out a libretto. In this project Balanchine intended to put into effect his ideas about ballet in movies. The possibilities of the medium intrigued him, and the opportunity to try out some of his conceptions had been one of the temptations that had lured him to Hollywood. A movie ballet, he felt, ought not to be merely a stage ballet on film. It need not be a continuous dance observed from a fixed angle, as the stage required, but could be a montage of dance shots, photographed from whatever angle or distance one wished. And it could employ effects the stage could never achieve, especially in the realm of fantasy, which seemed to Balanchine a quality particularly suited to the film medium.

The *American in Paris* ballet was conceived of as a fantasy quest. The milieu was to suggest the Paris Exposition, through which an American, portrayed by the tap dancer, George King, would search for Zorina, the girl of his dreams. Seductive, tantalizing, ever elusive, she would manifest herself now here, now there—at one moment in a Spanish pavilion, another time in a Ferris wheel, yet again high overhead among the stars of the zodiac in a planetarium—always just beyond reach, and vanishing each time just as the American was about to take her in his arms. It would be the first ballet that had been expressly designed to take advantage of the motion picture camera's resources.

After three weeks of preparation, the day came for Goldwyn to see a run-through of it. Goldwyn arrived at the studio's Stage 2, accompanied by his entourage. With him were Adolphe Menjou and the Ritz Brothers, who had roles in the picture, Alfred Newman, the musical director, and Fred Kohlmar, who was Goldwyn's assistant. Vernon Duke was also present, he having been hastily called to Hollywood from New York to complete the musical score. Kopeikine was at the piano. Balanchine, in shirt sleeves and slacks, was bustling about, making certain that all was in readiness. Little sets representing the various scenes were scattered here and there on the vast sound stage, and Balanchine moved about from one to another, arranging his ballet company members in various groupings.

Goldwyn sat down in his director's chair, and all settled back to enjoy the ballet. The music began. In about two minutes, Balanchine said briskly, "That's the first bit. Now the next part will be shot over here." All had to pick up their chairs and move to another of the little sets. A couple of minutes later they had to move again. Goldwyn tried to protest. He did not want to keep moving around, he said, his arm hurt him. His arm was in a sling, the result of an injury sustained—so rumor had it—by pounding on the desk while reprimanding a subordinate. But Balanchine, all afire with enthusiasm for his project, brushed Goldwyn's protestations aside. He insisted that Goldwyn had to see each scene exactly the way the camera would see it. Goldwyn was not used to having his wishes, or even his whims, ignored by his employees. "It was a rare sight," wrote Vernon Duke in his memoirs, vastly amused in retrospect, "to see the man, piloted by George, made to crouch and squat, the better to view a couple wriggling on the floor or peer straight into a dancer's navel—'that's where camerra vill be shott!' George would exclaim triumphantly."

As this went on, Goldwyn's face grew redder and grimmer. All at once, he said, "All right, thank you very much."

"But you have not seen it all," protested Balanchine.

"I've seen enough." And Goldwyn, trailed by his entourage, swept out.

Furious, Balanchine dismissed the company from the sound stage and followed, a few minutes afterward, to Goldwyn's office. There Goldwyn told him he simply could not comprehend what Balanchine was trying to do and that he did not intend to risk a hundred thousand dollars on an experiment. It might possibly turn out to be a very artistic and beautiful ballet and all that, Goldwyn said, but even so he was sure it was not for the general public. "The miners in Harrisburg wouldn't understand it," he said.

"I'm not President Roosevelt," Balanchine retorted. "What do I care about the miners in Harrisburg?" As an afterthought, he added, "Besides, there are no miners in Harrisburg. I know because I've been there."

With imperial finality, Goldwyn said that he was sorry but the ballet was out. With equal finality, Balanchine replied that then *he* was sorry but he was out, too; and stalked from the office.

For several days Balanchine went into seclusion while Goldwyn's staff sought vainly to find him. At last the designer Richard Day, a good friend of Balanchine's, managed to track him down and persuade him, for the sake of the whole ballet company, whose contracts depended on him, if for no other reason, to return to the studio and meet once more with Goldwyn. As far as the *American in Paris* ballet was concerned, the ensuing meeting with Goldwyn did not alter matters. Goldwyn was still reluctant to risk the experiment. Now, however, instead of handing down fiats to Balanchine, as a lowly subject of his empire, Goldwyn treated him as a respected colleague. As a favor, he begged Balanchine, for his first Hollywood effort, not to try to be too radical in his film techniques. "This time I'd like you to make for me a ballet I can put a chair in front of and enjoy, without having to worry

Zorina in the water nymph ballet in THE GOLDWYN FOLLIES.

about how it's going to work out and how much it will cost if it doesn't. Be guided by me this first time, George, and after that you can have all the freedom you want." Goldwyn could be very convincing when he tried.

The ballet which Balanchine made as a substitute for the Gershwin was the now-famous water nymph ballet, to music by Vernon Duke. An updated *Swan Lake* in concept, it began with the beauteous nymph, Zorina, suddenly emerging from a pool at a garden party. One of the guests, William Dollar, falls instantly in love with her. They have a *pas de deux* of a romance which, alas, must come to an end—as all such ballet romances must. In ballet, people are always falling in love with nymphs or birds, and having to suffer for it. The art form is better suited than any other for expressing the unconsummatable. So at the end the nymph returns to her watery element, and the human lover is left forlorn beside the pool. Numerous surrealistic effects were employed in the staging, but the whole thing, as Balanchine had promised, could take place before Goldwyn's eyes, without scene changes, and without his having to squat or squint. At the run-through, Goldwyn was extremely pleased with it. His only doubt came at the very start when, as he was taking his seat, his eyes fell on a large, non-naturalistic representation of a horse, which was the most prominent feature of the set's background. It was a touch which Balanchine had suggested to the designer, who had modeled it after the horse in Chirico's set for the Balanchine ballet, *Le Bal,* of the Diaghilev days.

Goldwyn grimaced at the sight of it. "I don't think I like that horse," he groaned. "It doesn't look human, somehow. Jascha, look at that horse," he said, turning to Jascha Heifetz, who happened to be present because he was performing in another film that the studio was making at that time. "What do you think?"

"I love it," Heifetz replied. "I think it's wonderful."

So the horse stayed.

During the filming of this ballet Balanchine was able to demonstrate that his conceptions were not the vague ambitions of an amateur. His acute eye and trained powers of visualization enabled him to plot with easy instinct the camera setups required. Working with the excellent cameraman Gregg Toland, he completed the filming of the ballet ahead of schedule in six days of shooting, with as many as eighteen camera setups a day, which the old hands on the lot considered very fast. So sure of himself was he that he never bothered, while filming a scene, to have protection shots made— that is, shots from more than one vantage point. This took nerve. It saved some time and money, but Balanchine would have been in trouble if the scenes had not turned out as well on film as he had imagined they would. Fortunately, they did.

Goldwyn was not only delighted with the results but to this day remains devoted to the water nymph ballet as the finest example of dance on film. He still shows it to guests at dinner parties and speaks proudly of his initiative in bringing the greatest choreographer of the age to Hollywood. The water nymph ballet has won much praise from ballet critics as well. Balanchine himself thinks that probably the best thing about it was the Chiricoesque horse and that otherwise, though pleasant, it was not particularly novel or exciting. It was not what *American in Paris* might have been or what Balanchine had hoped to do when he set out for Hollywood. He never did get the chance to experiment that Goldwyn had promised. This was the only Goldwyn movie he worked on. The producers of the other films he did dance numbers for in the years immediately following this proved even more unwilling than Goldwyn had been when it came to trying new techniques.

During those years when he was producing dances for Broadway and for Hollywood, Balanchine made lots of money and spent every cent. He drank the best champagne, tooled around town in one of the first MG's seen in America, bought two grand pianos for the living room of his posh apartment on Central Park South, built a house on Long Island, near Northport, and courted Vera Zorina with trinkets from Cartier. He spent a lot of his spare time with a racy, fast-quipping Broadway crowd—with Larry Hart, Vernon Duke and his agent, Milton Bender, who was known as Doc, having been a dentist before becoming a Broadway agent, a profession he had given up because, as he said, making a decent living at it was like pulling teeth. There would be noisy parties at Hart's apartment, where there was always something doing, or weekends at the Northport house, or at Westport or the Cape. He lived high and had a lot of fun. When he had a nightmare, as he occasionally did, he would call up Salvador Dali and tell him about it; and Dali would give him an expert opinion as to whether his nightmare was an interesting effort or just run-of-the-mill stuff.

On Christmas Eve of 1938 Balanchine and Zorina were married. The marriage came as something of a surprise, for the newspaper columnists had lately been linking her name with various glamorous figures, most particularly with Douglas Fairbanks, Jr. She was, that year, the toast of Broadway for her role in *I Married an Angel*—a Rodgers and Hart show, with choreography by Balanchine, which had great charm. Balanchine had fashioned her dances with imagination and loving care, to show her off to best advantage. He had also painted her dressing room at the theatre himself, because he thought it too dingy for her. There was no doubt about his adoration. He was moonstruck—as passionately in love as he had ever been in his life. Time and again he proposed, and then one night, to his astonishment, wonder and delight (in that order), she said yes. Without any public announcement, they slipped over to Staten Island on the ferry right after the Christmas Eve performance of *I Married an Angel* and were married by a judge in St. George.

A small Christmas party had been planned for that evening at the Manhattan apartment of Mrs. Hartwig, Zorina's mother. Zorina and Balanchine arrived long after the other guests had assembled, but they did not tell anybody present—not even any of Balanchine's Russian cronies—why they were late. Supper was served, with champagne, and then Christmas presents were exchanged. Balanchine's present to Zorina was a package which, when opened, was seen to be a raincoat—obviously a very cheap one, such as could be picked up at a Forty-second Street drugstore. "Oh, a raincoat!" Zorina exclaimed, trying her theatrical best not to look too disappointed. "Just what I wanted." Balanchine suggested that she try it on. As she unfolded the garment, there fell out from inside it an ermine coat, whose individual skins Balanchine had spent weeks selecting and matching, and which he had then had specially made up for her. Zorina found she liked it even better than the raincoat. The gesture of wrapping a precious gift in an unprepossessing exterior was an example of Balanchine's playfulness, but it also had its symbolic aspect. Whatever assurance he may have had about his inner worth, Balanchine was always surprisingly diffident about his outer appearance. He did not consider himself a handsome or romantic figure, even though the young girls in his ballet company had sighed over him. He thought of himself as rather a shrimp, with a beaky nose and rodent-like front teeth. He nicknamed himself Malaross, and would sign himself that way in some of his letters to Russian friends—on such rare occasions when he wrote. "Malaross" was a pun. The word is generally used to mean an inhabitant of "Little Russia" or the Ukraine, which Balanchine, a Georgian, never was. But literally it means "undersized," and that was how he regarded himself, though, in fact, he is of average height.

The bliss of Balanchine's conquest of Zorina did not last long. In fact, he found within a short time that, though he had won her hand, he had not conquered her affections. Their marriage in its essence was, one of Balanchine's friends has said, rather like Balanchine's *American in Paris* ballet, in which Zorina was an elusive will-o'-the-wisp, always just out of reach of her tormented lover. During the few years that this marriage lasted, Balanchine was as nearly wretched as he has ever been in his life. Frequently they would separate, and then he would beg her to try again. Sometimes he could be seen standing in the street outside her apartment for hours late at night, unshaven, haggard, thoroughly wretched, waiting for a glimpse of her. He was in such despair that some of his friends thought he might do himself harm. At one time he talked his problems over with a psychiatrist. The consultation took place in the fall of 1940 aboard a small steamer returning to New York from Cuba, whence Balanchine had gone to recuperate after the opening of *Cabin in the Sky,* and the psychiatrist— a Russian—was a fellow passenger with whom Balanchine had struck up an acquaintance. Vernon Duke, who had done the music for that show, accompanied Balanchine on the cruise and he noted with amusement one aspect of these shipboard psychiatric sessions: it was a rough voyage, and the doctor, whose stomach was queasy, lay down as well as the patient while they talked. Duke thought there might be a new analytic technique in the making there. From the psychiatrist, Balanchine got the advice that he needed to be more assertive toward his wife, whereupon he composed a long, high-handed letter to her, telling her what a great man and great choreographer he was and how lucky she should feel at being associated with him. This seemed to pique Zorina's interest, but Balanchine was not able to hold the high-handed pose for long. Such advice could not help him because it was false to his nature. Once back on dry land, he did not seek further psychiatric treatment, the process of introspection and self-contemplation being so alien to him. Eventually, by a route opposite to the one the psychiatrist had advised, he found a way of making some peace with his frustrated desires. This was the route of abnegation and humility, and it was shown to him by a friend of his father's, a Georgian, now living in America, to whom Balanchine once went for advice. This friend, a devout member of the Greek Orthodox faith, was an old man and, Balanchine thought, a wise one. "Aren't you selfish?", the old man said to him, after listening to Balanchine tell of his unhappiness. "You think only of yourself. What makes you think you have a right to be happy, anyway? And above all, what makes you think you have a right to demand that another person love you? No human being has a right to demand love from another— that is the height of conceit and arrogance." These words took hold, and they seemed to help.

To blame all of Balanchine's unhappiness during those years on un-requited conjugal love would be an over-simplification. That was an impor-tant element, but his unhappiness was compounded of many other ingredients as well. For one thing, he had begun to run into his share of Broadway flops—such forgettable shows as *Keep off the Grass, The Lady Comes Across* and *Dream with Music.* Zorina was featured in some of these flops, which did not help Balanchine's status with his wife. For another, though he had been fortunate in his colleagues in the first shows he had done—

people like Rodgers and Hart, and the producer Dwight Deere Wiman, who was a gentleman and who treated Balanchine with deference and respect— he now began to find himself working for much cruder Broadway types, who tried to push him around and meddle with his dances. Typical of this genre of Broadway producer was Harry Kaufman, of the Schubert enterprises, who produced *Keep off the Grass.* Kaufman came into a rehearsal once, during an adagio moment, and almost swallowed his cigar in horror. "George, what are you doing? Why the slow motion?" he exclaimed.

"I'm building toward a climax," Balanchine replied.

"Please, George, you're killing me with that slow motion," cried Kaufman. "I want you should start with the climax. Give me nothing but climaxes."

It did not make life pleasanter during those days to find himself suddenly, after having lived prosperously for several years, stone broke and having to borrow money from Larry Hart to live on. Naturally, he could not get rich from flop shows. And even on the hits now he had bad luck. *Cabin in the Sky,* for instance, won great acclaim and was considered a smashing triumph, but it did not earn much money over its investment. Balanchine not only was responsible for the choreography but he also directed the show and put several thousand dollars, his last savings, into it. He never did break even.

Even if he had kept on earning fat sums and had continued to find the most understanding and congenial of producers to work for, by that time such challenge and interest as the commercial theatre had originally posed had been exhausted for him. The whole epoch was not one he would care to relive. He had adapted himself philosophically, even light-heartedly, to Broadway and Hollywood much of the time, that being the way he is, but it was not the life he would have chosen by preference. "I'm like a potato," he has said, in one of the homely metaphors he produces from time to time. "A potato is pretty tough. It can grow anywhere. But even a potato has a soil in which it grows best. My soil is ballet."

Undoubtedly, the worst and most fundamental of all his frustrations during that time was not having a ballet company. Those years without a company were years in which it was simply impossible for him to work at what he did best. Without a troupe of trained dancers, a choreographer, it has been said, is as frustrated as a painter without brushes, oils or canvas. Balanchine, characteristically, prefers a less exalted comparison to describe this situation. He says it is like being a lion tamer with no lions. It seems strange now, when Balanchine's continued creativity in ballet has come to be regarded as one of the artistic wonders of our era, to recall that at the time he was working on his Broadway shows many people thought that he was finished as a serious artist—all washed up at the age of thirty-five. This would not have been a particularly unusual fate, for several of the most noted choreographers of our time have started out meteorically, only to run out of inspiration as they approach middle age. Agnes de Mille discusses this curious early fading in her autobiographical book, *Dance to the Piper*. She describes tellingly the unique nervous strain that choreographers are subjected to by having to compose with human beings as their medium, rather than inert matter; they are forced always to work with live ammunition, so to speak.

During the years that Balanchine was out of serious ballet, his absence was not mourned by ballet's powers-that-be as much as one might suppose. Kirstein, of course, regretted it and was bitterly disappointed at the waste of Balanchine's talents. A friend remembers Kirstein gloomily proclaiming to him one day—in French, for heightened effect, no doubt—*"Balanchine, cet un homme perdu."* But there were others who saw no reason to lament the way things had worked out. In 1938, for instance, when Balanchine staged the dances for *I Married an Angel,* John Martin wrote an article about it for the *Times* that lavishly praised the show's choreography and at the same time suggested that this light commercial stuff was the sort of thing that Balanchine was really cut out for. Late the following year, Balanchine found himself left on the sidelines when the Ballet Theatre was organized. Eleven European and American choreographers were invited to contribute ballets to the new company; he was not. Balanchine was the only choreographer of note in the Western world who was not asked to participate. The reasons why he was passed by have never been clarified. Power politics, with which the ballet world is rife, undoubtedly played a part, and the founders of Ballet Theatre may also have been motivated by the apprehension, one not entirely unwarranted, that Balanchine might prove too dominating a personality to work in tandem with other choreographers. All the more galling it must have been to Balanchine to be thus excluded, however, as he saw that ballet was beginning to catch on in the United States at last. The founding of the Ballet Theatre marked a big stride forward for ballet in the United States, and it was organized on a far larger scale than the humble

enterprise of Balanchine, Kirstein and Warburg five years before. Endowed by Lucia Chase, a New England heiress, who has over the years since then pumped about two million dollars into her venture, the Ballet Theatre was to prove the dominant company on the American scene for the next decade.

Throughout his Broadway years, Balanchine never ceased regarding himself as a ballet master, not a showman. He had a deeper allegiance to ballet than he had to the Shubert enterprises. Denby recalls meeting him on the street in New York one day and having a casual conversation, during which Balanchine suddenly said, "We must save ballet."

"But it is immortal," Denby replied.

"I don't mean the dance," said Balanchine. "I mean ballet."

It was then the age of Tudor. The psychological ballets Antony Tudor was doing for Ballet Theatre were being received with great excitement and acclaim. Tudor's work was a continuation of Fokine's revolt against the formalism of classical ballet. His productions stressed emotion and literary content, employing a style of movement that relied greatly on

BALLET IMPERIAL, *as performed by Britain's Royal Ballet.*

mimed gestures and that often effectively set up tensions by deliberately working against the recognized classical line or model of movement. In a Tudor ballet the characters whose steps were from the classical vocabulary were intended to be recognized as conventional, inhibited, cold people; and they always danced in a peculiarly rigid way. Balanchine's aims were the direct opposite of all this. To him the classical technique was not a constriction but a liberation—a way of freedom from the drabness and compromises of workaday reality. He wanted to show the grandeur and grace that was potential in the human form. "I would like to show," he said once, "that these bodies of ours, which most of the time are used for dull, ordinary things, can be beautiful—really beautiful." Least of all did he want to use ballet as a vehicle for self-expression. "If I were feeling suicidal," he remarked at one time, "I would never try to express this in a ballet. I would make as beautiful a variation as I could for a ballerina, and then— well, then I'd go and kill myself."

Always, during this period of his life, whenever he got the chance to do a ballet, he seized the opportunity eagerly. For a company known as the Original Ballet Russe, a schismatic offshoot of the Ballets Russes de Monte Carlo (when an enterprise feels the need to put "original" in its name, one may feel pretty sure that it is not), in 1941 Balanchine choreographed *Balustrade*. Its music was by Stravinsky, its sets and costumes were by Tchelitchev, and it enjoyed a grand total of one performance. The critics heaped scorn on it. John Martin wrote that it was a sad state of affairs that "while gifted American artists are starving in the effort to bring their work before the public, there is money available for the production of European importations of this calibre." Despite this reception, the making of *Balustrade* is remembered by Balanchine as a happy occasion, as he collaborated once again with artists he admired on a project to which he could give himself wholeheartedly.

Perhaps Balanchine's most fruitful interlude during the period of his stint in the world of the commercial theatre came later on in 1941 when the American Ballet Company was temporarily revived, for the purpose of carrying out a specific mission. The mission was a good-will tour of Latin America. The idea for this project came from Nelson Rockefeller, who had recently been given an appointment in the State Department as coordinator for Latin American affairs. He suggested it to his friend Lincoln Kirstein, who naturally recruited Balanchine. The aim of the project was to reveal to the people of South America, through a medium that transcended the language barrier, that the North American colossus had a soul and was not just a grasping imperialist. The government would agree to underwrite all the operating expenses of the tour if Kirstein could raise the production costs—which he readily promised to do. The dancers were recruited from the School of American Ballet and from a chamber dance group, Ballet Caravan, which Kirstein had been sponsoring and working closely with during the past three years. For the tour's repertory, Balanchine revived several of his ballets and choreographed two new works—*Concerto Barocco* and *Ballet Imperial*. These two ballets may be seen now as having been of considerable importance in Balanchine's development. This was the first time he dared to make ballets which were purely dance compositions, with no apologies and without even the hint of a plot. This was what he had been moving toward for some years. He has said it was, oddly enough, Fokine who gave him the courage to dispense with the last vestige of the plot element. Balanchine saw a Ballet Theatre production of *Les Sylphides* the previous year, one which Fokine himself had carefully supervised, and was struck once more by its beauty. "Of all the Fokine ballets," he told himself, "*this* is the one that really lasts—this one which is an exception to all of Fokine's theories. If he could do it, why can't I?"

The South American tour, which lasted four months, was only moderately successful. The South American audiences did not find the company or its repertory very glamorous. There were sizable deficits at the box office, and numerous petty difficulties and problems all along the way. Kirstein, in his gloomy fashion, once described the South American tour as "a disaster," but it was not. It was the first attempt the American government had made in the direction of sponsorship of the performing arts and, as such, laid some of the groundwork for the State Department's present cultural exchange programs. If nothing else, it provided the excuse and the conditions for the production of two notable Balanchine ballets.

After this tour, the company disbanded once more. Balanchine went

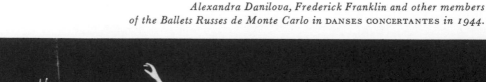

Alexandra Danilova, Frederick Franklin and other members of the Ballets Russes de Monte Carlo in DANSES CONCERTANTES *in 1944.*

back to work in the commercial theatre. His spirits were somewhat refreshed by the creative interlude; he was more at peace with himself now.
In the shows he was engaged to do after this, he found some that were
enjoyable enough, as well as lucrative—particularly a number of operettas,
such as *Rosalinda, The Merry Widow,* and the *Song of Norway,* which
allowed him more scope for dancing than the typical Broadway musical
and which, incidentally, were extremely successful.

From 1933 on, the Ballet Russe de Monte Carlo—the company that
Balanchine had helped to start and been fired from by de Basil—had been

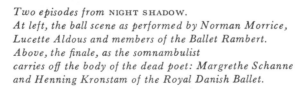

Two episodes from NIGHT SHADOW.
At left, the ball scene as performed by Norman Morrice,
Lucette Aldous and members of the Ballet Rambert.
Above, the finale, as the somnambulist
carries off the body of the dead poet: Margrethe Schanne
and Henning Kronstam of the Royal Danish Ballet.

making frequent tours of America, under the sponsorship of S. Hurok. By 1944, this company, now controlled by Serge Denham, was in rundown condition, and that year Denham asked Balanchine to help liven it up. Balanchine agreed. The effect on the company was that of a magic potion; the moribund company suddenly blossomed again. As George Amberg has written in his book *Ballet in America,* "The one single individual who miraculously rejuvenated the Ballet Russe de Monte Carlo was George Balanchine." In addition to supervising the staging of a number of his older works, he choreographed three new ballets—*Night Shadow, Danses Concertantes,* and a new version of *Bourgeois Gentilhomme*—and reformed the company's dancing in general, replacing about half of the old Russians with eager young Americans, most of them graduates of his ballet school, and letting the company know, in his authoritative way, quiet but formidable, that he did not wish to see any more of the shoddy, slack dancing it had been trying to get by with. For two years Balanchine worked enthusiastically with the Ballet Russe. It can be considered the return of that potato, Balanchine (to use his own figure of speech), to his native soil of ballet.

CHAPTER TEN

Balanchine never considered allying himself permanently with the Ballet Russe, because no matter how much the company improved its dancing, it was fundamentally oriented toward the box office. It picked up its living from one-night-stand tours of the country—a ballet dancer's idea of hell—and had to shape its repertory to compete successfully in the hinterlands with any traveling circuses which might be passing through or with the passions and melodramas of the local revival meeting; there had to be plenty of tried-and-true terpsichorean fireworks to give the customers their money's worth. Continual touring of this sort dictated the expediency of employing only a small orchestra most of the time, which severely limited the range of ballets the company could put on; it also made it difficult for the company to maintain peak standards of performance: the conditions were too trying. In addition, Balanchine did not find it very congenial to work for Serge Denham, the company's general director, who was a former banker. Their tastes differed; they had different conceptions of ballet; Denham could not resist exerting the prerogatives of a general director to assert himself in matters which Balanchine regarded as peculiarly his own province as ballet master—a province Balanchine had always guarded jealously even when, as a young man, he had worked for so towering a figure as Diaghilev. It was inevitable that eventually Denham and Balanchine would part. For some years after Balanchine left the Ballet Russe, in 1946, the company managed to go along in good style on the momentum he had given it, and then it deteriorated again.

The immediate reason for Balanchine's departure from the Ballet Russe early in 1946, however, was not any particular climactic disagreement with Denham but the fact that Lincoln Kirstein (who, for the past three years, had been in the Army, during which time, as a member of the Monuments and Fine Arts section, he had received a citation for his work in ferreting out art treasures the Nazis had hidden in salt mines and had risen gloriously from the rank of private to that of private first class) had now returned to civilian life, full of plans for a new venture into ballet and with about two hundred and fifty thousand dollars, a recent inheritance, burning a hole in his pocket. Kirstein immediately sought out Balanchine, the man who most of his life has epitomized ballet for him, to enlist his help in disposing of this money in the most stimulating and agreeable way. "As millionaires go," W. H. Auden has commented, "Lincoln Kirstein is really a very *poor* millionaire, but he's been more effective than many richer ones because he's used his money with such discrimination, as well as passion." Balanchine once said, after years of association with Kirstein, "Lincoln is a true Christian, even though he won't admit it. He gives you money and runs away before you can thank him."

Throughout the years since Kirstein had brought Balanchine to America, the two men had kept in touch, remaining in close rapport even during periods of time when they saw each other little. The strong, abiding link between them, after the American Ballet Company had collapsed in 1938, was provided by the school they had established together. The school, as it patiently went about its task of teaching an ancient code of movement to young American bodies, asserted their mutual faith in the future of ballet in America, regardless of individual setbacks or mischances. Kirstein had always maintained an office in the school building, and Balanchine had always been the chairman of its faculty, even though there had been stretches of time when, busy with musicals and movies, he had not done much teaching himself. The school had flourished. It had survived a crisis in 1940 when Kirstein had bought out the director, Dimitriev, with whose financial policies he had increasingly disagreed, and incorporated the school, as he had always wanted to do, as a nonprofit educational institution. Kirstein then became president and director, but its administration, for all practical purposes, was placed in the hands of its executive secretary, Eugenia Ouroussow, who had been with the school since its founding and who has continued to administer it to the present.

As part of its new policy, after its reorganization, the school in 1941 had instituted a scholarship competition—awarding scholarships to the five most promising of the one hundred and thirty children who applied. One of the scholarships went to a long-legged, eleven-year-old girl named Tanaquil LeClercq. Balanchine, chief judge at this competition, had been charmed by her poise and fine configuration. "She looks like a real ballerina already," Balanchine commented, "only very small, as if you were looking at her

Tanaquil LeClercq (at far right) taking class at the age of nine.

through the wrong end of a telescope." By 1946, the school's enrollment had grown to over two hundred, and it even included a handful of boys. There was an eleven-year-old lad, Jacques d'Amboise, now in his third year at the school, who could leap like a gazelle, had an open, ingratiating personality, and was considered most promising. His parents had not intended to enroll him as a ballet student, but at first had just sent him along to keep his sister, Ninette, company when she took her lessons. After class, though, it would turn out that young Jacques was able to demonstrate everything he had seen his sister trying to learn, and could do it easily and naturally, with a broad grin on his face. He did not know it was supposed to be hard; he thought it was just fun. So his parents bowed to his wishes and enrolled him as well as his sister. At the school, in whose classes he was doing his best to acquire, as was expected of him, the noble, elegant bearing of a courtier or prince, he could often be seen, when his own class was over and he was waiting for his sister to finish, lying slouched, his hair rumpled, on the floor in some corner reading comic books and looking like any American kid who has just come in from playing ball. Then there was another boy, a new lad—Edward Villella by name. He was ten and had just started taking classes. He was

Balanchine with pupils at the School of American Ballet in 1946.
The boy is Edward Villella, age ten.

small but handsome and had a sturdy, manly air. But it was too soon to
tell how he would develop.

Second beginnings are often more difficult than first tries. One has acquired more wisdom and experience, but often more inhibitions as well.
One sees all too clearly now along the path the pitfalls and booby traps of
which one had been blithely unaware when setting out in earlier days. Is it
worth all that pain and trouble? a man may ask himself at this point. Balanchine and Kirstein thought it was, but they were chary of repeating the
mistakes they had made a dozen years before. They wanted to avoid the
hazards and distracting preoccupations that went with box-office ventures
and the commercial theatre; they wanted nothing to do with that whole

Villella as he looks today, in the rehearsal studio with Carole Sumner.

rat race. So they decided to form an organization which would cater only to an élite subscription audience. Working with them in this project from the start was the excellent conductor Leon Barzin. This new organization, which was to be called Ballet Society, would have as its aim, as its announcement stated, "the encouragement of the lyric theatre by the production of new works." It would not perform works in the standard repertory, since it needed to make no concessions to mass tastes. In addition to new ballets, it would put on chamber operas and other kinds of dance beside the classical. Among the chamber operas it would present would be Gian-Carlo Menotti's

The Medium and *The Telephone*—the latter being a work which Ballet Society commissioned. The society also planned to publish books and monographs on the dance, to award fellowships to gifted young dancers or to choreographers and to commission dance films.

Ballet Society's first performance took place November 20, 1946. It was given in the auditorium of the Central High School of Needle Trades. It would have taken considerable effort to find a more unlikely setting than this bleak hall for the presentation of ballet or lyric theatre. The chairs were hard; the stage was merely a raised surface with a curtain; there was no orchestra pit. The fifty members of the orchestra were seated in full sight at floor level, partially obstructing the spectators' view of the stage, and the conductor, on a small raised platform, presented a further obstruction to vision. "The whole thing," recalls Anatole Chujoy, in his detailed history, *The New York City Ballet,* "looked hopelessly amateurish, provincial, and depressing." The audience was kept waiting for half an hour for the first curtain, during which time the sound of hammering and other construction work could be heard going on behind the curtain and the orchestra tuned up and practiced difficult passages over and over. "The evening was getting to be as uninspiring and untheatrical as one could imagine," wrote Chujoy. Then the curtain went up. "The long wait, the uncomfortable seats, all the impedimenta of the auditorium and stage were immediately forgotten, for there was magic on the stage: *The Spellbound Child* (*L'Enfant et les Sortilèges*) by Maurice Ravel."

An enchanting fantasy, in an English translation by Jane Barzin and Lincoln Kirstein of Colette's text, the opera was staged by Balanchine in a manner similar to what he had done at the Metropolitan Opera with Gluck's *Orpheus.* That is, the singers sat offstage with the musicians, and the action was portrayed by dancers. "There were forty-three dancers on the stage," noted Chujoy. "How they ever got on or, having got on, did not spill into the audience, will remain Balanchine's secret." The audience was captivated.

The other work on that first program, after the intermission, was the première of one of Balanchine's greatest ballets, *Four Temperaments.* The Hindemith score for this ballet—one of Hindemith's most impressive pieces of music—came into being in an interesting way. A few years before, during his musical comedy heyday, Balanchine at one point found himself running out of ideas as to how to spend all the money he was earning. He got to wondering how much it would cost to commission a piece of music—from

Paul Hindemith, say. Balanchine had no ballet company at the time and he was not looking for music he could choreograph, merely something for his own pleasure, that he would enjoy listening to and playing over on the piano. He inquired of Hindemith's agent how much that composer's fee would be for a work of perhaps half an hour in length for piano and strings. The agent's reply was something like five hundred dollars, which seemed to Balanchine a great bargain. Hindemith was too busy to undertake the commission at that moment; but one day, about a year after Balanchine had broached the matter, Balanchine got a letter from the agent saying that Hindemith now had some free time; if Balanchine still wished to have a composition, on the terms discussed, the first part could be delivered to him one week from that date. Promptly a week later the music arrived. It received its first hearing in the large apartment on East 52nd Street at Fifth Avenue, conveniently near to Cartier's, where Balanchine was then living, at one of the little Sunday afternoon "musicales" he liked to give. At the piano was Kopeikine. The "orchestra" was made up of a few of Balanchine's musician friends, who had dropped into the apartment for the occasion: Nathan Milstein, Samuel Dushkin, Leon Barzin, and Raya Garbousova. Edvard Fendler conducted. As could be imagined, with such musicians playing, the performance was a most exciting one. Balanchine felt he had got his five hundred dollars' worth right then and there. He first began seriously to think of using it for dance in 1941 when the temporarily revived American Ballet was preparing for its State Department sponsored tour of Latin America. At that time he and Tchelitchev worked out a conception quite different from the present one. It was to be called *The Cave of Sleep,* but it was abandoned because Hindemith objected to it and it would have been too expensive. The 1946 performance for Ballet Society used costumes designed by Kurt Seligmann. They were extremely elaborate and bizarre, though fascinating to look at. A few years later Balanchine got rid of them and found that this ballet made its best effect and showed up most clearly when danced simply in black-and-white practice clothes against a bare blue cyclorama.

Four Temperaments, as Balanchine's first ballet for Ballet Society, was a presage of things to come, the annunciation of a new era. It can be seen now as the precursor of *Opus 34, Agon, Episodes* and *Movements,* initiating one of Balanchine's most important lines of development. It was not like anything that had ever been seen in ballet before and opened a realm of new

Maria Tallchief in FOUR TEMPERAMENTS.

possibilities, which he has since been exploring. The intricate angularity of the steps and patterns of movement in *Four Temperaments* presented the dancers with the severest kind of challenge; the earlier American Ballet Company could never have coped with it; the present group, better trained and prepared, had their difficulties but eventually they would master the new style. It was an inexorable work, *Four Temperaments,* but not a gloomy one; it had grandeur. It manifested a kind of force new to ballet, a kind of ruthlessness even in its degree of concentration, and what was then a novel kind of impersonality which was not an absence of quality but a meaningful attitude toward life—one very much of our age. Balanchine's later ballets in this line have made this attitude more familiar to audiences of today. There also seemed to be in *Four Temperaments* a new sort of content—for the so-called "abstract" ballets of Balanchine do have real content even if they do not have plot, and even if Balanchine won't admit it except in unguarded moments. "Balanchine's ballets are all full of the most extraordinary encounters and events," Jerome Robbins once commented. "In *Apollo* the three Muses suddenly become horses pulling Apollo's chariot, and then an instant later they are lovely goddesses again. In *Four Temperaments* at the end, where there are those great soaring lifts, I always feel as if I am watching some momentous departure—like interplanetary travelers taking their leave of the world." Even without a metaphorical science fiction interpretation, *Four Temperaments* was a ballet of the future. The audience in the auditorium of the Central High School of Needle Trades that November evening in 1946, favorably disposed toward Balanchine, thought they rather liked what they saw; but it would be some years before *Four Temperaments* would be acknowledged as the masterpiece it is.

For the critics at the time, Ballet Society was a most peculiar venture in general, and they did not know what to make of it. Kirstein and Balanchine carried the exclusiveness of their policy so far that they did not even

FOUR TEMPERAMENTS, *as it looked after the Seligmann costumes were discarded.*

invite the press to attend their performances. This made for an odd situation, with the critics buying their own subscriptions, sneaking into the auditorium on performance nights and then, half apologetically, writing what were, on the whole, extremely laudatory reviews, which they were not at all sure the haughty management would welcome. *Time* magazine titled its article about the organization "Ballet Underground." A deliberately impractical venture, the Ballet Society was a typical expression of Kirstein's—and, to a lesser extent, Balanchine's—noble but unrealistic struggle to establish ballet on purely artistic terms, untainted by the box office. As a ballet impresario, Kirstein was no Hurok. Profits revolted him. When a booking agent once came to him and showed him how he could make money by taking his ballet company on tour with a reduced ensemble and orchestra and a popularized repertoire, Kirstein said caustically, "Sir, I am not in ballet to make money."

To many, then, Ballet Society appeared to be just another of Balanchine's and Kirstein's impetuous, quixotic forays. But a few observers saw that it was part of a grand plan and was potentially of considerable significance. Chujoy remembered that back in 1937 Kirstein had outlined to him a plan for an organization very similar to the Ballet Society he had now formed. Since 1934 Balanchine and Kirstein had worked together to de-Russianize ballet as an art—to establish it as something that American practitioners could do well and that American audiences could enjoy in a natural way. Now, as Denby noted, they were trying to decommercialize it as theatre—as the most effective, even if troublesome, way of keeping it civilized. "I have here reported the Society's lucky beginning at quite disproportionate length," Denby wrote in an article in April, 1947, "partly because it is a new, much talked of enterprise, partly because it may well, after several years of trial and error, turn out to have been the origin and foundation of the sensibly organized, exciting American ballet company we need now so badly."

Each new epoch of Balanchine's creative life seems to have been associated with a new wife or love—always a dancer under his aegis, always young, not yet fully formed, either as person or dancer. As a model does for a painter or sculptor, they served the choreographer as both reality and potentiality—with the poignant addition that they were also the raw material out of which the finished work of art would be formed. Patiently, willingly, they allowed themselves to be used by him in the explorations of his craft. It was their job; they were married to their work, as he was to his. That one young woman should be supplanted in this role by another in the course of time had begun to seem by then, as with Picasso's succession of wife-mistress-models, an outward manifestation of the constantly renewed youthfulness of the artist's creative powers. "Grow old along with me, the best is yet to be" was not a likely motto for Balanchine. The choreographer lives only in the present. Caring intensely, as he does, about physical beauty, as joined in the great dancers with an Olympic athlete's prowess, Balanchine has always suffered to see this masterful beauty fade. No Elizabethan sonneteer was ever more pained by time's encroachments and ravages than he. He has been known on some occasions to avoid meeting with beautiful dancers whom he once knew in a bygone era because he cherished a precise and acute image of their beauty in his memory which he could not bear to have spoiled for him by their present appearance.

For the era in his life initiated by his active return from the commercial theatre to the world of ballet, the young woman who would play the central part in his life was to be Maria Tallchief, whom he married on August 16, 1946. Their marriage lasted five years, ending with her being granted an annulment. The grounds for the annulment were that she wanted to have children but Balanchine did not. These grounds were generally assumed to be simply a convenient pretext for the legal action, but it is a fact that during her subsequent marriage, to a Chicago businessman, she did have a child; and it is also a well-known fact that Balanchine wishes that the ballerinas in his company would suppress the urge to procreate. "Any woman can become a mother," he says, "but not every woman can become a ballerina." This is a piece of evidence often cited by those who regard Balanchine as heartless and inhuman.

Maria Tallchief was twenty-one at the time of their marriage, a girl with black hair, pale olive skin and beautiful, large, dark eyes. Her young face had already developed a mysterious, somber gravity; it had the look sometimes of a Mayan mask. Born in Fairfax, Oklahoma, of an Osage Indian father and a mother who was of Irish, Scottish and Dutch ancestry, Maria grew up in Beverly Hills, California, where her family moved when she was eight. As a child she studied the piano intensively, as well as taking ballet lessons from Bronislava Nijinska in Hollywood. On her twelfth birthday she gave a recital at which, for the first half of the program, she played the Chopin E Minor Concerto and for the second half she danced. Her musicality was part of her attraction for Balanchine, a personal bond as well as a trait of crucial importance in one of his ballerinas. They often played four-hand piano together. He was also very taken by her Indian heritage. This charmed him. It made him feel that in marrying her he was becoming really American—John Smith marrying Pocahontas. When, a few months after their marriage, he crossed the country by train to join her in Los Angeles, where she was vacationing with her family, and to work with Stravinsky on a new ballet, Balanchine was quite agog when the train, passing through Oklahoma, went by an Indian reservation. "Look, those are my new relatives!" he proudly told Nicholas Nabokov, with whom he was making the trip, and then for hours regaled Nabokov with Indian lore—all this in Russian, of course. Most of all, in regard to Maria Tallchief, Balanchine was attracted by her appearance and her potential abilities, by the way she moved—and by the way he saw that she would move after he had worked with her. Still with a little tender plump flesh on her, not pared down to the bone yet, the way Balanchine likes his dancers, she had a high chest and straight back, and she moved like a tiger. Under Balanchine's tutelage and in his ballets, she would win world renown.

For her part, she stood in awe of Balanchine then. He was the master. She had said that she was astonished when he proposed, for he had not previously showed any lover's ardor, and when he had turned his eyes on her, in the rehearsal hall, she had not been aware that these might be melting glances he was bestowing, but was rather painfully conscious of all the flaws he must be noting. There was no thought of refusing him, just as in the rehearsal hall there would never be any thought of refusing to attempt whatever he demanded of her.

To the general public, by this time, Balanchine's marriages were beginning to be a subject of some fascination, viewed through the golden haze of glamour. The public had begun to picture Balanchine as having the personality of a Don Juan combined with a pinch or two of Pygmalion and more than a trace of Svengali. This reputation quite surprised him. He had never concealed his interest in beautiful women or his admiration for them—indeed, his ballets so glorified the ballerinas that he had been scolded by some critics for neglecting the male dancer—but he did not think of himself as a rake, or even as a particularly dashing figure. He did not leave any of his wives; it was they who left him, or so he said. Outside of the

Maria Tallchief in ORPHEUS.

world of ballet, where he moved with absolute assurance, he was often not merely reserved but diffident. Some of his friends suspected that a certain element of insecurity about himself in relation to women was what led him always to choose young girls from his company—as if he felt the need to bolster his role as lover by that of ballet master. But it may have been merely chance and propinquity which made for this pattern in his life. Balanchine himself once gave a reporter a more whimsical explanation of why he always married ballerinas. "If you marry a ballerina," he said,

"you never have to worry about whether she's running around with somebody else or anything like that. You always know exactly where she is—
in the studio, working." With all of his ex-wives, incidentally, he seems to
have maintained an unusually amicable relationship. A friend who dropped
into the school one day remembers seeing all the ex-wives lined up at the bar,
calmly taking class together.

If the cherished public image of Balanchine as a rake may be a
delusion, even more of a delusion may be the popular notion of how glamorous and fascinating it must be to be married to a ballerina. They are a
highly specialized breed, ballerinas—like borzoi or blue mink—selected
and developed for a rarefied, artificial purpose, in relation to which ordinary
human pursuits are likely to be subsidiary and peripheral. Their goal is to
move about on a stage with beauty, grace and mastery, and little else in
life matters to them. Offstage, many of them are quite unconcerned about
their appearance and may look undistinguished, even drab; many of them
dress indifferently and often have an ungainly gait (the turned-out-feet
style of movement so strangely suitable for the stage is less prepossessing
on the street). They work like dogs, with almost never a day off from
lessons and exercises, even when they are at the pinnacle of fame, and at
night come home from the theatre or rehearsal studio exhausted and
with sore feet. Long after she had separated from Balanchine, Maria
Tallchief still recalled with gratitude how glad she was during their marriage
that Balanchine liked to cook and was willing to prepare their meals at the
end of the day. "I've never had time to learn how to cook myself," she said,
"and besides, after eight hours of rehearsal, all I've ever wanted to do was
prop my aching feet up and fan them. George was simply wonderful
about it."

On February 26, 1947, shortly before the third program in Ballet Society's first season, Balanchine sailed for France on the *America*. He had
received an invitation to be guest ballet master at the Paris Opéra for the
coming season. Lifar had been dismissed after the liberation of Paris on
charges of collaborating with the Nazi occupation. For the Opéra, Balanchine staged his *Serenade, Apollo* and *Le Baiser de la Fée,* and he choreographed one new work, intended as a tribute to the Opéra ballet. Deeming
it only fitting that the music for this new ballet should be by a French composer, he decided to make use of a little-known work by Georges Bizet—

his Symphony in C Major, which Bizet had written at the age of seventeen but had never published for fear that it would be thought to derive too obviously from the symphony by his teacher, Gounod; it had only in recent years been discovered. Balanchine took just two weeks to choreograph this ballet—*Le Palais de Cristal,* or *Symphony in C,* as it is known elsewhere—but he caught ineffably its essential qualities: the youthful freshness of the allegro movements, the dreamy moon-drenched romanticism of the adagio movement. In this plotless, classical ballet the music supplies all the continuity required. Balanchine's musicality made for the happiest matching imaginable of music and dance. Few people who have seen this ballet can hear the music thereafter without seeing once again in their mind's eye some of the visual images Balanchine conjured up for it.

As guest ballerina that season, Balanchine had the services of Tamara Toumanova. A world-famous figure, she was no stranger to Paris, which had been applauding her performances since her "baby ballerina" days and hailed her now as "the black pearl." The other guest artist being presented was an unknown quantity to Paris—Balanchine's new wife and protégée, Maria Tallchief. She made her debut at the Opéra dancing Terpsichore in *Apollo* at a gala evening attended by King Gustav of Sweden, and she danced the Fairy in *Le Baiser de la Fée.* She was the first American to dance at the Paris Opéra since Augusta Maywood appeared there in 1839. Tallchief made a good impression on that great stage; she was recognized as showing great promise. Balanchine even told her that she had danced "not too badly"—which, from him, was high praise.

In addition to staging his ballets, Balanchine restored discipline, which had been deteriorating. As usual, wherever he goes, he kept a sharp eye out for new talent. He broke Paris Opéra protocol by giving such youngsters as Claude Bessy, Liane Daydé and Jacqueline Moreau more important parts to dance than their official rankings at the time indicated. At the Paris Opéra, as at the court of Louis XIV, it is not the custom of those of upper rank to dance on equal terms with those of lower. In general, the members of the Paris company respected Balanchine but were somewhat disconcerted by his reserve. They were used to Lifar making a great fuss over them, and some of them missed that kind of excitement. *"Il ne s'est pas pencher sur nous,"* one of the Opéra's ballerinas later said, when asked how Balanchine had treated them. He did not hover over them.

Once more, as in 1929, it is likely that Balanchine would have stayed on at the Paris Opéra permanently if he could have had his choice. Here it was, after all, that ballet had first been established and glorified from a code of manners into an art. Balanchine thought of himself by now as very much an American. He had received his citizenship papers in 1939 and, like his fellow naturalized American patriot, Stravinsky, would not permit any criticism of the United States to go unanswered; but he had to find a place to work, he had to have the opportunity to make his ballets and show them to a public. Ballet Society was giving only four programs a year to a small audience and was in precarious financial state. If it continued and he got the Paris post, he thought it might be possible to divide his time between Paris and New York.

But his wishes in regard to the Paris Opéra were once more of no consequence—fortunately for the future of American ballet perhaps. At the Opéra that season Balanchine found himself in the midst of a spider web of intrigue, buzzing with rumors, machinations, plots and counterplots. Lifar's adherents were constantly active in his behalf. Instead of Lifar being condemned as a collaborationist they felt he should be treated as a hero for having held the Opéra ballet together during the Occupation. Actually, Lifar was neither one nor the other; he was simply someone who needed at all times to bask in the applause of an audience. Not long after Balanchine arrived at the Opéra to take up his duties, a petition signed by nearly a thousand people was presented to the Minister of Fine Arts, asserting that the Opéra needed a permanent ballet master, not a guest, and not a foreigner. No names were mentioned but none needed to be: the message was clear. At the end of that season Lifar, cleared of all charges, was invited back to his old post at the Opéra. He returned in triumph, remaining in power there until his retirement in 1958.

Back in New York, Balanchine resumed his activities for Ballet Society. That 1948 season he choreographed *The Triumph of Bacchus and Ariadne,* a ballet-cantata with music by Rieti, his old colleague from Diaghilev days, and he also had the pleasure of preparing a new Stravinsky ballet. It was *Orpheus,* a composition especially commissioned by Ballet Society. To do a Stravinsky ballet would always be Balanchine's great delight; for him there could be no higher challenge or fulfillment than a Stravinsky score to choreograph. "All of Stravinsky's music can be danced," Balanchine once said, "every single note he has written." Best of all, of course, for Balanchine, were the occasions, such as with *Orpheus* now, when he and Stravinsky embarked on a new ballet together and collaborated in amity from the very start, before even a note of music had been put on paper.

The two men had by then become close friends. Though they had respected each other since the days of *Apollo,* the friendship had its real inception when they worked together on *Card Game* for the Stravinsky festival at the Met in 1937. As Russian émigrés, schooled in the subtle artistic ferment that was Paris after World War I, and now settled in America, the two men by nature had much in common. They shared, too, a similar outlook and aesthetic. For Balanchine, it was to be the most important personal relationship of his life. Throughout their friendship, it has always been Stravinsky, as the elder man (he was, after all, forty-six and Balanchine only twenty-four when they first met, to collaborate on *Apollo*) and by far the more articulate and formally intellectual of the two, who has played the dominant role. Balanchine has always deferred to him. One of Balanchine's friends has observed, "The only time Balanchine loses that air of calm, complete authority he has is when he's with Stravinsky. Then he's like a boy with his father. The two can respect each other's opinions, be gay and playful together, work together—but they never forget who is the father and who is the son." Balanchine would not wish it any other way. Their friendship has been aided by the respect in which each man holds the other's vocation. For Balanchine, music was always the supreme art. For Stravinsky, classical dancing was, as he has declared, "the perfect expression of the Apollonian principle," which since the mid-point of his life has been his guiding principle. He has written of his "profound admiration for classical ballet, which, in its very essence, by the beauty of its *ordonnance* and the aristocratic austerity of its forms, so closely corresponds to my conception of art. For here, in classical dancing, I see the triumph of studied conception over vagueness, of the rule over the haphazard."

When Balanchine and Stravinsky get together, there is apt to be quite a bit of merriment, ranging in expression from high wit to downright playfulness ("It's a pleasure to be with Stravinsky," Balanchine has said, "because he's a happy man"); a good deal of matter-of-fact, detailed discussion of such technical aspects of music and the dance as they happen to be concerned with at the time; and very little theorizing about art. Both men eschew the romantic conception of the soulful artist, producing his masterpieces out of agony and ecstasy. Rather, they pride themselves on being disciplined craftsmen, able to apply themselves to a job of work and produce it in good fashion and on time. They have made their share of what the world acclaims masterpieces, but they never admit, when they are engaged in creating a work, that they think of it as anything more than the task at hand. "If you set out deliberately to make a masterpiece, how will you ever get it finished?" Balanchine once said. Balanchine has said that he learned from Stravinsky the trait of being satisfied with what one had made, once it was done. Stravinsky says his own model for this attitude was God, who on the days that he created lovely flowers and trees and the birds of the heavens was satisfied, and was also just as satisfied on the day he created crawling insects and slimy reptiles.

When Balanchine and Stravinsky collaborate on a ballet, after they have agreed on the subject and the various sections the work will contain, they try to specify for each other, with the exactitude of a blueprint, the size that each section will be. "How much music will you want for the three dancers' first variation?" Stravinsky will ask Balanchine. "Thirty-one seconds, I would think," Balanchine might reply. To which Stravinsky might well respond, "Could you settle for thirty-two?" Such byplay has a humorous intent, of course, but less than one might think. Balanchine has never forgotten the reproof Stravinsky delivered him when they first began to work on *Orpheus* and Stravinsky asked him how long he thought the *pas de deux* of Orpheus and Eurydice should run. "Oh, about two and a half minutes," Balanchine replied. "Don't say 'about,' " Stravinsky said crisply. "There is no such thing as 'about.' Is it two minutes, two minutes and fifteen seconds, two minutes and thirty seconds, or something in between? Give me the exact time, please, and I'll come as close to it as possible." Once they have given each other such specifications and know that they understand each other about the course of the work, though there may be much consultation, there is little meddling. Each knows that he cannot really guess or predict quite what the other will produce and looks forward very happily to the surprises he is going to get.

The *Orpheus* première took place April 28, 1948. Stravinsky, who was to conduct the orchestra, arrived in New York three weeks early. Compact, dapper, authoritative, with his spectacles much of the time pushed up on his forehead like a racing driver's goggles and only in interludes of repose being returned to their perch on his large nose, Stravinsky threw himself eagerly into all aspect of the ballet's final preparations. He visited, together with Balanchine, Isamu Noguchi's studios to inspect the decor, worked meticulously with the orchestra, and attended nearly all the dance rehearsals. It was a happy and fruitful time for both him and Balanchine. The *Orpheus* they made together, a concentrated retelling of the legend, conveyed the grief of loss, but by the end, as in Greek tragedy, had purged the beholder of his grief and left him with a sense of acceptance and of awe. It was an impressive achievement. The choreography had many wonders. The *pas de deux* for Orpheus and Eurydice after he has rescued her from Hell, in which she twines herself about him beseechingly while he desperately strives to avoid looking at her, has been often singled out for praise. It is technically an extraordinary tour de force, but one in which the spectator's attention is so riveted on the poignancy of the situation that he is scarcely aware of the virtuosity of the choreography or dancing. Equally impressive, and perhaps even more unusual, was the long *pas de deux* for the two men —for Orpheus and his Dark Angel—which had a grave, supernatural tenderness. The cast—Nicholas Magallanes as Orpheus, Maria Tallchief as Eurydice, Francisco Moncion as the Dark Angel, Herbert Bliss as Apollo, Edward Bigelow as Pluto and Tanaquil LeClercq as the Leader of the Bacchantes—was superb. The performance was a memorable one.

Orpheus was a prime example of what Ballet Society sought to do. Everything was fine, except that Kirstein's money was going like water. The Society had about eight hundred subscribers, a number which was enough to cover just about half the costs. How much longer it could go on was doubtful. But at this point chance—that all-important agent of the classic plot—intervened. It so happened that the company's business agent, Frances Hawkins, overcoming Kirstein's reluctance, had persuaded him to schedule a few performances for the general public, in addition to the one for the subscribers, and had booked Ballet Society into New York City Center for four performances. It was thus that it came to the attention of a man named Morton Baum. As chairman of the City Center's finance committee, Baum was in charge of the policy and operation of this theatre on West Fifty-fifth Street—the former Mecca Temple, which the city had taken over from a fraternal lodge in 1941 for back taxes, and had converted into a center for popular-priced cultural events. Just to see what was going on around the place, Baum dropped into the City Center one evening when Ballet Society was performing. That night was the première of *Orpheus*. Baum was no ballet lover at that time—indeed, as a lawyer specializing in tax matters and a former alderman and Assistant United States

ORPHEUS: *Above, The Dark Angel
(Moncion) consoling the
bereaved Orpheus (Magallanes);
at right, Euridice (Tallchief)
with Pluto in Hades;
at far right, Euridice twines
about Orpheus,
beseeching him to look at her.*

Attorney, he was an eminently practical man—but that evening he quite lost his head. He went and found the house manager at the end of the evening, a man named Ben Ketcham. "Ben, who runs this? What is this all about?" Baum asked.

"Oh, it's an organization called Ballet Society. They rented the house for a couple of nights."

"Well, who runs it?"

"It's a fellow named Kirstein—Lincoln Kirstein—who runs it."

"Ben," said Baum earnestly, "I am in the presence of greatness."

As he recalls his feelings of that night, a touch of wonder and surprise is apt to come over Baum's countenance nowadays, like a middle-aged

man who should know better admitting to having fallen madly in love. He felt that he had to go right out and do something about it.

Baum's committee did not share this feeling. The City Center in those days sponsored the New York City Drama Company, which brought in some revenue, and the New York City Opera Company, which was a deficit operation, and the committee had no wish to upset the precarious balance by getting involved with a ballet company, which they knew could be a very costly toy. The committee member most vehemently opposed to the project was Gerald Warburg, Edward's brother. "You play around with Balanchine and Kirstein and you'll lose your shirt," he warned Baum. But Baum, using all his craft in support of his new passion, was somehow able to win the committee over.

Then Baum went to talk to Kirstein, whom he had never met. He remembers the scene that ensued as one of the strangest in his experience. Kirstein, who is a pessimist even when things are going well, was in a mood of black despair. He could not raise any more money, and Ballet Society was on the verge of collapse. To Baum, Kirstein, too, seemed to be on the verge of collapse. Not waiting for Baum to state his business, but automatically assuming that it boded ill, Kirstein launched into a tirade, talking, as he sometimes does, so fast that he appeared to be speaking a

*A Ballet Society performance
of* SYMPHONY CONCERTANTE, *to music by Mozart,
in 1947.*

foreign language. He raged against the whole ballet field—its managers, its politics, its repertoires, its audiences. At last, Baum managed to get in the question he had come to ask: "Mr. Kirstein, how would you like the idea of having Ballet Society become the New York City Ballet?"

Kirstein was flabbergasted. Then, as he perceived that Baum really meant it and had not come to thwart him in some new way, he burst out, "If you do that for us, I will give you in three years the finest ballet company in America!" They emotionally shook hands on it. Then Kirstein rushed off to tell Balanchine the news, and Baum went back to his office to try to figure out how he was going to finance this new affair he had got himself into. That autumn of 1948, Ballet Society's performing group officially became the New York City Ballet, with Balanchine as artistic director and Kirstein as general director (unsalaried positions, both of them), and thus was born the first ballet company in the United States to be accorded the status of a public institution.

It was, to be sure, a public institution with a not very prepossessing home. The City Center is a monstrous dump—a barn prettied up with quasi-Oriental decorations. The acoustics are poor. The orchestra pit is grubby and narrow—like a men's lavatory, as Stravinsky commented when he conducted *Orpheus* there. The sight lines are not good for many of the

Herbert Bliss in LA VALSE.

holders of orchestra seats; to those in the first dozen rows, the dancers' legs appear cut off at the ankles. The stage is small, and the backstage area is so cramped that the stagehands have to be fast on their feet to avoid the dancers' hurtling bodies as they make their spectacular exits into the wings. Nevertheless, for all the City Center's disadvantages, having the place as

a home it could call its own has been probably the decisive factor in the New York City Ballet's survival.

Kirstein, for his part, kept the promise he gave Baum. Within three years, the company was widely recognized not only as the finest ballet company in America but as one of the most important in the world, with a repertoire and a style of dancing quite unlike any other. Its reputation was established in 1950 when it attempted its first foreign engagement—seven weeks at Covent Garden, the home of Britain's Royal Ballet. The reception in England was not all pure glory. The galleries took the company to their heart, but many of the critics carped about the paucity of scenery and elaborate costume and the fact that some of the ballets did not have any stories to them. They called Balanchine gifted but cold and heartless—an artist without a soul. The company had its mishaps on Covent Garden's raked stage as well. In fact, the critic Richard Buckle humorously suggested that a memorial should be erected to all the gallant Americans who fell at Covent Garden. Despite all this, the British engagement made the company's reputation and, more important, tempered the company as an entity. If nothing else, the engagement gave them their first real opportunity to dance together for any extended period of time. The seven weeks at Covent Garden was the longest season they had had so far; up till then in New York it had not been financially possible to manage more than four weeks at a stretch. The New York City Ballet's position was consolidated for a good two

A performance at Covent Garden of CONCERTO BAROCCO,
with Diana Adams and Tanaquil LeClercq in the principal roles.

As Cecil Beaton saw Balanchine, during one of the New York company's sojourns in London.

years after this when it made its second journey abroad—a five months' tour of Europe, starting in Barcelona, which, again except for a mixed reception in England, was pretty much a procession of triumphs. The homage the company received at the conclusion of its three-week engagement at Barcelona's Teatro del Liceo exceeded anything that the young American dancers had dreamed of. While the applause went on and on, roses and laurel leaves rained down from the balconies and loges, baskets of flowers were brought in for the dancers until the stage resembled a garden, and a flight of doves went winging overhead about the theatre. The auditorium of the Central High School of Needle Trades had never been like that.

CHAPTER ELEVEN

The first words that Tanaquil LeClercq remembers hearing from her future husband, George Balanchine, were a reprimand. He told her that she was a naughty, saucy child, who was putting on gestures so mannered and affectedly pretty that he could not bear to look at her. Then he sent her out of the room. That was when she was twelve, and having just won a scholarship to the School of American Ballet, had begun taking classes there. For her part, on first impression, she thought the famous Mr. Balanchine something of an old fogy and a very dull teacher, and she could not see what was supposed to be so great about him. She was a high-spirited girl, with a quick wit and a quick tongue. She had long legs and a proud bearing; she was rather like a mettlesome young race horse. Clearly she had the makings of a fine dancer.

Before long she formed a more favorable impression of her mentor and, under his tutelage, she soon began to show herself an accomplished technician. At the age of seventeen she danced her first professional solo role, in *Four Temperaments*. At twenty, when she appeared with the New York City Ballet in its important first engagement at Covent Garden, she attracted much favorable attention. She and Balanchine were married on December 31, 1952, not long after the annulment of his marriage with Maria Tallchief. She was then twenty-three years old, and he forty-eight.

Of all the dancers who have risen to fame in the past few decades, Tanaquil LeClercq had become recognized by then as most nearly the ideal Balanchine dancer, the one who came closest to embodying his conceptions of form and technique, the one whose development he had most carefully nurtured. With her vivacity, her unbelievably long, svelte legs and her flawless sense of timing, she was a ballerina of unusual versatility and strikingly individual quality. In *Bourrée Fantasque* she showed a rare instinct for comedy, proving, as one critic wrote, that it was "possible to be simultaneously beautiful and funny." The adagio of *Symphony in C* she danced with such elegance and musicality that those who saw her performance

of it can scarcely bear to see anyone else dance it today. In *Orpheus* as the Leader of the Bacchantes she was powerfully dramatic, in *La Valse* delicate and touching. "What precocious sense of the transience of beauty and gaiety enabled her to dance this role with such infinite delicacy and penetration?" a critic wrote of her performance in *La Valse*. "Fleet, fragile, touchingly young, incredibly lovely, she brought it a haunting quality which lifted it into the realm of poetry." She was thought of as having a brighter future than any other young dancer of our day. But it abruptly came to an end in 1956 at the age of twenty-seven when, while the company was on tour in Copenhagen, she was felled by poliomyelitis. The doctors could do nothing to save her career. They barely saved her life.

Balanchine, a deeply mystical man, sometimes recalls now, with a kind of horrified awe, a ballet he made featuring Tanaquil when she was a girl of fifteen. It was a little ballet put on at the Waldorf-Astoria in 1944 for the benefit of the March of Dimes. The scene represented a ballet class-

LeClercq partnered by Moncion in the adagio movement of SYMPHONY IN C.

An Irving Penn study of Tanaquil LeClercq as Ariadne, and the three collaborators in the 1948 Ballet Society production of the ballet-cantata, THE TRIUMPH OF BACCHUS AND ARIADNE — *Corrado Cagli, the designer; Vittorio Rieti, the composer; and Balanchine.*

Some of Tanaquil LeClercq's roles.

METAMORPHOSES.
With Moncion in LA VALSE.
BOURRÉE FANTASQUE, with Jerome Robbins.
High jinks in WESTERN SYMPHONY with Jacques d'Amboise,
as Todd Bolender looks on, bemused.

room, where the young students were to be seen practicing their steps and
leaps with eager devotion, obviously rejoicing in the virtuosity of their agile
bodies. Suddenly there appeared among them a grotesque, black-clad
monster—the evil Polio. He reached out his foul hand and touched one
of the girls, and she fell paralyzed to the floor. The girl was Tanaquil.
Balanchine himself, he recalls with a grimace, danced the role of Polio.
"It was an omen," he says, looking as if he blamed himself somehow for
what, years later, came to pass. "It foretold the future." In this little ballet,
Tanaquil was then placed in a wheelchair, where, as the others hovered
about her in sorrow, she performed exquisite, pathetic variations to the
music with her arms and upper body. For the climax, there was a shower
of silver coins. Miraculously restored, she rose radiantly from her chair.
The others hastened to fetch her ballet slippers, and in a burst of joy she
danced gloriously across the floor and off the stage. "It was, alas, a balletic
finale," Balanchine says. "Nothing like that ending will happen in Tanny's
real life."

In her real life, Mrs. Balanchine has the use of her arms but is paralyzed
from the waist down. The doctors have declared that she will never walk
again. Balanchine, for a time, hoped for a miracle through prayers. He and
his wife found it hard to accept the opinions of the medical specialists
that nothing could be done to restore her body any further and that additional aid from then on would have to take the form of mechanical appliances
for the handicapped. "They've got marvelous appliances now, those doctors,
that will breathe for you and eat for you and everything else," Balanchine
said. "But that's not what a dancer like Tanny wants. She wants her own
body back, or even any little bit of it that she can get back. She will work,
she will do exercises endlessly. Tell Tanny to do this a hundred times—" he
flexed his wrist—"and she will do it with pleasure. The others do not really
understand exercises. They must do something—make a mat or weave a
basket. But a dancer knows that to move is already an accomplishment,
without making anything." Three times a week a therapist came to
Balanchine's apartment to work with his wife and help her recover her
wasted powers. The efforts of the therapist—a German woman who was
once a dancer herself and studied biomechanics with the famed Rudolf
von Laban—were devoted at first to trying to discover even the faintest
glimmer of life in muscles that have officially been pronounced dead. The
therapist still comes; Balanchine still prays; but there is little hope any

longer of reviving the muscles. Now the therapist's efforts are aimed at helping her keep in as good general physical condition and tone as possible.

When Mrs. Balanchine was first brought home in 1958, after doctors had arrested her condition as far as they considered possible, she saw a pair of ballet slippers in the closet and burst into tears. For months thereafter she never mentioned ballet, and those around her carefully avoided the subject. This phase of acute distress has passed. When ballet comes up now, she speaks freely and without obvious pain, even reminiscing, in a seemingly detached way, about parts she herself used to dance; and in 1962, when *La Valse* was revived, she took pleasure in coaching Patricia McBride in the role she had originally created. Visitors to the Balanchine apartment these days generally find her in good, often even gay spirits—apparently quite her former spontaneous, lighthearted self.

The Balanchines live in a spacious five-room apartment at Seventy-

The Balanchines at home.

ninth Street and Broadway. Balanchine decorated and furnished it himself, becoming in the process well known to the housewares departments of Bloomingdale's department store and elsewhere. The apartment, painted off-white, reflects Balanchine's own unclassifiable tastes, as well as, here and there, his own sometimes surprising feats of handiwork. An ornate French chandelier hangs from the ceiling; over the fireplace is an early-nineteenth-century New England weather vane of copper; and an Audubon eagle, lifesize, is enthroned on one of the walls, casting a piercing eye over the room. Dominating the living room are two grand pianos, on one of which is an inscribed photograph of Stravinsky. The sofa and two chairs —ornately carved pieces covered in blue Italian silk—are mid-nineteenth-century American, by Belter. It is the kind of furniture one sees in the salons of prosperous mustached Westerners in cowboy films. Years ago, when Balanchine first began seeing movies, he used to think how wonderful it would be to have furniture just like that; and when he was furnishing the present apartment, he was lucky enough to find these pieces in an antique shop specializing in the rental of theatrical props. On the floor of the room is a large, approximately oval black rug, which goes well with the room; it was oblong until Balanchine took a pair of shears and improved its shape. Adjoining the living room is a smaller sitting room, and this contains more of Balanchine's handicraft—a bar he carpentered. On the walls are some drawings given to them by Tchelitchev, and along the windows is a variegated garden of plants, which Mrs. Balanchine tends with a masterful green thumb. It is a serene and sunny apartment. On the broad wall of the sitting room is a great, gleaming brass pendulum clock, acquired by Balanchine in Paris. And on a wall of the kitchen—where Balanchine concocts his French sauces, his galantines, and his kulitch and pascha, the special treats he serves at an annual party for his Russian friends, which begins right after Midnight Mass on Easter—is another conspicuous timepiece, as big as a street clock. For a choreographer, as for a composer, time is of the essence. It is not surprising that Balanchine, in his everyday life, should be noted for his punctuality.

His annual Russian Easter party is always the main festivity of the year. For it he prepares his most lavish board—roasts, ptarmigans, fish in aspic, specially prepared horseradish and garnishes, salade Olivier, and, of course, the traditional pascha and kulitch, which contain all the rich ingredients and exotic tastes one dreams of during Lent: sweet butter by the pound, mounds of sugar, vanilla beans, saffron, cardamom, pressed almonds, raisins. Invariably, this event occurs in the midst of a ballet season. For three days before Easter he is apt to be choreographing all day and cooking virtually the whole night through. On the day the kulitch is to be baked, he will have to keep phoning home from the studio during breaks in the rehearsal sessions to find out if the dough has risen. As soon as he gets word it has, he rushes home to get it into the oven in proper shape.

In accordance with Mrs. Balanchine's preference, no household help lives at the apartment. A maid comes in to do the housecleaning. Much of the time the other chores—the shopping, the cooking, and all the rest—are done by Balanchine. Because his wife must watch her weight carefully, the daily fare that Balanchine prepares is succulent but unextravagant; only on party occasions now does he unbridle his fancy and produce the rich French and Russian specialties of which he is capable. He tries to be away from the apartment as little as possible, but there are tasks which take him out of town from time to time. While he is away, Mrs. Balanchine's mother or a friend may stay with her, or she may, again by preference, choose to remain alone, kept company by Murka, their white-and-ginger-colored cat, a pampered and much admired creature. Balanchine has trained this cat to perform brilliant *jetés* and *tours en l'air;* he says that at last he has a body worth choreographing for. On free evenings when Balanchine is home, he and his wife may have friends over to the apartment. If there is a good science fiction movie playing, they may drive out to a suburban drive-in; if not, they will stay home and watch television. On television, Balanchine's predilection is for Westerns. "That's my bad taste, I suppose," he once told an interviewer. "If you were to say to me, 'What's the best thing in America, artistically the best thing?', I would reply, 'Cowboys! Westerns!' The people are right for it, they know how to do what they're doing, and to me it all rings true. When I see on the screen that wonderful Nevada or Arizona space and horses galloping beautifully across it, I am instantly satisfied. I find no fault in it at all." With the ballet he sees on television, he is much less satisfied. He has, himself, had some good experiences with a few ballet programs he has put on for the Canadian Broadcasting Company, but his efforts for the American companies have been disappointments to him in one way or other. On television the dance programs that give him the most pleasure are those of Fred Astaire, whom he admires exceedingly. He has called him the best male dancer of the day.

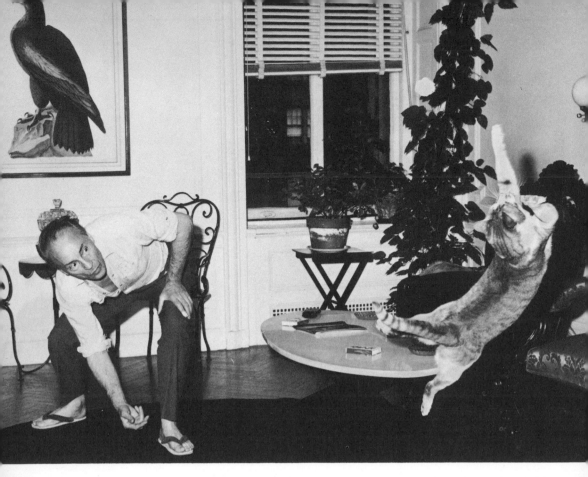

In the Balanchine apartment as Balanchine puts Murka through his paces.

Weekends and summers the Balanchines spend as much time as they can at a country place they own, eight acres in size, in Weston, Connecticut, where they have a number of ambitious horticultural projects under way, and where Balanchine enjoys mowing the lawn at breakneck speed with his power mower. The power mower is one of his favorite gadgets. His wife plans the strategies and tactics of the gardening, and he executes her commands. "Please dig four holes, George, near the lilacs, for some shrubs I've ordered," she will say. And he will dig. He is quite a good digger.

At the time his wife fell ill, Balanchine was absent from ballet for a full year—staying in Copenhagen during the months she was in the hospital there, and then going with her to Warm Springs, Georgia, where she underwent additional treatment. Rumors circulated that Balanchine was likely to retire from ballet altogether—that he did not have the heart to continue, and that even if he did, it might not be feasible. These rumors were con-

vincingly dispelled when he rejoined his company in the fall of 1957 and, within the space of a few weeks, choreographed *Agon, Square Dance, Gounod Symphony* and *Stars and Stripes*—a stunning feat of virtuosity. The company, which had sagged noticeably in his absence, responded immediately to his presence, and the season that ensued was hailed as the most brilliant and distinguished that the New York City Ballet had ever presented. After that, no more talk was heard of his retiring. When a reporter subsequently asked him if he had ever thought of quitting, Balanchine looked at him in astonishment. "How can I quit?" he said. "I'm a choreographer. All I know how to do is make ballets. As long as I can move around enough to show my dancers what I want them to dance, I expect to go on making ballets. That's my job."

Opus 34, Western Symphony, Ivesiana, Divertimento No. 15, Square

After the "performance."

Dance, Agon, Stars and Stripes, Episodes, Liebeslieder Walzer, A Midsummer Night's Dream, Movements—the ballets, these named and many others, came cascading from him, as happily and artfully as the play of Italian fountains, in the years after his company had become established. The sixth decade of his life, beginning in 1954, saw him choreographing more than thirty ballets, as well as staging three operas—for Hamburg, the Met, and for N.B.C.—and supervising the mounting of various of his works by ballet companies throughout the world, from Winnipeg to Milan. It was the most prolific era of his whole career. Lotte Lenya, who was in the 1933 performance of *The Seven Deadly Sins* and also in the 1958 production (which turned out to be virtually a new work in its choreography, rather than a revival), commented after the later occasion, "It was breathtaking to work with him again after twenty-five years and find him so full of ideas and energy still. With other creative people I've known, the time always comes when you can say to yourself, a little sadly, 'Well, that's it— there'll be no more surprises.' But with Balanchine you can't say that. Who knows what he's still got up his sleeve!" Balanchine, himself, has commented, when asked how it happens that he seems to gain in vigor as he grows older, "That's nothing. Old people don't get tired—it's only the young who tire. Confusion exhausts them. I've got more energy now than when I was younger because I know exactly what I want to do."

What he wants to do most, of course, is to keep his company going, which is no small task, and to continue to make ballets in which the dance predominates, exploring new possibilities in his old art all the time. The two objectives are inseparable in his mind, since he cannot conceive of choreography except in the tangible, living terms of the bodies of the dancers who assemble, on call, before him at rehearsal time. "My dancers, you might say, *are* my choreography, at the moment of performance."

His most distinctive contribution to ballet, as has long been recognized, has been his bold assertion of the dance element. Other elements had held the limelight previously—the virtuosity of the individual ballerina, the decor, the plot; sometimes the dancing got lost altogether. Balanchine has been the first to make the choreography, in effect, the star of the show, evolving what has been called perhaps the purest kind of ballet, in which all the drama is in the dance itself—in the pattern of movement unfolding in intimate relationship with the music. These ballets of his are sometimes called "abstract," but he considers this a misnomer, since he is not trying

*Balanchine zestfully throws himself
into the part of the sinister Drosselmeyer
during a television performance
of* THE NUTCRACKER.

to present any abstractions in his work, and prefers to call them "plotless" ballets. Plotless or not, there is always drama in them, and a recognizable attitude or outlook.

In addition to these pure dance ballets, he will generally, each season, do any of a number of quite different kinds of ballets, depending on what he thinks the repertory seems to need at the moment. In doing so, he describes himself as like a chef, or a restaurant owner, who has the obligation to present his patrons with a varied menu, so that they will feel satisfied and well dined and will want to come back again. Among the long roster of ballets he has made in his lifetime are to be found acknowledged masterworks in a wide range of categories: narrative ballets such as *Prodigal Son* and *Orpheus,* which are reckoned among the most powerful dramatic pieces in the contemporary ballet repertoire; romantic evocations of mood and atmosphere, like *Liebeslieder Walzer* or *Cotillon;* amusing novelties on the order of *Western Symphony* and *Square Dance;* and strange visions of indefinable nightmare, such as *Ivesiana* and *Opus 34*. In all of these he has sought to convey his ideas not in a literal way but in terms of dance metaphors. As Kirstein has said, "He has no interest in any effect that is not danced." When he chooses to do a ballet with a plot, he can tell a story

LIEBESLIEDER WALZER.

with masterly clarity and economy. He thinks it should not be necessary to have to learn the language of pantomime in order to follow what is taking place on the stage, as did the St. Petersburg balletomanes in the old days, who used to attend regular classes in the subject. Nor should it be necessary to read an involved synopsis in the program. "The curtain should just go up, and if the spectators understand what's going on, it's good—if not, not," Balanchine says. In a narrative ballet, the relationships should be such as can be grasped at sight. He once compressed the essence of his years of consideration of this matter into a nutshell of wisdom he called Balanchine's Law, which went: "There are no sisters-in-law in ballet." Yet when, in 1962, he choreographed *A Midsummer Night's Dream*, he was able to make clear, with no apparent strain, that whole complex tangle of

The butterflies grouped about Puck (Arthur Mitchell) in A MIDSUMMER NIGHT'S DREAM.

relationships, with all the humor, fantasy, romanticism and suspense one could wish—and to do it all through dance conceptions, not through mime.

Almost singlehanded, Balanchine has kept the classic tradition of ballet alive in our epoch. He carried out a revolt against the Fokine revolutionaries, but, as can be seen now, Balanchine's revolution was a new one, not a counter-revolution. For if he kept classic ballet alive, it was not through idolatry and archaeology, but through constant innovation, experiment and discovery. Always Balanchine has thought of ballet as a living art, not as a relic of the past to be worshipfully or academically preserved. The company's repertoire is not a museum; the only two traditional works Balanchine has mounted for it—*The Nutcracker* and the second act of *Swan Lake*—have both been freely staged by him to suit his company's personnel and his own preferences. Balanchine's classicism is a contemporary classicism—designed to be seen by twentieth-century eyes and make its effects on twentieth-century nerves. The classic vocabulary of steps is employed in a different way from Petipa: extensions are higher, movements may be faster and more staccato, combinations are apt to be more complicated and intense. Aside from the obvious fact of having jettisoned the plot and dispensed with the pantomime, Balanchine will differ from Petipa's approach in such respects as his employment of several ballerinas in a work, dancing parts of equal importance, or in the importance he gives to the corps de ballet as an element of the total dance composition. In Petipa's ballets the corps danced very little, but was mainly used for pictorial effects. In Balanchine's ballets the corps is expected to dance a great deal and perform demanding feats of skill: a Balanchine corps de ballet member will swoop easily through a chain of steps that a Petipa ballerina would have thought impossible to do. The same thing has happened in nearly all fields of physical attainment: the mile is now run twenty or thirty seconds faster than it was at the turn of the century. But despite the differences in technique, Balanchine shares with Petipa —and with the other great exponents of classicism, in all the arts, throughout the ages—a common outlook as to the relationship of his art to society, and to humanity. "The secrets of emotion Balanchine reveals," Denby has written in a discussion of Balanchine's classicism, "are like those of Mozart, tender, joyous and true. He leaves the audience with a civilized happiness. His art is peaceful and exciting, as classic art has always been."

Very different in appearance from his classic ballets have been Balanchine's ballets to contemporary music. In a line of ballets which begins with

Two moments from EPISODES. *Right, Jacques d'Amboise and Diana Adams.*
Above, among others, Allegra Kent and Nicholas Magallanes.

Four Temperaments in 1946 and whose high points have been perhaps
Ivesiana in 1954, *Agon* in 1957, *Episodes* in 1959 and *Movements* in 1963,
he has boldly explored realms of movement not seen before in ballet. These
works have each been quite different from the other in implicit content and
spirit. *Agon* was pert, witty, a high-wire act, a contemporary comment on
skill and danger, employing for effect in places a typically American kind
of understatement, like that of the astronaut saying, as he emerged from
the capsule in which he had just orbited the world, "Boy, what a ride!"
Episodes, to the music of Webern, seemed to be about alienation and de-
personalization, not in explicit terms of any plot but in its very essence—
in the way the dancers were manipulated, like so many manikins, as if
devoid of all will. *Movements,* which, like *Agon,* had a Stravinsky score, was
rarefied, remote, beyond good and evil, with an impersonal, godlike serenity.
But each of these works was hailed, as it appeared, as a landmark, a breakthrough—one of those rare productions that affect the course of dance
history. How advanced Balanchine's explorations have been was revealed,

MOVEMENTS, *with Jacques d'Amboise and Suzanne Farrell.*

whether the comparison was intentional or not, during the season of *Episodes'* première, at which time that work was danced in two parts, with the opening part choreographed and danced by Martha Graham and her company. The modern dance group, in handsome, ornate Elizabethan costumes, danced the story of the death of Mary, Queen of Scots; the classical ballet company went through its grim, strange paces in stark, black-and-white practice clothes. The critics wrote what a curious thing it was to see the two companies together this way, and noted inevitably that it was the modern dancers who seemed old-fashioned, the classic ballet company who looked modern.

In regard to the Balanchine ballets in the novelty category—these lighter offerings, which are intended, one might say, to fill a place similar in the repertory to that occupied by perhaps a baked Alaska in a chef's menu—they often take as their starting point some device or gimmick. In *Native Dancers* it was simply the conception of the girls as fillies, the boys as jockeys; in *Square Dance*, it was the perception of common musical forms in the country dances of today and the works of seventeenth-century classical composers; in *Western Symphony,* the amusement was in putting classical ballet steps to "Red River Valley" and "On Top of Old Smoky." Even in these, it will be noted that the gimmick is almost always a dance conception, not one imported from the world of mime; and it is also to be noted that Balanchine will often work more deeply than he sets out to do. In *Bugaku,* for instance, Balanchine goes beyond the Japanese setting, costumes and mannerisms which are the superficial aspects of the ballet, and achieves in his choreography, through tempos as slow and alien as those of a deep-sea diver on the ocean bottom, a profound and powerful sense of a culture completely different from our own.

To some, all this seems perhaps illicitly easy and facile. Balanchine's ability to work in many styles is a trait he shares with certain other contemporary artists—with Picasso and Stravinsky, for example. Perhaps ours is the age of the great chameleon, of the quick-change artist. No matter how diverse they are, though, a common thread runs through all of Balanchine's works. They all bear his strong stamp; it would not be possible to mistake them for the work of anybody else.

In all these ballets of his, whatever the genre, music has always been the platform for him—or, better yet, the sustaining element in which he swims. A friend who went backstage to congratulate Balanchine after the première, in 1952, of *Caracole,* a ballet to the music of Mozart's *Divertimento No. 15,* remembers finding Balanchine off to one side, by himself, in a kind of rapture. "Oh, that Mozart—that music!" he kept saying, and paid no heed to his admirer's compliments on the wonders of his choreography.

Even when the score that Balanchine choreographs for is not a masterpiece, it is always treated by him with affection and appropriate respect. This is not the same thing as being solemn about it. Some of the intellectuals in the City Center audience—the ones who flock reverently to the "twelve-tone nights" which in recent years have been a feature of every season, when all four ballets on the program will be to serial music and there will not be a single resolved cadence to be heard the whole evening long—were shocked when, in 1958, their admired Mr. Balanchine chose to do a ballet, *Stars and Stripes,* to the marches of John Philip Sousa. Boulez they would have been ready for, or Stockhausen—but *Sousa!* They decided finally that Balanchine must be spoofing, but he never said he was. His only comment was, "I like Sousa's music. It makes me feel good."

When Balanchine is engaged in making a ballet, he will sometimes offer prayers to the composer if he runs into difficulties. "Let us pray to Gounod," he was heard saying to some of the company when he was chore-ographing *Gounod Symphony,* "He will help us." This brought smiles to the lips of those who heard him. They assumed he was being whimsical, but he was not. He meant it—not symbolically, either, but simply and literally. He feels certain that the composers have often heard his prayers and have inter-ceded to help him assemble the materials of his ballet in suitable style— "assemble," not "create." Creation is an act performed only by God in his view. "God creates, woman inspires, and man assembles," he says.

Some critics have opined that Balanchine is actually too musical for his own good. They declare that what he does is closer to eurythmy than ballet, as they define ballet. The most distinguisted of the critics who take this line is Cyril Beaumont. Reviewing *Ballet Imperial* in 1950, Beaumont wrote, "The relation between music and choreography is almost automatic. It seems to me to be less creative choreography than the literal reproduction in terms of the dance of the rhythm, texture, and pattern of the music. It is a mathematical process rather than a creative one." Beaumont is once reported to have commented, in a discussion with Anatole Chujoy, that Balanchine always repeats his choreography when the music repeats, and that this is a fault because it leaves the audience with the impression that the choreographer could not think of any other steps to put in that place. Aside from the fact that this is surely a curious observation to make in regard to a choreographer who has proved himself to be as facile as any who ever lived, it misses the intention completely. Balanchine often likes to show a dance motif or section twice, because he knows that audiences often fail to grasp what they are seeing the first time. His choreographic repeat fre-quently serves a parallel function to that fulfilled by the musical repeat in the score. He knows that in dance, as in music—and in life, too, for that matter—a repeat is not a repeat, in its effect. One cannot bathe twice in the same stream, as the Greek philosopher said. One experiences the same thing differently the second time. Actually, there are to be found in Balan-chine's ballets many instances in which the music repeats and the choreog-raphy does not. The most obvious example that comes to mind is *Opus 34,* a ballet of grim, nightmarish quality to the music of Arnold Schönberg. The ballet consists of two parts. The score is played through twice. In the first part, the choreography is in Balanchine's characteristic plotless style;

the second part, to the same music, is a hallucinatory operating-room scene, and here the choreography is of a strange dance-mime character. Sometimes in his ballets Balanchine follows the music even more closely than those in the audience, including perhaps Cyril Beaumont, might be aware of. In *Episodes,* for instance, there occurs an unusual moment when the girls are turned upside down and do *entrechats* with head down, feet in the air. When asked about this, Balanchine replied gravely, "Oh, I have to do that. That's where Webern inverts the theme. See, it's right here in the score." But one may be certain that Balanchine would not have choreographed it that way if the action had not, first and foremost, pleased him visually and been in accord with his palette of movement for that particular

A scene from Balanchine's staging of EUGEN ONEGIN *for the Hamburg Opera.*

ballet. There are theme inversions in Bach's *Double Violin Concerto* but no upside-down *entrechats* to be found in the ballet Balanchine choreographed to that score. Similarly, in *Movements*: at the start Stravinsky exposes the sequence of notes in his tone row with great rapidity, and Balanchine deploys his dancers in the same way. Later in the piece, Stravinsky brings back the tone-row sequence, but this time in very leisurely fashion; Balanchine repeats his earlier choreographic deployment, but in the new leisurely tempo. Such turns and devices give Balanchine pleasure. They can be considered, since so few people in the audience are ever aware of them, the private games of a choreographer. Yet it is quite possible that such conjunctions of dance patterns to the musical patterns work in subtle, subliminal ways on even an uncomprehending audience to convey the overall effect characteristic of Balanchine ballets—of appropriateness and harmony, of surprises that are seldom gratuitous, and of fulfilled expectations. In any case, he does not do what he does in order to illustrate some theory. He has no theories about this, and he hopes the audience will not bother itself with theories. One should not need to be conscious of the inner workings to appreciate a ballet, just as it should not be necessary to have to read a ballet's plot beforehand in the program notes.

In regard to the question of whether Balanchine's musicality operates restrictively on him as a choreographer, one can hardly do better than cite the judgment of Igor Stravinsky, who has concerned himself more with the ballet than any first-rate composer in history and who, in the course of his phenomenal half-century and more of composing for the ballet, has had his works staged by almost every choreographer of the age. Stravinsky, of course, has long since expressed his preference for Balanchine as collaborator. "I don't see how anyone can be a choreographer unless, like Balanchine, he is a musician first," Stravinsky has written. Unfortunately, he adds wryly, very few choreographers have been musicians. In Stravinsky's opinion, Balanchine's musicality actually enables him to free himself from the obvious constrictions of the music, particularly the tyranny of the beat (which, Stravinsky thinks, trapped Nijinsky inextricably in his choreography for *Le Sacre du Printemps*), and to construct dance phrases that have a life of their own yet are always subtly linked with the musical phrases.

"Oh Brave New World that has such dancers in it!" So wrote, in a most un-British burst of enthusiasm, the critic of the London *Times* after spending a season in New York, attending all the performances of the New York City Ballet. The London *Times'* reports are always unsigned, but the voice in this case was clearly that of Clive Barnes, the liveliest and most knowledgeable of England's younger generation of critics. His visit to New York took place a decade after the American company had been last seen in London, and he was impressed to see how much the company had developed since then—"beyond expectation if not recognition." The company's senior ballerinas—Diana Adams, Melissa Hayden, Jillana, Allegra Kent, Violette Verdy and Patricia Wilde—had recently been joined, he said, by a remarkable influx of younger dancers, and he named as the most notable Patricia McBride, Suzanne Farrell, Gloria Govrin, Patricia Neary, Mimi

A rehearsal in 1957, as Balanchine and Stravinsky work together in AGON.

They begin with a discussion, in Russian, on tempi.
"The pianist says he doesn't know how to play it," says Balanchine.
"I don't either," replies Stravinsky.

A discussion on style with Bolender after the sarabande

*As the dancers crouch downward
for the ending of the coda
to their pas de trois
Balanchine snaps his fingers
and cries, "Now!"*

Barbara Walzack and Barbara Milberg dance the gaillard. Stravinsky,
who has by now shucked his jacket, claps out the rhythm. He said he thought
the last bars of their dance "beautiful but dangerous"
because they had complicated arm movements to a count of nine. "I'm afraid
I don't know how long nine is," Stravinsky said.
Balanchine has since simplified the ending.

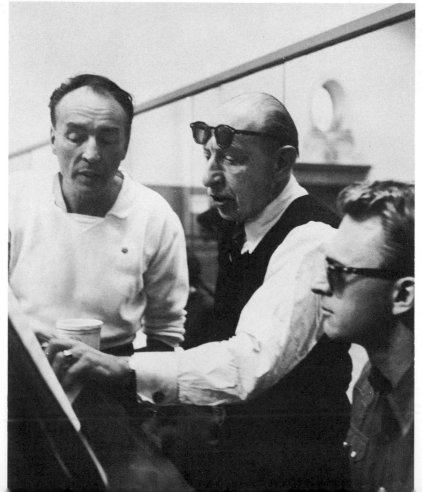

The exuberant conclusion of the bransle double, with Melissa Hayden,
Roy Tobias and Jonathan Watts. "Horosha!" said Stravinsky.

The adagio. In this section Balanchine seemed to have succeeded in his aim
of happily surprising Stravinsky, who clapped when it was finished
and said, "Wonderful! Wonderful!" He had never seen Arthur Mitchell before,
asked his name and complimented him. Diana Adams he knew and spoke
of admiringly. "She has legs like the Solingen scissors trademark," he said.

One of numerous forays to the piano. During this one, just before the adagio
pas de deux, Stravinsky wants to be sure that the first part of
the music here will be played in such a way as to bring out an echo
of the music at the end of the preceding section.

They discuss the ballet's conclusion. Stravinsky thinks that the four boys should swing their arms in more controlled and precise fashion than they were doing; otherwise it looks lazy. Balanchine agrees, and the four boys go through it again to everybody's satisfaction.

Stravinsky dances.

And Balanchine strikes a dynamic pose,
as he describes the quality one movement is to have.

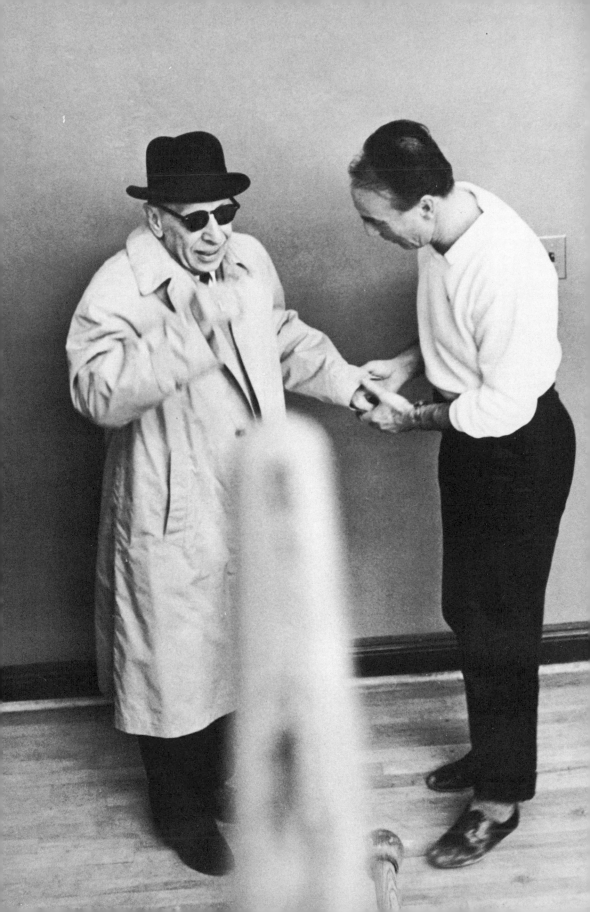

Paul and Suki Schorer. A splendid new generation was coming along. Perhaps the most significant change that had occurred in the past ten years was that the male members of the company—with such as Jacques d'Amboise, Edward Villella and Arthur Mitchell leading the way—were now just as impressive in their dancing as the women, whereas a decade before they had been completely overshadowed. New York, he wrote, has become the dance capital of the world, and the effect of seeing the New York City Ballet performing there is "as exhilarating as horses at Epsom or Mozart in Salzburg."

In carrying on the New York City Ballet, Balanchine and Kirstein continue to collaborate in amity and rare harmony. Their friendship was not shaken by their early failures and, what is perhaps even more rare, it seems even strong enough to survive success. Throughout the years, they have always approached matters in a very different way, as far as personality is concerned. Kirstein can be moody and irascible. Driven by the haunted energy of the insomniac, and perpetually bringing forth great plans for new projects, many of them quixotic, some of them inspired, Kirstein often exhibits the aggressiveness of a man who is innately shy, whereas Balanchine bears himself with the quiet ease of one who is supremely confident. Entering the company's studios when all is in chaos, Balanchine can calm matters simply by his untroubled presence. Kirstein, on the other hand, is apt to come in at a time when everything is going swimmingly, peer about him, and ask, with an agonized scowl, "Is anything wrong?" Nevertheless, there is seldom any divergence on matters of fundamental principle. Balanchine has often expressed his gratitude to Kirstein. He says that if it weren't for Kirstein, he not only might never have come to the United States but, for lack of a company, might never have created the ballets he has. When this is repeated to Kirstein, he glares as if he has been insulted, and snaps that it's nonsense—that such a talent as Balanchine's would have found a way of expressing itself, in a form not too different from the one it has taken, whether he had helped or not. Be that as it may, Kirstein has played his role of patron and impresario in an extraordinary way. As John Martin has written, "The General Director [of a ballet company] usually hires the Artistic Director to carry out his policies; Kirstein, on the other hand, has hired himself, so to speak, to carry out Balanchine's policy."

Certainly, there is never any question about whose influence pre-

Respectful farewell.

dominates in the New York City Ballet. The company reflects in such a multiplicity of ways the personality of its artistic director that it seems less an ensemble of skilled performers he has gathered than a kind of emanation from him. "Nowhere else in the world," to quote Martin again, "is there a ballet company that is similarly the creation of a single mind." Every dancer in the company either has been trained by Balanchine from an early stage or has been retrained according to Balanchine's principles of dance technique. The values and stylistic standards that prevail are those of Balanchine's neo-classicism—a mode that is grand and aristocratic in manner, but naturally so, without pomposity; full of invention yet lucid in quality; tearing no passion to tatters but, instead, enlivened by a constant play of subtle wit and irony and an unfeigned delight in the pleasures of the dance. And nearly all of the ballets in the repertory—three-quarters, at least —have been choreographed by Balanchine himself.

In its first year at the City Center, the New York City Ballet gave a total of only thirty performances. By the 1960's it was presenting, in an average year, a total of around a hundred and fifty performances, spread out over two or three seasons, in New York alone, plus whatever tours were made. In the course of a year's performances in New York, the New York City Ballet may be seen by a total audience of around three hundred thousand people. This, as even some devotees of the ballet may be surprised to realize, is at least five times as large an audience as Diaghilev's Ballets Russes commanded in the Twenties. That company did not dare risk more than a couple of weeks a year in Paris, even in a small theatre, holding no more than eight hundred people; in Monte Carlo, the theatre's capacity was only four hundred. Never in history has ballet enjoyed such wide favor as it does today. The growth of enthusiasm for this exotic, patently artificial and aristocratic entertainment is one of the sociological phenomena of the times, make what one will of it.

In New York nowadays, almost as many people attend ballet during the course of a year as baseball—a piece of information often cited by ballet writers, though almost never by baseball columnists. Nor is it New York alone that has taken to ballet. Still more significant is the fact that regional semi-professional ballet companies are springing up all over the United States, supported by small-town bankers, shopkeepers, and others who not long ago would have sneered at having anything to do with such a thing.

Over a hundred such ballet companies have come into existence. The dream that Balanchine and Kirstein discussed, back in 1933, of seeing ballet take root in America as a living, flourishing art would certainly seem to have become a reality.

As for Balanchine—"Mr. B.," as his dancers call him—during the decade of the 1950's he attained recognition and status on a new, grand scale..He had founded a school, a company, a style, a repertory—a range of achievements, as could be seen now, matched by few, if any, individuals in the history of ballet. He had become, without question, the dominant figure in ballet for the present era. His influence went far beyond that of his own company. In Germany, for example, where he had mounted some of his ballets and done some work with the ballet company of the Hamburg Opera, he was credited with having initiated a whole new interest in ballet. In the United States, in addition to supervising his school, directing his company, and choreographing several new ballets each season, he had become increasingly active in fostering ballet in general, and improving its standards. He traveled about the country, advising the regional ballet companies; conducted annually a free seminar for the ballet teachers of America; sent small groups of his dancers here and there on lecture-demonstration tours; organized free ballet performances for under-privileged children; and contributed of his experience and insight in a variety of other ways.

By now, the audience for his kind of ballet had grown considerably, and critics who, for many years after Balanchine began working in America, had been antipathetic to his efforts had become ardent advocates. The London *Times* critic noted, on his visit to New York, that Balanchine seemed to have trained his audience and his critics almost as carefully as he trained his dancers. When the New York State Theatre was built at Lincoln Center—a $19,000,000 gem of a theatre—it was Balanchine's advice that was most heeded as to what the theatre should be like. "I did the house with Balanchine in mind," said the architect, Philip Johnson. "I have always wanted to design a theatre for him." And the New York City Ballet agreed to formally open the threatre on April 23, 1964, and to be for the following two years the resident company, performing twenty weeks a year.

Beyond the world of ballet now, fame in its various characteristic manifestations had come to Balanchine—a *Time* cover story, a *New Yorker*

Profile, features in *Life* and other magazines, an invitation to the White House. The fame seems to have altered him little. He paid not much more heed to the praise being accorded him now than he had to the criticism he had received in earlier years. To a friend, who showed him a flattering article, Balanchine recently commented, "Publicity over-rates everything," and then, specifying to clinch his point, added, "Picasso's over-rated. I'm over-rated. Even Jack Benny's over-rated."

CHAPTER TWELVE

G. M. Balanchivadze had left Russia at the age of twenty, a little-known youth. As George Balanchine, he came back in 1962 at the age of fifty-eight, world-famous, at the head of a brilliant American ensemble, which was as much his creation as were the Balanchine ballets it performed.

On the basis of what was known of Russian taste in ballet, and of various advance indications and prior encounters with leading figures in the Russian ballet world, no great success was expected for Balanchine or his company. There had been, for instance, the interesting occasion in 1959, when the Bolshoi had made its first trip to the United States and was enjoying a spectacular triumph. Since the Bolshoi's schedule did not permit its members to attend a regular performance of the New York City Ballet, Balanchine arranged to put on a special rehearsal for the visitors while they were in New York. The event turned out to be something of a fiasco. The Russians were able to make little or nothing of what they saw the New York City Ballet do, and looked as if they were pretty sure they would not like it even if they did understand it. Their faces registered, variously, bewilderment, pain, boredom and stiff politeness.

The first ballet presented was *Agon,* then one of Balanchine's most recent works and probably as complex and sophisticated a piece of choreography as had ever been devised. "It was like giving *Finnegans Wake* to someone who has never gone beyond Galsworthy," commented one American witness of the Bolshoi troupe's baffled reaction both to the choreography and to Stravinsky's twelve-tone-technique score. The Russians were used to ballets that tell a tale or convey a readily understandable situation and, if possible, impart a moral. Nothing of that sort was to be found in *Agon.* Its entire orientation seemed to them incomprehensible. As his point of departure in the score, Stravinsky makes use of some seventeenth-century dance forms, and so does Balanchine when it suits him. At one point, a soloist goes through an elaborate, decorous saraband, but, as an observer has noted, "It recalls a court dance as much as a Cubist still life recalls a pipe

AGON

or guitar." A few introductory words by Balanchine about his intentions might have given some of the audience a clue to the way to look at the ballet, but Balanchine, sticking to his belief that if a ballet is any good, it does not require a program note or other explanation, told them only the title and the name of the composer. The Russians have a word which is similar in sound to *Agon* and means "fire"; throughout the ballet some of the Bolshoi members, who had misheard Balanchine's announcement, sat conscientiously trying to make some sort of fire dance out of the choreography. The title—*Agon*—is, in fact, the Greek word for "contest," but that knowledge would not have been of much help, either, to a spectator expecting to see a recognizable representation of some portion of "life." Within *Agon's* self-contained cosmos, presented to the audience with an air of cool, ironic detachment, there do occur, in a mysteriously coherent pattern, the most amazing events—sometimes intensely exciting and charged with drama, sometimes sparklingly witty or lucidly nonsensical—but the events are choreographic events; they could not happen in what we call the real world, though they seem inevitable in the world called *Agon*. Complex as *Agon* is, it had nevertheless delighted New York audiences and had received a great ovation at its première two years before. The New York audiences, of course, had been acquainted with Balanchine's way of organizing dance movement and Stravinsky's way of organizing sound, and they had also been prepared for *Agon* by all that had happened in art in the Western world during the past few decades—all the innovations and discoveries that had shaped the taste and outlook not just of sophisticates but of the broad public—to the point where Surrealism, for example, far from shocking anybody, had become a comfortable cliché of popular advertisements. At that City Center rehearsal for the Bolshoi in 1959, one was reminded how little the Soviet Union had been touched by such influences.

After *Agon,* the New York City Ballet danced two other plotless Balanchine ballets—*Symphony in C* and *Serenade*. These were somewhat better received than *Agon,* no doubt partly because the nineteenth-century music sounded less strange, and partly because in these ballets Balanchine's choreography makes more use of familiar steps. Even so, no great enthusiasm was discernible. And it must be said that the quality of the dancing did not help matters. The members of the New York company were visibly nervous, and some of them danced as awkwardly as they ever have danced in their lives. When they began making obvious mistakes, Balanchine, who had been sitting in the first row, went up on the stage to work with them, as patiently as if this were a routine rehearsal. If he felt any chagrin at the company's performance, he showed no signs of it.

An odd scene took place when Balanchine met with the Bolshoi's chief choreographer, Leonid Lavrovsky, at an informal reception that was held in the City Center's balcony lobby after the rehearsal. There was a long table heaped with food and drink in the middle of the lobby, and there the Russian and American dancers animatedly swapped information about their trade, chattering in snatches of English, Russian and French but communicating mainly by gesture—their hands swooping about in the air to describe steps and choreography in the manner of fighter pilots in a bull session showing what their planes had done. Off to one side, near a staircase, one of the New York City Ballet's ballerinas stood weeping, because she felt she had not performed as well as she should have. At the opposite side, Balanchine and Lavrovsky were to be seen in the center of a small group, smiling and talking vivaciously. It was well known that Balanchine and Lavrovsky had once been classmates at the Imperial Ballet School in St. Petersburg, and that this was a kind of reunion for them. As movie and still cameras focused on them and flash bulbs popped, they embraced and kissed each other heartily on the cheek. From a distance it looked like a tableau symbolizing the end of the Cold War and the kind of understanding and mutual affection that cultural exchanges can bring. But what the two men were actually saying to each other, as those who understood Russian discovered on approaching the group, was that they had no use for each other's conception of art.

Lavrovsky, a chunky, shaggy-haired man given to blunt, forceful gestures, was heard saying as he beamed at Balanchine, "You know, in the Soviet Union work such as yours would be condemned as mere formalism, as inhuman."

To this, Balanchine—fully as forceful, under his elegance, as the other—replied, beaming back at Lavrovsky, "Well, I'm certainly not interested in using beautiful dance movement and gesture as merely a caption for some silly story."

Tolerantly, Lavrovsky said, "Ah, well, someday you'll come around to our way of doing things."

With equal assurance, Balanchine retorted, "What do you mean 'come around'? I went through all that and left it behind me long ago—thirty-five years ago, to be exact." This last, as both were fully aware, was a reference to the date when Balanchine had left the Soviet Union.

"Just one more, please!" a cameraman called, whereupon the two men embraced again and once more kissed each other mightily on the cheek.

After that visit, there was little reason to expect that the New York City Ballet would ever be invited to perform in the Soviet Union, or that Balanchine would go if he were invited—or, unlikeliest of all, if these eventualities should come about, that the company would enjoy a great triumph there.

Two years after that, in the fall of 1961, another Russian troupe came to the United States. This was the Kirov Ballet Company, from Leningrad —the troupe that, under the name of the Maryinsky, had been the company into which, as a youth, Balanchine had graduated at the end of his school training. The members of the Kirov company attended numerous performances of the New York City Ballet and several class demonstrations. Though they did not like everything equally, they were much more receptive than the Bolshoi to the Balanchine ballets they saw. It was noticeable that they seemed more sophisticated in their tastes than the Bolshoi and expressed themselves more freely; they mingled more readily with the Americans and did not appear to be quite so compulsive about echoing the party line in their aesthetic judgments. This difference reflected to some extent, in Balanchine's opinion, the greater cosmopolitanism of Leningrad, in comparison to which Moscow has always been more rigid and provincial in outlook; but it was also a reflection of the fact that, during the two years that had elapsed between the two visits, the thaw had been continuing in Russia's intellectual and cultural life. It was ceasing to be treason to be interested in Western art forms, and it was conceivable even to like some.

Following this, increased speculation was heard about the possibility of a Russian tour by the New York City Ballet. It began to seem vaguely possible, then expedient, and then, in the way many projects have of gaining momentum, an absolute must—a solution, somehow to all the State Department's unsolved problems. The State Department was in favor of it; the impresario Hurok favored it, so he could have a *quid pro quo* to offer Russia in connection with his bargaining to bring the Bolshoi back to the United States for a second time; the press wanted it because it seemed like a great story. Everybody assumed that Balanchine would naturally be eager to go and that he must feel that his life was not really complete until he had revealed to his Russian compatriots what he had achieved, and gained their approval of it. Well, possibly. But if Balanchine did feel that way, under his guarded exterior, he certainly did not show it. Profoundly and strenuously anti-Communist in his politics and in his entire orientation, he kept saying that he would never go to Russia. At first, he asserted that the company also would not go. Later, as all the various intangible pressures increased, he could be heard to declare that the company might go, if the State Department wanted it to, but that it could go without him. By the spring of 1962, he was becoming less firm. By then it had begun to seem, as the Marxists might put it, an absolute historical necessity that the New York City Ballet be transported five thousand miles to the land of Lenin and dialectical materialism to show that Americans were just as capable as the Russians in the production of fantasy and enchantment. Once this assumption was granted, and the corollary assumption that all this was somehow relevant to the cementing of peace and amity between the two countries, then it was unthinkable that the New York company should go without Balanchine. That would have been a mortal insult. Balanchine was made to see that his duty as an American citizen was to go back to Russia, and he acquiesced.

An eight weeks' tour was planned. Preceding the Russian tour there would be a five weeks' tour of Europe. In negotiations with the State Department the company's administrators had insisted that this be part of the arrangement, in order to provide the company with as many weeks of work as possible. This is an abiding factor every year in the company's considerations: how to put together enough weeks of work every year to keep the dancers alive. The European tour went exceedingly well, though its beginning, which was at Hamburg, was disastrous. There, the singers, who had been picked up in Germany to perform *Liebeslieder Walzer* with the company, turned out to be incompetent. Hardly had the performance commenced when the audience began to laugh and to applaud sarcastically. The dancers, appalled, could not at first understand what was happening; then it became clear that it was the singing, not the ballet or the dancing, which was being ridiculed. Needless to say, though, *Liebeslieder,* one of the loveliest romantic ballets ever made, never got a chance to cast its hypnotic spell. After that, *Liebeslieder* was dropped from the repertory for the rest of the tour, which was a pity.

In Hamburg also there occurred, the next day, a grave accident.

Jacques d'Amboise and Victoria Simon were struck by a streetcar in front of the theatre. Both were seriously injured. D'Amboise was not able to dance again until the middle of the Russian engagement, about eight weeks later, and even then had not recovered his full strength.

Despite these setbacks the company, as a whole, looked magnificent during the European preliminaries to the Russian tour that was to be, whether Balanchine saw it that way or not, the main event. The London *Times* printed in September two reports on it from Zurich. A theme of the *Times'* reports, as well as those of other British reviewers who made the trip to the Continent to see the New York City Ballet in action, was what a shame it was, verging on the scandalous, that so many years had gone by without London's powers-that-be in the realm of ballet making the effort necessary to arrange for an appearance of the New York company there. Meanwhile the New York City Ballet was off to Russia. "The Russian ballet world will certainly be startled," wrote the *Times*. "One hopes it will also be enchanted, for America, and perhaps the western world, is sending what is probably its strongest cultural ambassador."

On the evening of October 6 the plane carrying Balanchine and the ninety other members of the New York City Ballet organization landed at Sheremetyevo Airport in Moscow. A host of dignitaries and officials were waiting to greet the party. There were speeches and an interview for Radio Moscow. "Welcome to Moscow, home of the classic ballet!" the interviewer said to Balanchine.

"I beg your pardon," replied Balanchine. "Russia is the home of romantic ballet. The home of classic ballet is now America."

Among the crowd present at the airport was Balanchine's brother, Andrei, who was now the leading Georgian composer and of high repute throughout the Soviet Union. It was their first meeting in forty-three years. The two embraced warmly. Balanchine was quite surprised to find that he was several inches taller than his brother. "He's short," Balanchine subsequently remarked, when asked by an acquaintance to describe what his brother was like. "He's a very short brother." The two men had not much chance to talk at the airport, but they spent much time together in succeeding days. They had never corresponded during their long separation, but each had been aware of the main facts of the other's life. Andrei was the only one of the immediate family left alive in Russia. Their father had died

In Moscow—Balanchine with members of his company.

in 1937 at the age of seventy-six, their mother, also at an advanced age, just a few years ago. Balanchine had been informed of these deaths at the time they had happened. He had kept in touch with his mother, and for years after his departure from Russia had sent her food parcels from time to time, until the authorities put an end to all private exchanges between Russia and the outside world. Their sister, Tamara, was also dead. She was the one whom Balanchine had accompanied on the day she tried out for the Imperial Ballet School in St. Petersburg that day when, to his surprise and dismay, they had accepted him instead. Turned down by the school then, she had tried again the following year and had been admitted but was dropped at the end of her probationary year. After going to the Caucasus with her parents, she had become an architect and returned to Leningrad. She was killed during a German air raid in World War II. From his brother, Balanchine also learned the details of how his father had died, which he had not known. His father, it seemed, had developed gangrene in one leg and was told that an amputation was required in order to save his life. "What?" he answered, "I, Meliton Balanchivadze, stump about on one leg? Never!"

"But it's absolutely necessary. If you don't have an operation, you'll be dead within two days."

"So be it then," his father said lightly, with a shrug of his shoulders. "Death is a beautiful girl, who is going to come and take me in her arms. I look forward to the experience." Two days later he died. This account, as Balanchine heard it from his brother, made a deep impression on him, for it seemed so in keeping with his memories of his father's character.

The company was to open at the Bolshoi three days after their arrival in Moscow—the first American ballet company ever to appear on that stage. Then, for the bulk of their three weeks' Moscow engagement, they would shift over to the Palace of Congresses in the Kremlin, an immense theatre seating six thousand people, which is well over twice as many as the Bolshoi holds, and with a far larger stage. A new glass and concrete building, rather like the halls recently constructed in New York's Lincoln Center, it is one of the few pieces of modern architecture to be seen in Moscow, and makes a curious contrast with the dominant Slavic medieval style of the Kremlin buildings around it. During this time the company would have an interlude of one more performance at the Bolshoi in order to free the Palace of Congresses for the scheduled celebration of the 150th anniversary of Napoleon's retreat from Moscow, and the company's final performance of the engagement would also be given in the more glamorous Bolshoi. All seats for all the performances had been sold out in advance.

The repertory brought to Russia consisted of eighteen ballets, out of which five different programs were made up. The program for the opening night, October 9, was *Serenade,* Jerome Robbins' *Interplay, Agon* and *Western Symphony.* In the audience that night were the Foreign Minister, the Minister of Culture, the American Ambassador and numerous other dignitaries and functionaries. It was a boiled-shirt, bureaucratic audience, and it responded bureaucratically—with politeness, tinged with puzzlement and suspicion. They might not know much about art, the bureaucrats in that opening night audience, but they knew, down to the least tittle, what they were supposed to like, and in ballet it was not this—not these stark or wispy bits of nothing, with no story and no scenery and, except for the last ballet, the simplest of costumes.

The critics next day expounded officially the response the audience had made manifest. To be sure, the company was recognized immediately as an extraordinarily brilliant ensemble, who had mastered to a point of virtuosity the classic technique. In *Izvestia* Aram Khachaturian wrote of "the impeccable classic technique of which the artists are in brilliant possession." And the Soviet choreographer Rostislav Zakharov wrote: "Their strict discipline, precision and deep sense of the musical rhythm, which is often very intricate, combined with a fine classic dance technique, produce a highly gratifying impression. George Balanchine, the company's artistic director, has managed to instill in the young dancers an exacting attitude toward their art." Also recognized from the first was Balanchine's remarkable choreographic abilities and ingenuity, but his conception of art was deplored. What a sad waste of talent and effort! "G. Balanchine in his creative practice adheres to the principle of plotlessness," wrote Khachaturian. "This principle is foreign to Soviet artists and spectators. Without an idea, without a subject, there cannot be true emotional art." One critic went so far as to call Balanchine a fanatic who had frivolously sacrificed ballet's great tradition to his own vision of the dance.

All this was just about what one might have predicted. What no one had expected, though, was what happened subsequently. In the huge Palace of Congresses, one began to be aware quite early in the engagement of a sense of growing interest on the part of the audience, a sort of deepened hush of concentration. Then spontaneous murmurs of appreciation began to be heard here and there which grew, one evening, into an outburst of enthusiasm. The breakthrough came quite suddenly. John Martin, who had accompanied the New York City Ballet's party to Russia, wrote back to the *New York Times* that the point where the tide of understanding turned was with the first presentation of the Bizet *Symphony in C*. "Though the program had opened with the 'Raymonda Variations,' received in all but stony silence," he wrote, "the Bizet work brought forth not only applause throughout and repeated curtain calls at the end but also rhythmic cries of 'Bal-an-chine' until the choreographer was forced to come forward and bow his acknowledgment." Martin thought that a possible explanation for the audience reaction might have been that the frank titling of this ballet as a symphony eliminated all possibility of confusion as to whether or not it had a plot or subject to be puzzled over. Be that as it may, nearly all Russian critics who saw it were to agree that *Symphony in C* was sheer joy—"a life-affirming" ballet, as Golovashenko hailed it, "a true festival of dancing . . . agile and light, diversified and wonderfully harmonious." Even Petipa, wrote one, could not have invented such a breath-taking display of classical choreography as Balanchine had done in this work.

After that night, regardless of whatever the critics might write, whether

in praise or blame—and the critics would always have their doubts and reservations and dutiful scruples—the spectators were unequivocal in their enthusiasm. Night after night excitement was sustained at a high pitch. Now nearly every ballet in the repertory went over well, including those which were supposed to be the most difficult and alien. *Agon* made a great impression whenever given. Undoubtedly the biggest surprise of all was the tumultuous favor which *Episodes* won from the time of its first presentation. In New York, as Martin recalled, this ballet, "perhaps the most puzzling avant-garde work in the repertory," had not always fared too well; many Balanchine fans in America found the style of dance, with its distortions and strange, impersonal manipulations, and Webern's twelve-tone music disconcerting and unpalatable. But here in Moscow there were storms of applause between each of the individual sections. Balanchine was particularly pleased that the Muscovites did not laugh during the brief "Five Pieces" section; in New York during that part, with its curious dramas compressed into just a few seconds of time, there are often nervous titters to be heard.

In discussing the New York City Ballet, the Russians noted, generally with approval, that the company had succeeded in abolishing the star system—the cult of personality. In practice, spectators soon developed their own favorites among the dancers. Probably the most admired were Allegra Kent, who, one critic said, had something of the flavor of Ulanova, and Edward Villella. The Russians did not have the opportunity to see Diana

Adams and Jacques d'Amboise at their best, because of the effect of injuries and disabilities. Arthur Mitchell won everybody's favor. As the one Negro in the company, he was naturally the subject of special interest to the Russians, but beyond that, they much admired the way he moved and carried himself. Among the lesser soloists there was praise for Mimi Paul and Suki Schorer. The latter reminded the Russians of the Bolshoi's Ekaterina Maximova.

The greatest ovations nightly were always for the choreographer. They called for him until he appeared. Then they would often shout their thanks and gratitude: *"Spa-si-bo! Spa-si-bo!"* Balanchine seemed at first delighted, even euphoric, at the reception. Some of the members of the company remarked that they had never before seen him so ready to take a curtain call. But even then he was, one may gather, in a complicated state of emotions, a more complicated state than, perhaps, he himself realized. There was one evening when Balanchine stood in the wings at the end of the performance, making no move to go forward, while the applause for him went on and on. Francisco Moncion, who was nearby, said, "Mr. Balanchine, they're calling for you. Aren't you going to take a bow?"

Balanchine turned a haggard look on him and said, "Well, what if I were dead!" And he did not appear.

During his stay in Moscow, Balanchine did not go about the city much for pleasure. What he saw of Moscow, under the bleak October skies, he did not like; this was hardly surprising, for nobody who has been brought up in Leningrad finds Moscow appealing. He felt that he was not there for his own amusement or edification, but to fulfill a duty; so he put it, anyway. Whatever the American Embassy asked of him, he did. He gave interviews to the press and made whatever appearances were required, no matter how much time they took. Daily he conducted a company class, which many dancers and teachers from the Bolshoi attended. The Russians recorded some of these sessions on 16 millimeter film for future study. There was considerable amazement expressed by some of the Russian teachers, as they watched his company's classes, as to how he got human bodies to move in such complicated yet harmonious patterns. In the detailed technical analyses and appreciations made by the Russians, the American dancers always rated the highest commendation for their clean-cut footwork; if they had any outstanding common fault, the Russians felt, it was that they did not work enough on developing the lyrical and expressive use of their arms and shoulders. In return for Balanchine's efforts, the Bolshoi school put on a demonstration class for him and the company. It was conducted by Elizaveta Gerdt, now a woman of over seventy, who had been Balanchine's favorite ballerina when he was a boy, and the wife of his revered teacher, Andreyanov.

One evening, while in Moscow, Balanchine was excited to discover that a new ballet by the man who had been his first choreographic inspiration—Kasyan Goleizovsky—was being performed. Goleizovsky, after languishing in obscurity for a long time, had in post-Stalinist years been reinstated. Balanchine went to see a rehearsal of the ballet—*Scriabiniana*, it was called—but was disappointed. It seemed to contain nothing new— just stereotyped repetitions of ideas which forty years ago had seemed daring. He had intended to call on Goleizovsky, but after seeing this ballet could not bring himself to do so. If he met Goleizovsky, he would have to say he had seen his work, and he knew that he would not be able to bring himself to praise it, because he is incapable by nature of feigning an enthusiasm he does not feel. In addition, he found himself most reluctant to spoil his

Members of the New York City Ballet taking their daily class while in Russia. This photograph is taken at a rehearsal hall in Leningrad — one that Balanchine himself had rehearsed in as a boy.

cherished memories of the magnificent young Goleizovsky by seeing him as he would look now. He left Moscow without calling on him.

Near the end of the company's engagement in Moscow the Cuban crisis erupted; the United States and the Soviet Union were suddenly at the brink of war over the Soviet missile emplacements in Cuba. On October 29, when the company was scheduled to give its closing performance in Moscow, the crisis was at its peak. The American Embassy issued a warning to the company that demonstrations could be expected, and it was rehearsed in the procedures that were to be taken if trouble broke out in the theatre. There were, in fact, demonstrations at the Bolshoi that night, but not of the sort that dancers would wish to fend off. That night the audience gave the New York City Ballet the greatest ovation, according to Bolshoi personnel, ever given at that theatre. It only ceased after Balanchine came forward and made a short speech, inviting those who wished to see more to follow the company to Leningrad. Outside the stage door a large crowd were gathered. Many of them had attended every one of the twenty-four performances given in Moscow. "Come back," they cried, as the company's bus started off for the hotel. "Come back, come back, come back!"

Early the first morning in Leningrad, Balanchine said eagerly to Nathalie Molostwoff, a Russian expatriate like himself, who is on the staff of the School of American Ballet and is one of his good friends, "Let's go see my old house!" Now he was in his home town, and for the first time seemed to find zest in looking about him. They went out to his old neighborhood and stood for a long time before the house. "It all looks much as I remember it," Balanchine said. Putting his finger to his forehead, he said, "But I didn't need to come here to be reminded of it. I've always had a picture of it right here." They went around the corner in search of the neighborhood church, where he had been taken every Sunday when he was small. That was changed. The building still stood, but its cross had been taken down, and it was now a factory. As for the great Cathedral of Our Lady of Kazan, for which his father had written chorales and where he had seen his uncle consecrated, that had been converted into Leningrad's Anti-God Museum. Balanchine did not have the heart to go in and see what it was like. He did manage to find that morning a small church that was still in use, and he went in, made his devotions and lit a candle to his patron

On the following pages, curtain call at the Maryinsky Theatre —
with Allegra Kent, after a performance of NIGHT SHADOW.

saint. In each city in Russia where the company stayed Balanchine managed
to find a church where he could practice his faith.

In Leningrad, the New York City Ballet had no initial coolness to
overcome. Here all was triumph, from the rise of the first curtain in the
lovely Kirov Theatre—the old Maryinsky, where Balanchine, as a boy of
eleven, had made his first appearance on any stage. This was the place, this
gold and royal blue jewel of a house, that always haunted his memory as
the ideal theatre. Many of his former classmates were in the audience that
first night to cheer for Balanchine and his company. "But," as Martin wrote,
"there was more involved in the evening's success than nostalgia and senti-
ment." The ballets made their own impression on a sensitive and aware
audience. In Leningrad, even the critics paid only a brief lip service to the
official line about plotless ballets being of necessity cold and inferior. The
intellectuals were by now very well aware of what Balanchine was driving
at and, coming as this did just at a time when an aesthetic revolution was
stirring against Socialist realism in all the arts, they were hit very hard by it.
One of the most important events of the whole Soviet tour was a meeting
with Balanchine which the choreographers of Leningrad requested. They
gathered around a table in a room next to the Ballet School's museum, a
room in which Balanchine had once taken classes, and listened intently as
he talked to them about the principles of his art. "Why should we do
Shakespeare?" he said. "Shakespeare's already done Shakespeare." Some of
the older choreographers seemed to be left in despair by Balanchine's words,
but the younger ones listened eagerly and they requested another meeting
with him, which was held two days later.

Another high point of the trip was a matinee to which the New York
City Ballet had invited the artists of the city—dancers, theatrical people,
painters, writers, students. At the end of that program, Konstantin Sergeyev,
the Kirov's artistic director, led ten young ballerinas of the Kirov Ballet
onto the stage, where they presented bouquets to each of the New York
company's leading dancers and to Balanchine. Sergeyev made a gracious
speech, proudly claiming Balanchine as a native of this city. Balanchine
accepted the honors being bestowed, on behalf not of himself, he said, but
of America and the city of New York.

By this time, the Russians—the Russian authorities, at any rate—seeing
Balanchine's success in their country, were picturing him as a sort of Prodigal
Son. Not that penitence was expected from him, but perhaps there might

Surrounded by the teachers of the ballet school in Leningrad.

be tears of joy and kinship and reconciliation, ending with Balanchine being picked up and tenderly wrapped in Father Russia's cloak. Politely but adamantly Balanchine rejected the role of the Prodigal Son. In his frontier-style garb—with string ties and pearl-button vests—which he wore most of the time during the tour, he looked more like someone out of *Western Symphony.* Every time he was hailed as a great fellow Russian, whose achievements were part of the great Russian culture, he would always interrupt the speaker to demur and, in the old-fashioned Russian he had learned as a boy in St. Petersburg, would insist that he was not a Russian, he was an American. In a certain fundamental way, perhaps, he showed himself never more Russian than those times when, resisting the flattery of his admiring hosts, he proclaimed himself an American through and through. To resist proffered affection is not an American trait. Describing Balanchine's response to the admiration of the Russians, Lincoln Kirstein afterward recalled the coronation scene in Eisenstein's *Ivan the Terrible.* "Do you remember that scene?" he said to the friend with whom he was talking. "Ivan is on his throne. The nobles bow down before him; they heap gold upon him. And he sits there, implacable—he is absolutely implacable." Lincoln Kirstein's reports are often as much descriptions of his own interior state of mind as of the outside, but in either case they are of interest.

Here Balanchine was, having what most observers would call the greatest triumph of his life, but he insisted that it meant nothing to him, and that it was of no great moment to him to be back in the country of his birth from which he had fled nearly forty years before. By now he had become so accustomed to concealing his feelings that perhaps he convinced himself that he was really feeling as little as he said. Yet those around him could see that he was visibly affected by what was happening, and seemed to be suffering from an increasing strain, of which the physical demands on his energy were only a part. He began to lose weight and look gaunt. And he began to have nightmares again, such as he had not had for years—night-

mares that he had lost his passport, that he had been thrown into prison, that he was suffocating. At last, he felt he could stand the strain no more. So when the company ended its two weeks' stay in Leningrad, instead of going on to Kiev with it, he flew back to the United States for a week's respite.

Balanchine rejoined the company in time to go on with it to Georgia, where it would scarcely have dared show up without him. As the son of Georgia's honored composer, he was treated as a Georgian national hero. Crowds mobbed him wherever he went. There were endless toasts to be drunk, all—as is the Georgian custom—from a brimming full glass, and there were endless flowery speeches. The only moments that Balanchine was

In the wings of the theatre at Leningrad, watching his company perform his ballets.

allowed to spend by himself were at his father's grave at Kutais. What the Georgians would have loved best, as they kept letting him know, would be to see him, as the son of Georgia's great composer, now do a ballet to Georgian music—to the music, for instance, of his own brother. Resisting this politely was something of a problem. He could hardly come out and say that he did not care for his brother's music, but it was not possible for him to praise it.

There was one harrowing evening Mrs. Molostwoff remembers when they had dinner at Andrei Balanchivadze's home in Tbilisi. All evening she had enjoyed seeing the warm family feeling and comradeship between the two reunited brothers. Then Andrei suggested that he would like to play some of his recent compositions for his brother, and put a record on the phonograph. During the next two hours Andrei played one record after another. Balanchine sat, with his head in his hands, looking down at the floor. Mrs. Molostwoff found the situation unbearable, and she found herself praying that Balanchine would say just one kind word to his brother about his music. But he said nothing, and at last Andrei, passing the awkwardness off with a jest, stopped the phonograph. Afterward, Mrs. Molostwoff berated Balanchine for his silence.

"Would it have hurt you so much to make some small compliment about his music?" she said.

"I couldn't," Balanchine replied, looking remorseful and unhappy. "I just couldn't."

So, crowned with laurels, Balanchine and the New York City Ballet returned early in December to New York. He rested and convalesced, recovering his strength and health, while the company prepared its annual pre-Christmas performance of *The Nutcracker;* and then Balanchine settled down to choreograph two new works for the forthcoming spring season.

THE ESSENTIAL TRADITION

For its rehearsals, the New York City Ballet uses the same studios as the School of American Ballet. These studios now occupy the upper floor of a two-story building at Eighty-third Street and Broadway, the Madison Avenue location having been given up in 1956. It is just four blocks north of the apartment where Balanchine lives, and he may go back and forth between the two places several times a day. As he walks briskly along Broadway, he is continually being greeted—by dancers in the company, young students of the school, ballet mothers on the way to pick up their children after class, and students and faculty of other ballet schools in the vicinity, of which there must be at least five. He responds with courtly bows left and right as he goes. The block containing the studios is the usual upper-Broadway mélange—a shoe store, a Schrafft's, a discount house, some apartment buildings, a delicatessen. The scene is one that might well perplex a visiting balletomane of another era—Degas, say, or Théophile Gautier, or Czar Alexander III, or Louis XIV—but once inside Balanchine's studios, watching a class or a rehearsal in progress in one of the large practice rooms, the visitor would feel himself quite at home. Degas's painter's eye would be as fascinated by what goes on here as it was by the compositions it caught at the Paris Opéra ballet three-quarters of a century ago. In their essential quality, ballet studios have changed less than most things in the three hundred years since the basic principles of ballet technique were worked out at the court of Louis XIV. To see Balanchine in this environment is to be reminded how much tradition means to him and how much a part of tradition he is, for all his contemporaneity and his innovations—to see him take his place in a line of ballet masters extending back in time through Petipa, and Didelot before him, to Noverre and Lully. One discerns Balanchine's traditionalism most clearly, perhaps, in his attitude toward his school, for the curriculum he has established is much like the one he went through as a boy in St. Petersburg. That, in turn, though it stressed accelerated tempos and bravura movements, was much like the system of training that

Teaching class at the School of American Ballet — as recorded by Henri Cartier-Bresson in this and the photographs on the following pages. The group being taught are the C Class, advanced students but not professionals.

Didelot had brought from France to Russia a hundred years before. Some of the teachers Balanchine employs—such as Felia Doubrovska and Pierre Vladimirov, two of the last great dancers of the Imperial Ballet, whom the youthful Balanchine used to watch with awe on the stage of the Maryinsky Theatre—are themselves a living link with the past. Another of that rare breed, until his death in 1962, was Anatole Oboukhoff.

Balanchine himself teaches advanced student groups at times and conducts a class for the company between seasons. When he does, the other teachers often gather to watch. On one typical recent occasion, he was observed teaching an advanced class of about twenty pupils, several of them —Diana Adams and Violette Verdy, for instance—leading dancers of the New York City Ballet. Ballet stars never get to be too good to take lessons; they take them every day. For the space of an hour and a half, Balanchine worked this class intensively through the fundamental positions and steps that are the vocabulary of ballet; he walked about the room from one dancer to another, correcting now this one's stance in the fourth position, now that one's *arabesque,* and tossed off piquant comments to the group as he moved about. He was good-humored, agreeable, yet demanding. Praise from Balanchine is so rare as to be almost nonexistent. Instead, he holds before even the most superlative of his dancers a vision of perfection toward which they are expected to strive. Stopping before Diana Adams, who was wearing a plain black leotard, he sought to get her to increase the turnout of hips, legs, and feet that is the curiously satisfying basis of ballet technique. "Push the heel forward—more, still more! Open the hips!" he told her. Then, assuming a natural position, with toes pointed forward, he said to the group as a whole, "Anybody can stand like this. But when you force it, like this—" and he forced his toes and hips outward —"then you feel you've done something." With a smile, he told a small, very young-looking brunette in the second row, "Don't ask why it must be like this. Don't analyze. Just do it." He moved on to the movement known as *développé à la seconde*—a sidewise unfolding and extending of the leg that, he said, must be as elegantly continuous as the movement of an elephant's trunk, and he illustrated this with a gesture of the arm that at once made it uncannily both a leg and a trunk. Then the dancers went on to leaps, and he reminded them of how the upflung arms pull the body into the air, and of the composition they must make in space at the top of their leap, and of the crucial importance of coming down softly. He had them line up and go separately across the room in a sequence combining a gliding step, a leap, an intermediate step and another leap. When Violette Verdy had done this, he called her back and had her try it again, telling her that she must push forward on the glide, not rest on it. Miss Verdy, who was dressed in a bright-blue sweater and black tights, with her golden hair in a shining topknot, nodded eagerly as she listened. As she went through it again, Balanchine cried at the start of her second leap, "Stay up in the air!" and, incredibly, she seemed to obey this impossible command, hovering momentarily in space like a hummingbird. There were gasps of appreciation from the other dancers. Balanchine nodded, the faintest trace of a smile on his lips. "Tha-at's right," he said. "You're getting it."

While working on this book, I once complained to Balanchine about the comparative scarcity of documentary materials pertaining to his life. I had just been reading some biographies of literary figures—abounding in quotations from the subjects' diaries, letters, journals and memoirs—and, as a biographer, I was feeling deprived. Balanchine had never journalized, had written perhaps fewer letters than the number of ballets he had choreographed, and had kept no scrapbooks to preserve what other people had had to say about him. Balanchine listened to my complaint, and then replied, "You should think of your task as if you were writing the biography of a race horse. A race horse doesn't keep a diary." This is quite close to the way he regards himself, as one of a highly developed physical breed, whose inner life is of little interest to others.

In the course of doing this book, I had many conversations with Balanchine, though very few formal interviews. This is not what is called an authorized biography. When I was in doubt about some point or other, I would question Balanchine closely and he responded patiently and graciously, but I was not expected to submit the manuscript to him for approval. It goes to press without his seeing it. I must express my thankfulness to him for not interfering. He never once tried to suggest what I should say or how I should evaluate or present the facts of his life. "It's *your* biography, not mine," he said. Ultimately, I sought to treat the materials of his life with the same detachment and objectivity as he treats his dancers while choreographing a ballet. I think I learned some lessons from him in this respect.

During the last few years I watched him choreographing many ballets. In this engrossing occupation I spent hundreds of hours in his studio. These hours were the most important research I did for this book.

For the rest of the research it was the familiar procedure of interviewing hundreds of people, reading all the references that could be found, sifting, evaluating, and then setting it down on paper. I have tried to indicate my major sources and references in the body of the text, so as to avoid the necessity for footnotes. I will not try to list the several hundred people whom I interviewed or who assisted me in one way or another, but I would like at this time to thank them collectively for their kindness, patience, and interest. Many contributed perceptive insights as well as information. I am most grateful to them, and beholden.

B. T.

A Chronological List of Balanchine's Ballets

1920– As a youth, before leaving Russia at the age of twenty, Balanchine choreo-
1924 graphed a number of works, including *La Nuit,* to music by Anton Rubinstein;
A Poem, to music by Fibich; *Valse,* to a composition of his own; *Enigma,* to
Arensky's music; *Marche Funèbre* by Chopin; a dance to one of Ravel's
Valses Nobles et Sentimentales; and dances to the music of Scriabin and
other composers. In addition he choreographed a mimed action to Alexander
Blok's poem *The Twelve;* a pantomime ballet to the Cocteau-Milhaud *Le
Boeuf sur le Toit;* and did dances for the State Opera's production of
Coq d'Or and for theatrical productions of Shaw's *Caesar and Cleopatra,* and
Toller's *The Broken Bow.* His duets were generally danced by himself, with
Alexandra Danilova as partner, or with Lydia Ivanova. In the larger works
they were joined by, among others, V. Kostrovitskaya, H. Stoukolkine, Tamara
Gevergeva, Leonid Lavrovsky, and Pyotr Gusev.

1925 LE CHANT DU ROSSIGNOL
MUSIC: *Igor Stravinsky.* DECOR AND COSTUMES: *Henri Matisse.*
PREMIÈRE: *June 17, 1925, Gaîté Lyrique Théâtre, Paris, by Les Ballets Russes
de Diaghilev.*
CAST: *Alicia Markova, Lydia Sokolova, Serge Grigoriev, Nicolas Kremnev,
et al.*

BARABAU
MUSIC: *Vittorio Rieti.* DECOR: *Maurice Utrillo.* LIBRETTO: *Vittorio Rieti.*
PREMIÈRE: *Dec. 11, 1925, The Coliseum, London, by Les Ballets Russes de
Diaghilev.*
CAST: *Léon Woizikowsky, Serge Lifar, Alice Nikitina, Alexandra Danilova,
Tamara Gevergeva, et al.*

1926 ROMEO AND JULIET ENTR'ACTE
MUSIC: *Constant Lambert.* PAINTING: *Max Ernst and Joan Miró.*
PREMIÈRE: *May 4, 1926, Théâtre de Monte Carlo.*
CAST: *Tamara Karsavina, Serge Lifar, et al.*

LA PASTORALE
MUSIC: *Georges Auric.* DECOR AND COSTUMES: *Pedro Pruna.* LIBRETTO: *Boris
Kochno.*
PREMIÈRE: *May 29, 1926, Théâtre Sarah Bernhardt, Paris, by Les Ballets
Russes de Diaghilev.*

CAST: *Felia Doubrovska, Alexandra Danilova, Serge Lifar, Léon Woizikowsky, et al.*

JACK IN THE BOX
MUSIC: *Erik Satie.* DECOR AND COSTUMES: *André Derain*
PREMIÈRE: *June 3, 1926, Théâtre Sarah Bernhardt, Paris, by Les Ballets Russes de Diaghilev.*
CAST: *Alexandra Danilova, Lubov Tchernicheva, Felia Doubrovska, Stanislas Idzikovsky, et al.*

THE TRIUMPH OF NEPTUNE
MUSIC: *Lord Berners.* DECOR: *Prince A. Shervashidze.*
PREMIÈRE: *Dec. 3, 1926, Lyceum, London, by Les Ballets Russes de Diaghilev.*
CAST: *Alexandra Danilova, Lubov Tchernicheva, Lydia Sokolova, Serge Lifar, George Balanchine, Constantin Tcherkas, et al.*

1927   ## LA CHATTE
MUSIC: *Henri Sauguet. Architectural and sculptural constructions by Gabo and Pevsner.* LIBRETTO: *Sobeka (Boris Kochno), based on a fable by Aesop.*
PREMIÈRE: *April 30, 1927, Monte Carlo, by Les Ballets Russes de Diaghilev.*
CAST: *Serge Lifar, Olga Spessivtseva, et al.*

1928   ## APOLLO (originally APOLLON MUSAGETE)
MUSIC: *Igor Stravinsky.* DECOR AND COSTUMES: *André Bauchant. (In 1929, Gabrielle Chanel designed new costumes.)*
PREMIÈRE: *June 12, 1928, Théâtre Sarah Bernhardt, Paris, by Les Ballets Russes de Diaghilev.*
CAST: *Serge Lifar, Lubov Tchernicheva, Felia Doubrovska, Alice Nikitina, et al. (Alexandra Danilova alternated with Nikitina as Terpsichore).*

THE GODS GO A-BEGGING
MUSIC: *Georg Friedrich Handel, arranged by Sir Thomas Beecham.* DECOR: *Léon Bakst, originally used for* Daphnis et Chloé. LIBRETTO: *Sobeka (Boris Kochno).*
PREMIÈRE: *July 16, 1928, His Majesty's Theatre, London, by Les Ballets Russes de Diaghilev.*
CAST: *Alexandra Danilova, Lubov Tchernicheva, Felia Doubrovska, Léon Woizikowsky, Constantin Tcherkas, et al.*

1929   ## LE BAL
MUSIC: *Vittorio Rieti.* DECOR: *Giorgio de Chirico.* LIBRETTO: *Boris Kochno.*
PREMIÈRE: *May 7, 1929, Monte Carlo, by Les Ballets Russes de Diaghilev.*
CAST: *Alexandra Danilova, Felia Doubrovska, Eugenia Lipkovska, Anton Dolin, André Bobrov, Léon Woizikowsky, George Balanchine, Serge Lifar, et al.*

PRODIGAL SON (or LE FILS PRODIGUE)
MUSIC: *Serge Prokofiev.* DECOR AND COSTUMES: *Georges Rouault.* LIBRETTO: *Boris Kochno.*
PREMIÈRE: *May 20, 1929, Théâtre Sarah Bernhardt, Paris, by Les Ballets Russes de Diaghilev.*
CAST: *Serge Lifar, Léon Woizikowsky, Anton Dolin, Felia Doubrovska, et al.*

1930   AUBADE
        MUSIC: *Francis Poulenc*. DECOR AND COSTUMES: *Angeles Ortiz.*
        PREMIÈRE: *Jan. 21, 1930, Théâtre des Champs-Élysées, Paris, by Les Ballets
        Russes Vera Nemtchinova.*

1931   JOSEF-LEGENDE
        MUSIC: *Richard Strauss*. DECOR AND COSTUMES: *Kjeld Abell*
        PREMIÈRE: *The Royal Theatre, Copenhagen, by the Royal Danish Ballet.*
        CAST: *Ulla Poulsen, Børge Ralov, et al.*

1932   LE BOURGEOIS GENTILHOMME
        MUSIC: *Richard Strauss*. DECOR: *Alexandre Benois.*
        PREMIÈRE: *Mar. 3, 1932, Monte Carlo, by the Ballets Russes de Monte Carlo.*
        CAST: *Tamara Toumanova, David Lichine, et al.*

        LA CONCURRENCE
        MUSIC: *Georges Auric*. CURTAIN, DECOR AND COSTUMES: *André Derain.*
        LIBRETTO: *André Derain.*
        PREMIÈRE: *April 12, 1932, Théâtre de Monte Carlo, by the Ballets Russes de
        Monte Carlo.*
        CAST: *Léon Woizikowsky, Tamara Toumanova, Lubov Rostova, Tatiana
        Riabouchinska, et al.*

        COTILLON
        MUSIC: *Emmanuel Chabrier*. DECOR AND COSTUMES: *Christian Bérard.*
        LIBRETTO: *Boris Kochno.*
        PREMIÈRE: *April 12, 1932, Théâtre de Monte Carlo, by the Ballets Russes de
        Monte Carlo.*
        CAST: *Tamara Toumanova, David Lichine, Léon Woizikowsky, et al.*

1933   SONGES
        MUSIC: *Darius Milhaud*. DECOR AND COSTUMES: *André Derain.* LIBRETTO:
        André Derain.
        PREMIÈRE: *June 7, 1933, Théâtre des Champs-Élysées, Paris, by Les Ballets
        1933.*
        CAST: *Tamara Toumanova, Roman Jasinsky, et al.*

        MOZARTIANA
        MUSIC: *Mozart-Tchaikovsky (Suite No. 4)*. DECOR AND COSTUMES: *Christian
        Bérard.*
        PREMIÈRE: *June 7, 1933, Théâtre des Champs-Élysées, Paris, by Les Ballets
        1933.*
        CAST: *Tamara Toumanova, Roman Jasinsky, et al.*

        THE SEVEN DEADLY SINS (LES SEPT PECHES CAPITAUX),
        Ballet-Cantata.
        MUSIC: *Kurt Weill*. DECOR: *Caspar Neher.* LIBRETTO: *Berthold Brecht.*
        PREMIÈRE: *June 7, 1933, Théâtre des Champs-Elysées, Paris, by Les Ballets
        1933.*
        CAST: *Tilly Losch, Lotte Lenya, et al.*

ERRANTE

MUSIC: *Franz Schubert, transcribed by Franz Liszt, orchestrated by Charles Koechlin.* DECOR AND COSTUMES: *Pavel Tchelitchev.* LIBRETTO: *George Balanchine and Pavel Tchelitchev.*
PREMIÈRE: *June 10, 1933, Théâtre des Champs-Élysées, Paris, by Les Ballets 1933.*
CAST: *Tilly Losch, Roman Jasinsky, et al.*

FASTES

MUSIC: *Henri Sauget.* DECOR AND COSTUMES: *André Derain.*
PREMIÈRE: *June 10, 1933, Théâtre des Champs-Élysées, Paris, by Les Ballets 1933.*
CAST: *Tilly Losch, Tamara Toumanova, Roman Jasinsky, et al.*

LES VALSES DE BEETHOVEN

MUSIC: *Ludwig von Beethoven.* DECOR AND COSTUMES: *Emilio Terry.*
PREMIÈRE: *June 10, 1933, Théâtre des Champs-Élysées, Paris, by Les Ballets 1933.*

1934   ### ALMA MATER

MUSIC: *Kay Swift, arranged by Morton Gould.* DECOR: *Eugene Dunkel.*
COSTUMES: *John Held, Jr.* LIBRETTO: *Edward M. M. Warburg.*
PREMIÈRE: *Dec. 6, 1934, Hartford, Conn., by Producing Company of the School of American Ballet. Presented by the American Ballet, March 1, 1935, at the Adelphi Theatre, N.Y.*
CAST: *Leyda Anchutina, Ruthanna Boris, Gisella Caccialanza, Kathryn Mullowny, Heidi Vosseler, William Dollar, Charles Laskey, Eugene Loring, et al.*

1935   ### REMINISCENCE

MUSIC: *Benjamin Godard, orchestrated by Henry Brand.* DECOR AND COSTUMES: *Serge Soudeikine.*
PREMIÈRE: *Mar. 1, 1935, Adelphi Theatre, New York, by the American Ballet.*
CAST: *Leyda Anchutina, Ruthanna Boris, Gisella Caccialanza, Elena de Rivas, Holly Howard, Annabelle Lyon, Elise Reiman, William Dollar, Paul Haakon, et al.*

SERENADE

MUSIC: *Peter Tchaikovsky.* DECOR: *Gaston Longchamp.* COSTUMES: *Jean Lurçat.*
PREMIÈRE: *Mar. 1, 1935, Adelphi Theatre, New York, by the American Ballet.*
CAST: *Leyda Anchutina, Ruthanna Boris, Gisella Caccialanza, Kathryn Mullowny, William Dollar, Charles Laskey, et al.*

DREAMS

MUSIC: *George Antheil.* DECOR AND COSTUMES: *André Derain.* LIBRETTO: *André Derain.*
PREMIÈRE: *Mar. 4, 1935, Adelphi Theatre, New York, by the American Ballet.*
CAST: *Leyda Anchutina, Ruthanna Boris, Paul Haakon, et al.*

TRANSCENDENCE

MUSIC: *Franz Liszt, orchestrated by George Antheil.* DECOR: *Gaston Long-*

champ. COSTUMES: *Franklin Watkins.* LIBRETTO: *Lincoln Kirstein.*
PREMIÈRE: *Mar. 5, 1935, Adelphi Theater, New York, by the American Ballet.*
CAST: *Elise Reiman, William Dollar, et al.*

1936   THE BAT
MUSIC: *Johann Strauss (Overture to* Die Fledermaus). COSTUMES: *Keith Martin.* LIBRETTO: *Lincoln Kirstein.*
PREMIÈRE: *May 20, 1936, Metropolitan Opera House, New York, by the American Ballet.*
CAST: *Leyda Anchutina, Rabana Hasburgh, Annabelle Lyon, Lew Christensen, Charles Laskey, et al.*

ORPHEUS AND EURYDICE
MUSIC: *Christoph Willibald Gluck.* DECOR AND COSTUMES: *Pavel Tchelitchev.*
PREMIÈRE: *May 22, 1936, Metropolitan Opera House, New York, by the American Ballet.*
CAST: *Lew Christensen, Daphne Vane, William Dollar, et al.*

MAGIC
MUSIC: *Wolfgang Amadeus Mozart.* DECOR: *Pavel Tchelitchev.*
PREMIÈRE: *Hartford, Conn., by the American Ballet.*

1937   LE BAISER DE LA FEE
MUSIC: *Igor Stravinsky ("inspired by the music of Tchaikovsky").* COSTUMES: *Alice Halicka.* LIBRETTO: *Igor Stravinsky (based on "The Virgin of the Lake").*
PREMIÈRE: *April 27, 1937, Metropolitan Opera House, by the American Ballet.*
CAST: *Kathryn Mullowny, Rabana Hasburgh, Gisella Caccialanza, Leyda Anchutina, William Dollar, Annabelle Lyon, et al.*

CARD GAME (or CARD PARTY)
MUSIC: *Igor Stravinsky.* DECOR AND COSTUMES: *Irene Sharaff.* LIBRETTO: *Igor Stravinsky and M. Malaieff.*
PREMIÈRE: *April 27, 1937, Metropolitan Opera House, by the American Ballet.*
CAST: *William Dollar, Lew Christensen, Annabelle Lyon, Charles Laskey, Leyda Anchutina, et al.*

1941   BALUSTRADE
MUSIC: *Igor Stravinsky (Concerto for Violin and Orchestra).* DECOR AND COSTUMES: *Pavel Tchelitchev.*
PREMIÈRE: *Jan. 22, 1941, Fifty-first Street Theatre, New York, by Original Ballet Russe.*
CAST: *Tamara Toumanova, Paul Petroff, Roman Jasinsky, et al.*

CONCERTO BAROCCO
MUSIC: *Johann Sebastian Bach (Double Violin Concerto in D Minor).* DECOR AND COSTUMES: *Eugene Berman.*
PREMIÈRE: *May 28, 1941, Hunter College Playhouse, New York, by the American Ballet.*
CAST: *Marie-Jeanne, Mary Jane Shea, William Dollar, et al.*

BALLET IMPERIAL
MUSIC: *Peter Tchaikovsky (Piano Concerto No. 2 in G Major)*. DECOR AND COSTUMES: *Mstislav Doboujinsky*.
PREMIÈRE: *May 29, 1941, Hunter College Playhouse, New York, by the American Ballet.*
CAST: *Marie-Jeanne, Gisella Caccialanza, William Dollar, Nicholas Magallanes, Fred Danieli, et al.*

FANTASIA BRASILEIRA
MUSIC: *Francisco Mignone*. DECOR AND COSTUMES: *Erico Bianco*.
PREMIÈRE: *Lima, Peru, by the American Ballet.*

1942 PAS DE TROIS FOR PIANO AND TWO DANCERS
MUSIC: *Theodore Chanler*. COSTUMES: *Pavel Tchelitchev*.
PREMIÈRE: *May 10, 1942, Alvin Theatre, New York, "Music at Work" benefit program for Russian War Relief.*
CAST: *Mary Ellen Moylan, Nicholas Magallanes.*

CONCERTO
MUSIC: *Mozart (Concerto for Violin and Orchestra)*. DECOR AND COSTUMES: *Pavel Tchelitchev*.
PREMIÈRE: *Teatro Colón, Buenos Aires, Argentina, by the Ballet of the Teatro Colón.*
CAST: *Maria Ruanova, Yurek Shabelevsky, Metek Borovsky, et al.*

1944 DANSES CONCERTANTES
MUSIC: *Igor Stravinsky*. DECOR AND COSTUMES: *Eugene Berman*.
PREMIÈRE: *Sept. 10, 1944, New York City Center, by the Ballet Russe de Monte Carlo.*
CAST: *Alexandra Danilova, Frederic Franklin, et al.*

WALTZ ACADEMY
MUSIC: *Vittorio Rieti*. COSTUMES: *Alvin Colt*. DECOR: *Oliver Smith*.
PREMIÈRE: *Oct. 11, 1944, Metropolitan Opera House, by Ballet Theatre.*
CAST: *Nana Gollner, Nora Kaye, Janet Reed, John Kriza, et al.*

1945 PAS DE DEUX
MUSIC: *Peter Tchaikovsky (Sleeping Beauty entr'acte).*
PREMIÈRE: *Mar. 14, 1945, New York City Center, by the Ballet Russe de Monte Carlo.*
CAST: *Alexandra Danilova, Frederic Franklin.*

ELEGIE
MUSIC: *Igor Stravinsky.*
PREMIÈRE: *Nov. 5, 1945, Carnegie Hall, New York, by Advanced Students of the School of American Ballet.*

1946 NIGHT SHADOW (LA SONNAMBULA)
MUSIC: *Vittorio Rieti (arranged from music of Bellini)*. DECOR AND COSTUMES: *Dorothea Tanning.*

PREMIÈRE: *Feb. 27, 1946, New York City Center, by the Ballet Russe de Monte Carlo.*
CAST: *Alexandra Danilova, Nicholas Magallanes, Maria Tallchief, Ruthanna Boris, Robert Lindgren, Marie-Jeanne, et al.*

RAYMONDA (*Choreographed with Alexandra Danilova*).
MUSIC: *Alexander Glazunov.* DECOR AND COSTUMES: *Alexandre Benois.*
PREMIÈRE: *Mar. 12, 1946, New York City Center, by the Ballet Russe de Monte Carlo.*
CAST: *Alexandra Danilova, Nicholas Magallanes, Nikita Talin, Leon Danielian, Julia Horvath, Pauline Goddard, Yvonne Chouteau, Herbert Bliss, Marie-Jeanne, Maria Tallchief, Gertrude Tyven, et al.*

THE FOUR TEMPERAMENTS
MUSIC: *Paul Hindemith.* DECOR AND COSTUMES: *Kurt Seligmann.*
PREMIÈRE: *Nov. 20, 1946, Central High School of Needle Trades, New York, by Ballet Society.*
CAST: *Gisella Caccialanza, Georgia Hiden, Rita Karlin, Tanaquil LeClercq, Mary Ellen Moylan, Elise Reiman, Beatrice Tompkins, Todd Bolender, Lew Christensen, Fred Danieli, William Dollar, José Martinez, Francisco Moncion, et al.*

THE SPELLBOUND CHILD
MUSIC: *Maurice Ravel* (L'Enfant et les Sortilèges). DECOR AND COSTUMES: *Aline Bernstein.* POEM: *Colette.*
PREMIÈRE: *Nov. 20, 1946, Central High School of Needle Trades, New York, by Ballet Society.*
CAST: *Gisella Caccialanza, Ruth Gilbert, Georgia Hiden, Tanaquil LeClercq, Elise Reiman, Beatrice Tompkins, Paul d'Amboise, William Dollar, et al.*

1947 DIVERTIMENTO
MUSIC: *Alexei Haieff.*
PREMIÈRE: *Jan. 13, 1947, Hunter College Playhouse, New York, by Ballet Society.*
CAST: *Gisella Caccialanza, Tanaquil LeClercq, Mary Ellen Moylan, Elise Reiman, Beatrice Tompkins, Todd Bolender, Lew Christensen, Fred Danieli, Francisco Moncion, John Taras, et al.*

RENARD
MUSIC: *Igor Stravinsky.* DECOR AND COSTUMES: *Esteban Francés.* LIBRETTO: *Igor Stravinsky.*
PREMIÈRE: *Jan. 13, 1947, Hunter College Playhouse, New York, by Ballet Society.*
CAST: *Todd Bolender, Lew Christensen, Fred Danieli, John Taras, et al.*

SYMPHONY IN C (originally LE PALAIS DE CRISTAL)
MUSIC: *Georges Bizet.* DECOR AND COSTUMES: *Léonor Fini.*
PREMIÈRE: *July 28, 1947, Paris Opéra, by the Ballet de l'Opéra.*
CAST: *Lycette Darsonval, Tamara Toumanova, Micheline Bardin, Madeleine Lafon, Alexandre Kalioujny, Roger Ritz, Michel Renault, Max Bozzoni.*

FIRST NEW YORK PERFORMANCE: *Mar. 22, 1948*, as Symphony in C, *without decor.*

CAST: *Maria Tallchief, Tanaquil LeClercq, Nicholas Magallanes, Francisco Moncion, et al.*

SYMPHONIE CONCERTANTE

MUSIC: *Mozart (Symphonie Concertante in E Flat, K. 364).* COSTUMES AND DECOR: *James Stewart Morcom.*

PREMIÈRE: *Nov. 12, 1947, New York City Center, by the New York City Ballet.*

CAST: *Maria Tallchief, Tanaquil LeClercq, Dorothy Dushok, Ruth Gilbert, Georgia Hiden, Rita Karlin, Pat McBride, Irma Sandré, Todd Bolender, et al.*

THEME AND VARIATIONS

MUSIC: *Peter Tchaikovsky (Suite No. 3 for Orchestra).* DECOR AND COSTUMES: *Woodman Thompson.*

PREMIÈRE: *Nov. 26, 1947, New York City Center, by Ballet Theatre.*

CAST: *Alicia Alonso, Igor Youskevitch, et al.*

THE TRIUMPH OF BACCHUS AND ARIADNE (ballet-cantata)

MUSIC: *Vittorio Rieti.* DECOR AND COSTUMES: *Corrado Cagli.*

PREMIÈRE: *Feb. 9, 1948, New York City Center, by the New York City Ballet.*

CAST: *Lew Christensen, Nicholas Magallanes, Tanaquil LeClercq, Herbert Bliss, Marie-Jeanne, Charles Laskey, Francisco Moncion, Claudia Hall, Pat McBride, et al.*

ORPHEUS

MUSIC: *Igor Stravinsky.* DECOR AND COSTUMES: *Isamu Noguchi.*

PREMIÈRE: *April 28, 1948, New York City Center, by Ballet Society.*

CAST: *Nicholas Magallanes, Francisco Moncion, Maria Tallchief, Herbert Bliss, Tanaquil LeClercq, et al.*

PAS DE TROIS CLASSIQUE

MUSIC: *Ludwig Minkus (Paquita).* COSTUMES: *Pierre Balmain.*

PREMIÈRE: *1948, Monte Carlo, by the Grand Ballet of the Marquis de Cuevas.*

CAST: *Rosella Hightower, Marjorie Tallchief, André Eglevsky.*

1949   ## THE FIREBIRD

MUSIC: *Igor Stravinsky.* DECOR AND COSTUMES: *Marc Chagall.*

PREMIÈRE: *Nov. 27, 1949, New York City Center, by the New York City Ballet.*

CAST: *Maria Tallchief, Francisco Moncion, Pat McBride, et al.*

BOURREE FANTASQUE

MUSIC: *Emmanuel Chabrier.* DECOR AND COSTUMES: *Karinska.*

PREMIÈRE: *Dec. 1, 1949, New York City Center, by the New York City Ballet.*

CAST: *Tanaquil LeClercq, Maria Tallchief, Janet Reed, Jerome Robbins, Nicholas Magallanes, Herbert Bliss, et al.*

1950   ## PAS DE DEUX ROMANTIQUE

MUSIC: *Carl Maria von Weber.* COSTUMES: *Robert Stevenson.*

PREMIÈRE: *Mar. 3, 1950, New York City Center, by the New York City Ballet.*

CAST: *Janet Reed, Herbert Bliss.*

JONES BEACH (*Choreographed with Jerome Robbins*)
MUSIC: *Jurriaan Andriessen.* COSTUMES: *Swimsuits by Jantzen.*
PREMIÈRE: *Mar. 9, 1950, New York City Center, by the New York City Ballet.*
CAST: *Maria Tallchief, Melissa Hayden, Tanaquil LeClercq, Jerome Robbins, Nicholas Magallanes, Frank Hobi, William Dollar, et al.*

MAZURKA
MUSIC: *Mikhail Glinka* (A Life for the Tsar).
PREMIÈRE: *Nov. 30, 1950, New York City Center, by the New York City Ballet.*
CAST: *Janet Reed, Yurek Lazowski, Vida Brown, George Balanchine, Barbara Walczak, Harold Lang, Dorothy Dushok, Frank Hobi.*

SYLVIA: PAS DE DEUX
MUSIC: *Léo Delibes.* COSTUMES: *Karinska.*
PREMIÈRE: *Dec. 1, 1950, New York City Center, by the New York City Ballet.*
CAST: *Maria Tallchief, Nicholas Magallanes.*

TRUMPET CONCERTO
MUSIC: *Franz Joseph Haydn.* DECOR AND COSTUMES: *Vivienne Kernot.*
PREMIÈRE: *Sept. 14, 1950, Manchester, England, by the Sadler's Wells Theatre Ballet.*
CAST: *Svetlana Beriosova, David Poole, David Blair, Elaine Fifield, Pirmin Trecu, Maryon Lane, et al.*

1951   PAS DE TROIS
MUSIC: *Ludwig Minkus.* COSTUMES: *Karinska.*
PREMIÈRE: *Feb. 18, 1951, New York City Center, by the New York City Ballet.*
CAST: *Maria Tallchief, Nora Kaye, André Eglevsky.*

LA VALSE
MUSIC: *Maurice Ravel* (Valses Nobles et Sentimentales, *and* La Valse). COSTUMES: *Karinska.*
PREMIÈRE: *Feb. 20, 1951, New York City Center, by the New York City Ballet.*
CAST: *Diana Adams, Tanaquil LeClercq, Yvonne Mounsey, Patricia Wilde, Herbert Bliss, Frank Hobi, Nicholas Magallanes, Francisco Moncion, et al.*

CAPRICCIO BRILLANT
MUSIC: *Felix Mendelssohn.* COSTUMES: *Karinska.*
PREMIÈRE: *June 7, 1951, New York City Center, by the New York City Ballet.*
CAST: *Maria Tallchief, André Eglevsky, et al.*

A LA FRANCAIX
MUSIC: *Jean Françaix* (Serenade for Small Orchestra).
PREMIÈRE: *Sept. 11, 1951, New York City Center, by New York City Ballet.*
CAST: *Maria Tallchief, André Eglevsky, Janet Reed, Frank Hobi, Roy Tobias.*

TYL ULENSPIEGEL
MUSIC: *Richard Strauss.* DECOR AND COSTUMES: *Esteban Francés.*
PREMIÈRE: *Nov. 14, 1951, New York City Center, by the New York City Ballet.*
CAST: *Albert Grant, Susan Kovnat, Jerome Robbins, Ruth Sobotka, Brooks Jackson, Frank Hobi, Beatrice Tompkins, Tomi Worthham, et al.*

SWAN LAKE (ACT TWO)

MUSIC: *Peter Tchaikovsky.* DECOR AND COSTUMES: *Cecil Beaton.*
PREMIÈRE: *Nov. 20, 1951, New York City Center, by the New York City Ballet.*
CAST: *Maria Tallchief, André Eglevsky, et al.*

1952   CARACOLE

MUSIC: *Wolfgang Amadeus Mozart (Divertimento No. 15).* COSTUMES: *Christian Bérard.*
PREMIÈRE: *Feb. 19, 1952, New York City Center, by the New York City Ballet.*
CAST: *Diana Adams, Melissa Hayden, Tanaquil LeClercq, Maria Tallchief, Patricia Wilde, André Eglevsky, Jerome Robbins, Nicholas Magallanes, et al.*

BAYOU

MUSIC: *Virgil Thomson* (Acadian Songs and Dances). DECOR AND COSTUMES: *Dorothea Tanning.*
PREMIÈRE: *Feb. 21, 1952, New York City Center, by New York City Ballet.*
CAST: *Francisco Moncion, Doris Breckenridge, Melissa Hayden, Hugh Laing, Diana Adams, Herbert Bliss, et al.*

SCOTCH SYMPHONY

MUSIC: *Felix Mendelssohn (Symphony No. 3).* DECOR: *Horace Armistead.*
COSTUMES: *Karinska, David Ffolkes.*
PREMIÈRE: *Nov. 11, 1952, New York City Center, by the New York City Ballet.*
CAST: *Maria Tallchief, André Eglevsky, Patricia Wilde, Frank Hobi, et al.*

METAMORPHOSES

MUSIC: *Paul Hindemith* (Symphonic Metamorphoses on Themes of Carl Maria von Weber). COSTUMES: *Karinska.*
PREMIÈRE: *Nov. 25, 1952, New York City Center, by the New York City Ballet.*
CAST: *Tanaquil LeClercq, Nicholas Magallanes, Todd Bolender, et al.*

HARLEQUINADE PAS DE DEUX

MUSIC: *Riccardo Drigs.* COSTUMES: *Karinska.*
PREMIÈRE: *Dec. 16, 1952, New York City Center, by the New York City Ballet.*
CAST: *Maria Tallchief and André Eglevsky.*

CONCERTINO

MUSIC: *Jean Françaix.* COSTUMES: *Karinska.*
PREMIÈRE: *Dec. 30, 1952, New York City Center, by the New York City Ballet.*
CAST: *André Eglevsky, Diana Adams, Tanaquil LeClercq.*

1953   VALSE FANTAISIE

MUSIC: *Mikhail Glinka.* COSTUMES: *Karinska.*
PREMIÈRE: *Jan. 6, 1953, New York City Center, by the New York City Ballet.*
CAST: *Tanaquil LeClercq, Melissa Hayden, Diana Adams, Nicholas Magallanes.*

1954   OPUS 34
MUSIC: *Arnold Schönberg.* DECOR AND LIGHTING: *Jean Rosenthal.* COSTUMES: *Esteban Francés.*
PREMIÈRE: *Jan. 19, 1954, New York City Center, by the New York City Ballet.*
CAST: *Tanaquil LeClercq, Herbert Bliss, Diana Adams, Patricia Wilde, Nicholas Magallanes, Francisco Moncion, et al.*

THE NUTCRACKER
MUSIC: *Peter Tchaikovsky.* DECOR: *Horace Armistead.* COSTUMES: *Karinska.*
LIGHTING: *Jean Rosenthal.*
PREMIÈRE: *Feb. 2, 1954, New York City Center, by the New York City Ballet.*
CAST: *Maria Tallchief, Nicholas Magallanes, Roy Tobias, Francisco Moncion, George Li, Robert Barnett, Janet Reed, Tanaquil LeClercq, Yvonne Mounsey, Herbert Bliss, et al.*

WESTERN SYMPHONY
MUSIC: *Hershy Kay. First presented without decor and danced in practice clothes. The following year, costumes by Karinska and decor by John Boyt were added.*
PREMIÈRE: *Sept. 7, 1954, New York City Center, by the New York City Ballet.*
CAST: *Diana Adams, Herbert Bliss, Janet Reed, Nicholas Magallanes, Patricia Wilde, Jacques d'Amboise, Tanaquil LeClercq, et al.*

IVESIANA
MUSIC: *Charles Ives.*
PREMIÈRE: *Sept. 14, 1954, New York City Center, by the New York City Ballet.*
CAST: *Janet Reed, Francisco Moncion, Patricia Wilde, Jacques d'Amboise, Allegra Kent, Tanaquil LeClercq, Todd Bolender, Diana Adams, Herbert Bliss, et al.*

1955   ROMA
MUSIC: *Georges Bizet.* DECOR AND COSTUMES: *Eugene Berman.*
PREMIÈRE: *Feb. 23, 1955, New York City Center, by the New York City Ballet.*
CAST: *Tanaquil LeClercq, André Eglevsky, et al.*

PAS DE TROIS II
MUSIC: *Mikhail Glinka* (Russlan and Ludmila). COSTUMES: *Karinska.*
PREMIÈRE: *Mar. 1, 1955, New York City Center, by the New York City Ballet.*
CAST: *Melissa Hayden, Patricia Wilde, André Eglevsky.*

PAS DE DIX
MUSIC: *Alexander Glazunov.* COSTUMES: *Esteban Francés.*
PREMIÈRE: *Nov. 9, 1955, New York City Center, by the New York City Ballet.*
CAST: *Maria Tallchief, André Eglevsky, et al.*

JEUX D'ENFANTS (*Choreographed with Barbara Milberg and Francisco Moncion*)
MUSIC: *Georges Bizet.* DECOR AND COSTUMES: *Esteban Francés.*
PREMIÈRE: *Nov. 22, 1955, New York City Center, by the New York City Ballet.*

CAST: *Melissa Hayden, Roy Tobias, Barbara Walczak, Robert Barnett, Barbara Fallis, et al.*

1956   ## ALLEGRO BRILLANTE
MUSIC: *Peter Tchaikovsky (Opus 75, Third Piano Concerto).*
LIGHTING: *Jean Rosenthal.*
PREMIÈRE: *Mar. 1, 1956, New York City Center, by the New York City Ballet.*
CAST: *Maria Tallchief, Nicholas Magallanes, Carolyn George, Barbara Fallis, Barbara Milberg, Barbara Walczak, Arthur Mitchell, Richard Rapp, Jonathan Watts, Roland Vasquez.*

DIVERTIMENTO NO. 15
MUSIC: *Wolfgang Amadeus Mozart.* DECOR: *James Stuart Morcom.* COSTUMES: *Karinska*
PREMIÈRE: *May 31, 1956, American Shakespeare Festival Theatre, Stratford, Conn., by the New York City Ballet.*
CAST: *Diana Adams, Tanaquil LeClercq, Patricia Wilde, Melissa Hayden, Allegra Kent, Herbert Bliss, Nicholas Magallanes, Francisco Moncion, et al.*
FIRST NEW YORK PERFORMANCE: *Dec. 19, 1956, New York City Center.*

A MUSICAL JOKE
MUSIC: *Wolfgang Amadeus Mozart.* COSTUMES: *Karinska.*
PREMIÈRE: *May 31, 1956, American Shakespeare Festival Theatre, Stratford, Conn., by the New York City Ballet.*
CAST: *Diana Adams, Tanaquil LeClercq, Patricia Wilde, Herbert Bliss, Nicholas Magallanes, Francisco Moncion.*

SQUARE DANCE
MUSIC: *Antonio Vivaldi and Arcangelo Corelli.*
PREMIÈRE: *Nov. 21, 1957, New York City Center, by the New York City Ballet.*
CAST: *Patricia Wilde, Nicholas Magallanes, et al.*

AGON
MUSIC: *Igor Stravinsky.*
PREMIÈRE: *Dec. 1, 1957, New York City Center, by the New York City Ballet.*
CAST: *Diana Adams, Melissa Hayden, Arthur Mitchell, Todd Bolender, Roy Tobias, Jonathan Watts, et al.*

1958   ## GOUNOD SYMPHONY
MUSIC: *Charles Gounod.* DECOR: *Horace Armistead (designed for* Lilac Garden). COSTUMES: *Karinska.*
PREMIÈRE: *Jan. 8, 1958, New York City Center, by the New York City Ballet.*
CAST: *Maria Tallchief, Jacques d'Amboise, et al.*

STARS AND STRIPES
MUSIC: *John Philip Sousa, arr. by Hershy Kay.* COSTUMES: *Karinska.*
DECOR: *David Hays.*
PREMIÈRE: *Jan. 17, 1958, New York City Center, by the New York City Ballet.*

CAST: *Allegra Kent, Melissa Hayden, Robert Barnett, Jacques d'Amboise, et al.*

WALTZ–SCHERZO
MUSIC: *Peter Tchaikovsky.* COSTUMES: *Karinska.*
PREMIÈRE: *Sept. 9, 1958, New York City Center, by the New York City Ballet.*
CAST: *Patricia Wilde and André Eglevsky.*

SEVEN DEADLY SINS
MUSIC: *Kurt Weill.* DECOR AND COSTUMES: *Rouben Ter-Arutinian.* LIBRETTO: *Berthold Brecht (translated by W. H. Auden and Chester Kallman).*
PREMIÈRE: *Dec. 4, 1958, New York City Center, by the New York City Ballet.*
CAST: *Allegra Kent, et al., with Lotte Lenya singing the role of Annie.*

1959   ## NATIVE DANCERS
MUSIC: *Vittorio Rieti (Symphony No. 5).* DECOR: *David Hays.* COSTUMES: *Peter Larkin.*
PREMIÈRE: *Jan. 14, 1959, New York City Center, by the New York City Ballet.*
CAST: *Patricia Wilde, Jacques d'Amboise, et al.*

EPISODES
MUSIC: *Anton Webern. Choreographed with Martha Graham, who choreographed and danced in the first half of the work. The Balanchine section, later presented independently was then called* Episodes, Part II.
PREMIÈRE: *May 14, 1959, New York City Center, by the New York City Ballet.*
CAST (in the Balanchine section): *Violette Verdy, Jonathan Watts, Diana Adams, Jacques d'Amboise, Allegra Kent, Nicholas Magallanes, Melissa Hayden, Francisco Moncion, Paul Taylor, et al.*

1960   ## MODERN JAZZ: VARIANTS
MUSIC: *Gunther Schuller.* DECOR AND COSTUMES: *David Hays.*
PREMIÈRE: *Jan. 4, 1960, New York City Center, by the New York City Ballet.*
CAST: *Diana Adams, Melissa Hayden, John Jones, Arthur Mitchell, et al.*

PANAMERICA
MUSIC: *Section II, Luis Escobar,* Preludios para Percusion; *Section IV, Carlos Chavez, Sinfonia No. 5 for String Orchestra; Section VIII, Julian Orbon,* Danzas Sinfonicas. DECOR: *David Hays.* COSTUMES: *Esteban Francés.*
PREMIÈRE: *Jan. 20, 1960, New York City Center, by the New York City Ballet.*
CAST: *Patricia Wilde, Erik Bruhn, Diana Adams, Nicholas Magallanes, Francisco Moncion, Maria Tallchief, Arthur Mitchell, Conrad Ludlow, Edward Villella, et al.*

PAS DE DEUX (SWAN LAKE)
MUSIC: *Peter Tchaikovsky.* COSTUMES: *Karinska.*
PREMIÈRE: *Mar. 29, 1960, New York City Center, by the New York City Ballet.*
CAST: *Violette Verdy, Conrad Ludlow.*

THE FIGURE IN THE CARPET
MUSIC: *George Frederick Handel.* DECOR AND COSTUMES: *Esteban Francés.*
PREMIÈRE: *April 13, 1960, New York City Center, by the New York City Ballet.*
CAST: *Violette Verdy, Edward Villella, Judith Green, Francisco Moncion, Francia Russell, Patricia McBride, Nicholas Magallanes, Mary Hinkson, Arthur Mitchell, Diana Adams, Melissa Hayden, Jacques d'Amboise, et al.*

MONUMENTUM PRO GESUALDO
MUSIC: *Igor Stravinsky (Three madrigals by Gesualdo di Venosa recomposed for instruments).* DECOR: *David Hays.*
PREMIÈRE: *Nov. 16, 1960, New York City Center, by the New York City Ballet.*
CAST: *Diana Adams, Conrad Ludlow, et al.*

VARIATIONS FROM DON SEBASTIAN
MUSIC: *Gaetano Donizetti.* COSTUMES: *Karinska and Esteban Francés.* DECOR: *David Hays.*
PREMIÈRE: *Nov. 16, 1960, New York City Center, by the New York City Ballet.*
CAST: *Melissa Hayden, Jonathan Watts, Suki Schorer, William Weslow, et al.*

LIEBESLIEDER WALZER
MUSIC: *Johannes Brahms* (Liebeslieder Walzer, *Opus 52, Opus 65*). DECOR: *David Hays.* COSTUMES: *Karinska.*
PREMIÈRE: *Nov. 22, 1960, New York City Center, by the New York City Ballet.*
CAST: *Diana Adams, Bill Carter, Melissa Hayden, Conrad Ludlow, Jillana, Nicholas Magallanes, Violette Verdy, Jonathan Watts.*

JAZZ CONCERT: RAGTIME
MUSIC: *Igor Stravinsky.* COSTUMES: *Karinska.*
PREMIÈRE: *Dec. 7, 1960, New York City Center, by the New York City Ballet.*
CAST: *Diana Adams and Bill Carter.*

1961   ### ELECTRONICS
MUSIC: *Electronic score by Remi Gassmann and Oskar Sala.* DECOR AND COSTUMES: *David Hays.*
PREMIÈRE: *Mar. 22, 1961, New York City Center, by the New York City Ballet.*
CAST: *Diana Adams, Jacques d'Amboise, Violette Verdy, Edward Villella, et al.*

VALSES ET VARIATIONS
MUSIC: *Alexander Glazunov (Raymonda).* COSTUMES: *Karinska.* DECOR: *Horace Armistead (backdrop for Lilac Garden).*
PREMIÈRE: *Dec. 7, 1961, New York City Center, by the New York City Ballet.*
CAST: *Patricia Wilde, Victoria Simon, Suki Schorer, Gloria Govrin, Carol Sumner, Patricia Neary, Jacques d'Amboise, et al.*

1962   ### A MIDSUMMER NIGHT'S DREAM
MUSIC: *Felix Mendelssohn.* DECOR: *David Hays.* COSTUMES: *Karinska.*

PREMIÈRE: *Jan. 17, 1962, New York City Center, by the New York City Ballet.*
CAST: *Melissa Hayden, Edward Villella, Arthur Mitchell, Jillana, Patricia McBride, Nicholas Magallanes, Bill Carter, Roland Vasquez, Gloria Govrin, Francisco Moncion, Violette Verdy, Conrad Ludlow, et al.*

NOAH AND THE FLOOD (*a ballet-oratorio for television*)
MUSIC: *Igor Stravinsky.* DECOR AND COSTUMES: *Rouben Ter-Arutinian.*
PREMIÈRE: *June 14, 1962, on the CBS Television Network.*
CAST: *Edward Villella, Jacques d'Amboise, Jillana, et al. Narrated by Laurence Harvey.*

1963   BUGAKU
MUSIC: *Toshiro Mayuzumi.* DECOR: *David Hays.* COSTUMES: *Karinska.*
PREMIÈRE: *Mar. 20, 1963, New York City Center, by the New York City Ballet.*
CAST: *Allegra Kent, Edward Villella, et al.*

MOVEMENTS FOR PIANO AND ORCHESTRA
MUSIC: *Igor Stravinsky.*
PREMIÈRE: *April 9, 1963, New York City Center, by the New York City Ballet.*
CAST: *Suzanne Farrell, Jacques d'Amboise, et al.*

Musicals with Choreography by Balanchine

WAKE UP AND DREAM. PREMIÈRE: *Mar. 29, 1929, London.* PRINCIPAL DANCER: *Tilly Losch.*
COCHRAN'S 1930 REVIEW. PREMIÈRE: *June, 1930, London.*
ORPHEE AUX ENFERS. MUSIC: *Jacques Offenbach.* PREMIÈRE: *Dec. 24, 1932, Théâtre Mogador, Paris.* CAST: *Felia Doubrovska, Anatole Vilzac, Irina Baronova, et al.*
ZIEGFELD FOLLIES, 1935.
ON YOUR TOES. N.Y. PREMIÈRE: *April 11, 1936.* PRINCIPAL DANCERS: *Tamara Geva, Ray Bolger.*
BABES IN ARMS. N.Y. PREMIÈRE: *April 14, 1937.* PRINCIPAL DANCER: *Duke McHale.*
I MARRIED AN ANGEL. N.Y. PREMIÈRE: *May 11, 1938.* PRINCIPAL DANCER: *Zorina.*
THE BOYS FROM SYRACUSE. N.Y. PREMIÈRE: *Nov. 23, 1938.* PRINCIPAL DANCERS: *George Church, Betty Bruce.*
LOUISIANA PURCHASE. N.Y. PREMIÈRE: *May 28, 1940.* PRINCIPAL DANCERS: *Charles Laskey, Zorina.*
KEEP OFF THE GRASS. N.Y. PREMIÈRE: *May 23, 1940.* PRINCIPAL DANCERS: *Ray Bolger, José Limón, Daphne Vane, Betty Bruce.*
CABIN IN THE SKY. (*Entire production directed by George Balanchine.*) N.Y. PREMIÈRE: *Oct. 25, 1940.* PRINCIPAL DANCERS: *Katherine Dunham and troupe.*

LADY COMES ACROSS. N.Y. PREMIÈRE: *Jan. 9, 1942*. PRINCIPAL DANCERS: *Eugenia Delarova, Lubova Rostova, Marc Platt.*

ROSALINDA (Die Fledermaus). N.Y. PREMIÈRE: *Oct. 28, 1942*. PRINCIPAL DANCERS: *José Limón and Mary Ellen Moylan.*

THE MERRY WIDOW. N.Y. PREMIÈRE: *Aug. 4, 1943*. PRINCIPAL DANCERS: *Lubov Roudenko, Milada Mladova.*

WHAT'S UP? N.Y. PREMIÈRE: *Nov. 11, 1943.*

DREAM WITH MUSIC. N.Y. PREMIÈRE: *May 18, 1944.*

SONG OF NORWAY. N.Y. PREMIÈRE: *Aug. 21, 1944*. DANCERS: *Unit from the Ballet Russe of Monte Carlo.*

MR. STRAUSS GOES TO BOSTON. N.Y. PREMIÈRE: *Sept. 6, 1945*. PRINCIPAL DANCERS: *Harold Lang, Babs Heath, Margit Dekova.*

THE CHOCOLATE SOLDIER. N.Y. PREMIÈRE: *Mar. 12, 1947*. PRINCIPAL DANCERS: *Mary Ellen Moylan, Francisco Moncion.*

WHERE'S CHARLEY? N.Y. PREMIÈRE: *Oct. 11, 1948*. PRINCIPAL DANCER: *Ray Bolger.*

COURTIN' TIME. N.Y. PREMIÈRE: *June 13, 1951.*

Motion Pictures with Choreography by Balanchine

DARK RED ROSES (*1929*). DANCERS: *Lydia Lopokova, George Balanchine, Anton Dolin.*

THE GOLDWYN FOLLIES (*United Artists, 1938*). DANCERS: *Zorina and the American Ballet.*

ON YOUR TOES (*Warner Bros., 1939*).

I WAS AN ADVENTURESS (*20th Century-Fox, 1940*). DANCERS: *Zorina, Lew Christensen.*

STAR-SPANGLED RHYTHM (*Paramount, 1942*). DANCER: *Zorina.*

PICTURE CREDITS

The sources of photographs used in this book are listed below in alphabetical order.

Cecil Beaton, 244
Patrick Campbell, Courtesy Dance Collection, NYPL, 240, 241
Henri Cartier-Bresson, 306, 308, 309, 310, 311
Courtesy of Anatole Chujoy, 166
Courtesy Dance Collection, NYPL, 78, 151, 155, 185, 215, 216, 217
Courtesy of Dobrovska, 112, 114
Fred Fehl, 12, 106, 107, 108, 109, 152, 153, 226, 227, 247, 258, 259, 260, 263, 282, 283, 284, 285, 294
Felix Fonteyn, Courtesy of Richard Buckle, 127
Courtesy of Grigoriev, 111
Courtesy Collection GV, 192, 197
Courtesy Hachette, 86, 147
Courtesy The Hamburg State Opera Company, 266
Kochno, Courtesy Hachette, 97
Tanaquil LeClercq, 183
George Platt Lynes, 174, 231, 238, 239, 242, 248
— Courtesy Dance Collection, NYPL, 158
Maharadze, 186, 187
Courtesy of W. B. Morris, 124
Walter E. Owen, 248, 249
Courtesy of *Paris-Match,* 299
Irving Penn, 246
Courtesy Radio Times Hulton Picture Library, 88, 138, 139
Sasha, Courtesy Dance Collection, NYPL, 121, 122
— Courtesy Radio Times Hulton Picture Library, 93, 94, 103
Courtesy Sovfoto, 291, 301
Bert Stern, 296, 298, 299, 302, 303
Martha Swope, Frontispiece, 1, 2, 5, 6, 7, 13, 16, 18, 20, 21, 22, 25, 108, 109, 167, 170, 171, 223, 254, 255, 256, 262, 270, 271, 272, 273, 274, 275, 276
Richard Tucker, Courtesy Dance Collection, NYPL, 106
Courtesy The Wadsworth Atheneum, 81, 102
Roger Wood, 118, 119, 123, 212, 213, 243

INDEX